Mary Forman Rice received her MA in education at the University of Maryland. She also draws on her experience as a wife and mother of two children and as a volunteer for several years with Pittsburgh School Volunteer Association in writing this book.

Charles H. Flatter, Ed.D., an associate professor of human development with the Institute for Child Studies at the University of Maryland, was responsible for content development and consultation for the parent education television series *Footsteps.*

Help Me Learn

A handbook for teaching children from birth to third grade

Mary Forman Rice
Charles H. Flatter

line drawings by Margaret Cole
photographs by Judith Goodman

A SPECTRUM BOOK

PRENTICE-HALL, INC., *Englewood Cliffs, New Jersey 07632*

Library of Congress Cataloging in Publication Data

Rice, Mary Forman.
   Help me learn.

   (A Spectrum Book)
   Includes index.
   1. Child development. 2. Parent and child.
3. Learning, Psychology of. 4. Education, Preschool.
I. Flatter, Charles H., joint author. II. Title.
LB1115.R445 1979   372.21   78-25781
ISBN 0-13-386292-5
ISBN 0-13-386284-4 pbk.

Editorial/production supervision
and interior design by Claudia Citarella
Manufacturing buyer: Cathie Lenard

A SPECTRUM BOOK

Printed in the United States of America

10 9 8 7 6 5 4 3 2

PRENTICE-HALL INTERNATIONAL, INC., *London*
PRENTICE-HALL OF AUSTRALIA PTY. LIMITED, *Sydney*
PRENTICE-HALL OF CANADA, LTD., *Toronto*
PRENTICE-HALL OF INDIA PRIVATE LIMITED, *New Delhi*
PRENTICE-HALL OF JAPAN, INC., *Tokyo*
PRENTICE-HALL OF SOUTHEAST ASIA PTE. LTD., *Singapore*
WHITEHALL BOOKS LIMITED, *Wellington, New Zealand*

To all Children,
and naturally, with special love and concern,
to Laurie Rice Saunders, Jim Rice,
and Christopher and Julie Flatter.

contents

7

Learning How to Learn   103

8

Everyday Teaching   119

CHARACTER AND PERSONALITY DEVELOPMENT   179

9

SPECIAL TOPICS   181

acknowledgments

Writing this book has been an extraordinary experience because of the many friends, old and new, who have spent time enthusiastically discussing their specialties and making recommendations within the context of teaching young children. We are very grateful to all the teachers, librarians, shopkeepers, hobbyists, indeed, to people from all walks of life who have contributed their thoughts and expertise. The authors are enthusiastic about the broad interest they have found in the education of young children. And they have warm feelings about the generosity of people.

We want to express sincere appreciation to Barbara Baer and Sue Hyde for their dedication in the preparation of the manuscript, to Steve Arnold for his help at the inception of the project, to Lynne Lumsden for her invaluable editorial guidance, and to Claudia Citarella, our kind and patient production editor.

And, of course, our families are an integral part of our lives. Everyone will know, from the content of this book, how much we value the love and support of those who are so near and dear to us.

introduction

This book is primarily for parents. It is for young adults who want lives of their own, yet who also want the quality of the time they spend with their children to be excellent. It is also for parents—either one or both—who want to stay home with their young children in order to savor every moment of those early childhood years.

This book is for grandfathers and grandmothers and for aunts and uncles—because of their special relationship to young children. They are the child's gentle introduction to the world of different personalities.

It can be useful as a resource to teachers, volunteer tutors, teachers' aides, babysitters, neighbors, and all friends of children. Parents have the primary responsibility for deciding how a child is to be educated, and it is important for everyone in the child's environment to understand the parents' approach. If this book helps to clarify the direction of the child's early training for parents and helps to communicate that direction to everyone involved with the child, then it will have served a good purpose.

This is a handbook created for easy reference to a variety of child training subjects. During its creation, however, it became apparent that there is much crossover between subjects. It is our suggestion, therefore, that you read quickly through the entire book to get interrelationships and shades of meaning that run through the whole work. It is hoped that when you finish you will have a valuable overview, an understanding that the authors would not have been able to channel into each section without interminable repetition.

Sometimes we follow roads that have been pointed out to us by people whose values are different from our own, only to find out later that these are not the roads and values we had in mind. It is impossible to write a book without incorporating points of view, so the authors of this book admit that, no matter how objective they have tried to be, there is a point of view. It seems only fair to you, the readers, that the authors state the assumptions which have influenced their approach. Look them over and consider them as you read the book.

- Love and respect and the development of a positive self-image are basic to the development of a person—education is built on this foundation.
- Parents have the ultimate responsibility for their children's education and development.
- Children inherit different tendencies and abilities and, therefore, even in one family, have to be respected for their differences.
- The development of a sense of personhood is crucial to all aspects of growing up.
- Children think and learn differently at different stages of their development, which means that parents should learn about children in order to be able to enhance their full development at each stage.
- Parents are not expected to be perfect, but they need to try to be honest, sincere, and respectful with their children.

Preschool children love to learn. Watch them exercising, trying to develop muscle control; observe them looking at adults, trying to figure out what they are doing; see how they learn about objects, not only with their eyes, but by feeling them, by making them operate, by trying to take them apart; listen to them experimenting with language and trying to relate words to things. A classical philosopher said: "The mind is not a vessel to be filled, but a fire to be lit." Actually, parents do not so much need to light the fire of desire for learning as they need to keep it going.

How much the preschool child learns depends directly on the richness of his home life—not "rich" in the money sense, but rich in love, encouragement, and experiences. Before reading and writing can mean anything to a child, he must have some experience with the things he will be reading and writing about. Jacques Barzun says: "Without the image, the words remain only so much mumbo jumbo."[1]

All the things a child actually does (more than what he is told) make up his preschool learning. Piaget says: "The [young] child's understanding of the world does not go beyond those properties of objects and events *which arise directly from his actions relating to them*"[2] [author's emphasis].

When the child enters school and begins to learn how printed words are symbols for spoken words (which are, in turn, symbols for real things), he still needs to be connected to the real things to which the words refer. It must not be permitted that words and numbers become so much mumbo jumbo. When we try to teach a child something that he is not ready to learn, something for which he has no background or foundation in reality, we damage his love of learning because what we are trying to teach him means nothing.

Although well-organized curricula are necessary for learning certain skills in school, they cannot substitute for the experience that must precede and go along with formal education. This is why home and parents are so important.

---

[1]Jacques Barzun, *Teacher in America* (New York: Doubleday Anchor Books, 1954), p. 60.

[2]P.G. Richmond, *An Introduction to Piaget* (New York: Basic Books, Inc., Publishers, 1970), p. 13.

I

understanding
young
children

At each stage of a child's development, there are things on his agenda that he wants to do.[1] He is ready for them, and he is not ready, physically or mentally, for anything more advanced. It is not so important when, chronologically, your child begins to perform activities as it is to help him to get the most out of each kind of activity when he is ready. For example, when a child is ready to creep, he should get all he can out of creeping rather than be hurried into walking, even if other children his age are walking. All the activities in this book are based on developmental abilities and on the activities that enrich each stage of development to the fullest. Each stage, developed to the fullest, then forms the foundation for the next.

So much development takes place in infants and young children that it would be impossible to present a thorough treatment of the subject in this book. For such a treatment, you will want to read one of the excellent books listed at the end of this section. It is very important, however, to use the age references in most child development books only as general guidelines. Rather than expecting certain actions at certain ages, observe your child and let him tell you what he is ready to learn. This book avoids using specific age groupings for that reason.

[1]Throughout this book we use what we call the "universal he." We tried to invent a non-sexual pronoun for people, but having failed because of our literary limitations, will have to leave that creative charge to someone else.

1

infants

If we think of a newborn baby as the same person who was so recently suspended in the amniotic fluid of the womb, we can imagine what he will be learning during infancy. He is born not knowing gravity, breathing, swallowing or the state of being awake. His muscles are weak from being supported, his eyes don't focus, and his own hands and feet are unknown to him.

Very early, the infant shows an effort to hold up his head and to focus his eyes on his own hand. Before long, he is able to be propped in a sitting position for short periods of time so he can enjoy the new experience of seeing the world from a vertical position. He also likes to be held so he can look over your shoulder at windows, lights, and shapes, the likes of which he has literally never seen before in his life. Seeing things makes him want to focus his eyes, turn his head, and, a little later, to reach out and touch.

The hands are tightly fisted in the early weeks and open only when the baby is ready to reach for what he sees. At first, the hand reaches in an awkward way because the muscles of the wrist and fingers are not functioning. The coordination of the hand with the eyes is a great accomplishment. At this stage, any fingering is done unconsciously, not in coordination with the eyes, yet preparation is under way for coordinating the movements of the finger muscles with the eyes. In time, the index finger begins to poke and probe; then the thumb and forefinger accomplish a pincer-like movement. The baby can now pick up bits of food and carry them to his mouth. This is another feat of coordination and brings with it new sensations. The baby learns about his *two* hands; he lies on his back and clasps them together over his chest and plays with his fingers. Later he discovers that he can pass a toy from one hand to the other. Up to this time, everything looked like flat shapes to him, but now that he can feel as well as see things, he wants to learn all about the weight, shape, and texture of everything. He picks, pulls, pokes, turns, rubs, squeezes, lifts, and drops. After he gets a thorough grounding in all the qualities of things, he discovers that he can use objects to do things with other objects. He learns to put toys into boxes, pour water out of a cup, make a mark in the snow with a stick, put colors on a paper with a crayon. Still another fascinating discovery is the idea of letting go; and once he gets the hang of it, he practices vigorously, letting fly everything he can get his hands on. And, to everyone's pleasure, he uses his hands to caress.

Tiny eye muscles pull the eyes into focus within a couple of months; and, from then on, the baby seems to want to take in everything. He cannot relate what he sees to prior experience because he hasn't had any, but he is building his set of mental connections from scratch at a rapid rate. He reaches out for objects with his eyes before he realizes that he can direct his hand at what he sees. He sees his own hands and feet and watches them move, not realizing, at first, that they belong to him.

Vocalizing in early infancy is most often limited to crying when the child is hungry, uncomfortable, or fearful of falling. The baby's crying during the first few days of life also helps to clear his lungs of fluid. There is no variation in the quality of his cry. Before very long, however, different cries develop—cries of hunger, of frustration and rage, and of boredom; crying as a request for company and play, and crying for the sake of hearing the sound (once the baby makes the startling discovery that *he* is making it). Crying is part of the new experience of controlling his vocal cords. He learns to coo, gurgle, and make noises with a German accent, all the while listening to himself. Later the sounds become recognizable vowels and consonants, though at first, they are not words. The baby learns to imitate sounds that others make and begins to connect sounds with meaning as those around him respond to what he says. Without people talking with and to him, the baby would not learn to speak in recognizable words.

Social interest in the newborn is difficult to assess; but logic tells us that, since he has been inside a person until the trauma of separation at birth, the infant surely must find comfort in the familiar heartbeat and the soft moving warmth of a human body. Next to eating when he is hungry, being held close and rocked is his greatest pleasure. When the baby develops periods of really being awake and learns to focus his eyes, he makes it very apparent that he enjoys people. Wakeful time and social hour usually fall in the late afternoon and early evening. His smiles and body movements show his pleasure when being bathed, fed, played with, and snuggled. When stimulated by attention, the infant smiles, his eyes widen, and he moves his arms and legs vigorously, showing a wonderful sense of well-being. He soon begins, with great effort, to make sounds which burst forth in pleasure, almost unexpectedly. When he learns to reach out, he reaches toward the human face, explores it, and soon caresses it. He likes to play games with people—"so big" and "peek-a-boo." When he learns to creep, he likes people to chase him, catch him, pick him up, and hug him. All of this socializing is with adults and older children. He does not often socialize with other babies; he is, at most, curious about them.

Getting ready to walk requires learning how to get to a standing position, which the baby learns to do before he learns how to sit down again. In the meantime, he stands until exhausted and has to call for help. In time (how much time depends on the individual child), he learns that to drop back down isn't too much of a bump. He finds, too, that, while holding on, he can pick up first one foot and then the other and move sideways with boxlike steps. No one can do all these things for a child. Parents, by not rushing him into walking, will allow their child to experience the thrill of accomplishing each step in the walking process as his mind and body are ready, so that when he does step out alone, he will do so with confidence.

2

toddlers

It would seem natural that the toddler should be wildly enthusiastic about getting about on his own two feet. What we might overlook is the fact that this new experience is also pretty frightening. The toddler's behavior shows us that he is exhilarated yet he has fears because of his inexperience. Almost everything is unknown to him—what happens when he steps off a wall, pulls a hot pot from the stove, sticks a piece of metal in a wall socket. He does battle when parents stop him from hurting himself, yet he panics when they are not around.

Toddlerhood is a time to avoid separation from your child as much as possible, especially if you have not accustomed him to another person earlier. The toddler knows enough to understand being left, but he does not understand that you will return, and he doesn't trust people he doesn't know. He needs to have the security of the familiar in order to learn what toddlers are supposed to accomplish.

First of all, he needs to learn to run about, climb, and explore, developing his large muscles and his balance. He needs to learn how things around him really are, how they act when he pushes, bites, stomps, pulls, lifts, or pats them. Activities such as craftwork, requiring small muscle coordination, frustrate him and deprive him of the pleasure of success. Learning to talk is one of the few non-active items on his agenda.

Language during toddlerhood develops from single words to two word sentences. Some toddlers add a lot of words to their vocabularies and some are so busy with other activities that their language develops later.

Toddlers often seem cantankerous because they are going through a rapidly changing period of mental development. Alternatives are just dawning on the toddler, and he does not know how to handle them. Deciding to do *this* instead of *that* is hard for the toddler: he does not understand giving up one in favor of the other.

Toddlers are very fussy about schedules because they are just beginning to acquire a sense of time—eating times, story time, bath time, and sleep time. They seem to find security in regularity, in having the same thing happen at the same time in the same way, even though they may fuss unless they are lured into an activity.

The toddler does not so much decide on an activity as he reacts to what he sees and hears, which is why it is easier to distract him than it is to confront him when he is on a dangerous course. Since he is supposed to be developing his large muscles, sitting still is hard for him and settling down at bedtime becomes more and more difficult. He will run till he is exhausted, yet he needs about twelve hours of sleep at night as well as a nap in the afternoon. During toddlerhood, the child's muscle development will make it possible to begin toilet training.

Appetite may slow down in toddlerhood because growth slows; and other exciting activities make mealtime a drag if it lasts too long. Foods that were not accepted earlier may not be accepted now because of the toddler's insistence on the familiar. The toddler likes his same old blanket, his same old doll, his same old food— and he also likes the same old people and things and wants them to be in the same old places. He is beginning to understand *ownership* and is very definite about what is his and about what belongs to each and every other member of the family.

The toddler goes to extremes with all of his activities and in all of his concepts because they are so new to him. In a very short time, if allowed to develop himself with the appropriate activities mentioned earlier, he will have sorted things out for himself and will settle down into the comparatively cooperative preschool stage.

3

preschoolers

The preschooler has developmental limitations which sometimes cause him trouble and worry, but generally he is no longer as erratic as the toddler.

Walking now is more like adult walking. With practice and natural development, the large muscles have become better coordinated, allowing the child to stay on his feet, to run up and down stairs, to jump and kick, to change direction easily, and to ride a tricycle. His fine muscle coordination allows him to enjoy some quiet pastimes.

At this stage the child becomes intrigued with language; so, with encouragement, his speech should develop rapidly. Although sentences are getting longer, the preschooler, in an effort to "get it all together," may stutter for a while. He asks thousands of questions, as much to hear people make words as to gain information.

The preschooler is aware of the pleasures of companionship and, after the ups and downs of learning to get along, he is able to cooperate reasonably well. The toddler did not play *with* other children. Even when he was with other children, he played by himself or just watched others. The preschooler likes to talk with his peers and often makes jokes, which is something way beyond the toddler, whose sense of humor was strictly physical. The pre-schooler is also beginning to understand time; he can wait for short periods and, as a result, can be more patient. He begins to ask, "When is it *time* to go to the park?" "When is it *time* for Janie to come over?"

One of the most characteristic developments in this stage is the advent of fantasy. Actually, the preschool child understands little about cause and effect: He observes that things happen, but he does not know why. Because his little universe revolves around himself, he connects himself with everything that happens. He is becoming aware of himself as a person; he is also more aware of his thoughts and of the effects of his actions. Yet he knows very little about all this in the formal sense. This is why young children often present adults with refreshing approaches to the truth of a matter. However, the child is also apt to make some bizarre mental connections which are real to him and can be very frightening. All of a sudden your child may start to have nightmares or he may revert to earlier behavior patterns because of some fearful misunderstanding—some fantasy. Parents have to play detective in order to piece together what has happened to cause the misunderstanding. It is important to get at the source of the mental connection in order to dispel the fears. Not all the child's fantasies are frightening; this is the age of love for fairies and elves, for Santa Claus and the Easter Bunny.

Preschoolers seem to be in love with life. They approach with gusto all the things they are finding they can do. They can learn to sing simple songs (most likely off-key) and to recite short nursery rhymes. They paint pictures that sometimes look like things, and their abstract pictures have some design. They make things out of sand and clay instead of just pushing materials around. They begin to focus their attention for short periods of time and become interested in flowers, insects, animals, people doing jobs, other children, books, simple games, neighbors, playing "grown-ups," building and making things, playing with words, cooking, and housekeeping. However, the preschooler's understanding is still limited and very concrete; he does not understand that words are representations of persons and things. This is why it is not wise to rush children into reading, writing, and arithmetic until they have had rich preschool experiences doing real things. The preschooler learns best by direct observation, by manipulating things, playing simple games with parents and friends, talking at his own level of understanding, and by role-playing with friends. Nursery school curricula are based on these activities, which fit with the preschooler's level of mental development and thus are the best preparation for school.

4

school age children

The important changes that take place between first and fourth grade are often overlooked because physical growth slows and gives way to rapid mental development which is not as obvious to the casual observer. During these years, a child goes through three phases of working his way through a great many important life concepts. He comes to understand himself and the world partly through his own mental maturation and partly through what he learns in school; but his ultimate success depends a great deal on help he gets from his parents.

As he starts school, a child's own developmental changes, combined with the unsettling new experience of school, can cause him to be quite disoriented. He has a natural growing desire to move out from home, but he also feels the insecurity everyone feels in a new situation. What results may be a drastic change in behavior. Parents sometimes can't imagine what has happened to their sweet child and may conclude that there is something wrong with the school. It is understandable that the first grader, no matter how sympathetic his teacher is, will be jittery until he becomes familiar with school life. He may make faces, tweak his hair, chew his collar, suck his fingers, or wiggle constantly. He had thought that school was the "fun place" where the big kids go. He probably looked forward to it with enthusiasm; but once there, he may have changed his mind after finding everything so different from home. He may also have trouble understanding what is going on. His desire to succeed may keep him from admitting, even to himself, that his failures have anything to do with him. He wants to be "good"—to be the best. He has grand ideas and may tackle things he can't possibly finish.

In the early grades, your child may have a lot of colds, sore throats, and ear problems. His appetite is fairly good, though he is fussier about new foods. He craves the comfort of familiar foods and rituals. When the young school child comes home, he wants his mother or a familiar caregiver *there* to serve the ritual snack and to hear his tales of what went on at school. He adores his mother; but, to her chagrin, if she is not tactful in asking him to do something, she gets the "Who's going to make me?" treatment.

By the time he begins his second year in school, the child begins to mellow. His response now to his mother is apt to be a disgruntled, "Do I *have* to?" The second grader is quieter and is more likely to leave a fracas than to try to be a hero or win a point. He seems to need time to himself to think over all the experience he has been muddling through for the past year or so. It seems as though he has realized that it is time for him to really get down to figuring out how to move out into the world on his own. There is a wistful quality to this age.

The second grader still wants desperately to be "good"; but he is also thinking about some of the new ideas of "good" he is encountering outside his home. He wants to succeed in a game, and he will want to play it over and over till he learns how to win. He still has only a meager understanding of such generalities as "honesty," "generosity," and "loyalty," although he may think about what they can or do mean. He is comparatively kind to younger brothers and sisters and to grandparents. He has heroes in the eleven- to twelve-year-old age group, from whom he seems to be trying to learn what is considered right and wrong in the peer world. This is the age of deep and sensitive questions, an age during which parents can offer much guidance and will see patterns of developing maturity.

By the time your child is in his third year in school, he will have again gotten up a full head of steam. He will have pretty good control of his actions; and he will be stronger and more adept physically. His thinking will have become more logical, and his interests will have broadened to include other places and past times. He will begin to really enjoy and understand group games like baseball and soccer, both to watch and to play. He is amenable to learning skills like cooking, carpentry, and so on.

At this age, boys and girls like separate activities. However, both like to collect, trade, and borrow. The comic book stage is descending. Because third graders are so busy socializing and doing things, they have less time to read than before, but they still like to be read to.

We can see from the foregoing that the development of the young school child does not follow a steady course. It moves from disorientation to introspection to socialization, all within a couple of years. A great deal is going on within the young school child. Nothing is more discouraging at this time than insensitive misunderstanding on the part of parents, and nothing is more devastating than being ridiculed. It *is* serious business to learn about the world, practice skills, and develop individuality, and to still be able to fit in with the peer group. By the time he reaches fourth grade, your child's character and personality will be well developed; you will see many personal characteristics which will carry through adolescence and into adulthood.

RESOURCES

Books

AMES, LOUISE BATES. *Child Care and Development.* Philadelphia: L. B. Lippincott and Co., 1970.

BRAZELTON, T. BERRY. *Infants and Mothers.* New York: Dell, 1972.

BRAZELTON, T. BERRY. *Toddlers and Parents: A Declaration of Independence.* New York: Delacorte Press, 1974.

COMER, JAMES P. and ALVIN F. POUSSAINT, eds. *Black Child Care.* New York: Simon and Schuster, 1975.

GESELL, ARNOLD, FRANCES L. ILG and LOUISE BATES AMES. *Infant and Child in the Culture of Today.* New York: Harper and Row, 1974.

HARRISON-ROSS, PHYLLIS, and BARBARA WYDEN. *Black Child: A Parents Guide.* New York: Berkeley Publishing, 1974.

HYMES, JAMES. *The Child Under Six.* Englewood Cliffs, N.J.: Prentice-Hall, Inc., 1963.

McLAUGHLIN, CLARA J. *The Black Parents' Handbook.* New York: Harcourt Brace Jovanovich, 1976.

SALK, LEE. *Preparing for Parenthood.* New York: Bantam Books, 1975.

SPOCK, BENJAMIN. *Baby and Child Care.* New York: Pocket Books, 1976.

WHITE, BURTON L. *The First Three Years of Life.* Englewood Cliffs, N.J.: Prentice-Hall, Inc., 1976.

WHITE, BURTON L. *Bibliography.* Available from Dr. Burton L. White, Harvard University, Graduate School of Education, Roy E. Larsen Hall, Appian Way, Cambridge, Massachusetts, 02138.

Government Publications

Order from the Assistant Public Printer (Superintendent of Documents), U.S. Government Printing Office, Washington, D.C., 20402.

Bibliography, Children and Youth. Form SB–035. This form lists subjects and prices and can be used as an order form. Free.

A Child's World. 1974. HE 20.8002:C43, 017–024–00380–8.

Your Baby's First Year. 1975. HE 21.110:400, 017–091–00082–4.

Your Child from 1 to 3. 1973. HE 21.110:413, 017–091–00019–1. Spanish edition: HE 21.110:413/Span, 017–091–00088–3.

Magazines

Children Today. U.S. Department of Health Education and Welfare, Office of Child Development. DHEW (OHD)74–14. Assistant Public Printer (Superintendent of Documents), U.S. Government Printing Office, Washington, D.C., 20402.

the
fertile
environment

The foundation of a fertile environment, an environment in which a child can flourish and learn, is parental love. All the other surrounding features, important as they can be to intellectual development if judiciously selected, will, without love, be "as a sounding brass, or a tinkling cymbal." *

*I Corinthians, 13:1

5

tangibles

CHILDREN'S BOOKS

Supply your child with good quality reading material, whether you are reading to him or he is reading to himself. Help him find books and magazines that fit his developmental level and tie in with his current interests. Included in this chapter you will find lists of books arranged alphabetically by subject matter. When you notice that your child has developed a specific interest or is troubled about something he doesn't understand, refer to the lists for relevant suggestions. A list of magazines is also included. Your child's interests and choice of books will give you clues to his inclinations, and your knowing his inclinations will help you motivate him to read. Many children's books get right to the heart of children's concerns and anxieties, so you can use them to encourage your child to express his worries.

You will note that your child will respond to certain storybook characters and that he may even choose them for his imaginary friends. Since many children's authors have produced series of books with the same characters, your child will have the opportunity to follow his friends through several adventures. Introduce relatives and friends to your child's favorite series for gift ideas. In addition to fiction, your school age child will enjoy books about his favorite hobbies and sports.

Pride of ownership will enhance your child's interest in books. You may want to inscribe each of his books with his name, perhaps adding a fond note and the date. You can buy children's book plates at a book or stationery store; or, as an art project, you and your child may want to design and make his book plates.

Start your child's own library early so he will have a collection of favorites to read and reread when he starts school. Use the public library to introduce a variety of books and magazines, then buy those he especially likes for his own collection. You will find lists of current and choice books at the library; and the children's librarian will be very helpful. Two prizes are presented each year for outstanding children's books. The Newbery Award is presented to the best author and the Caldecott Award to the the best illustrator. The choices may not be favorites of yours or your child's, but they offer one guidepost for book selection. Many libraries present free story reading for preschool and school age children; some show children's and family films. Some lend tapes, records, and films, several of which are based on children's books.

The children's book list on pages 21–43 is arranged by subject and age, so you may easily locate a few ideas to fit your child's needs, interests, and developmental level. Be sure to talk with your children's librarian, because there are too many excellent books to list. New ones are published every day, so keep in contact with your library and book store.

In the following lists, where a book is coded P, it is intended to indicate that the book's subject matter should be appropriate for preschool children. The numbers indicate roughly the grade level at which your child may find the subject matter of the book interesting. K indicates kindergarten interest level. Some of the books will be above your child's reading level, so they will have to be read to him; others are written at that grade reading level. The subject lists have evolved out of children's interests and concerns and with the idea of enriching their experience with quality reading material appropriate to each developmental stage.

SEE ALSO: Reading with Children; Speech; Writing (creative); Reading.

ABC Books

BURNINGHAM, JOHN. *ABC*. New York: The Bobbs-Merrill Company, Inc., 1964. (P/2)

GREENAWAY, KATE. *Kate Greenaway's Alphabet*. New York: Putnam, 1973. Facsimile of the first edition in 1885. (P/2)

GRETZ, SUSANNA. *Teddy Bears ABC*. Chicago: Follet, 1975. Letters and words acted out in a very amusing way by a group of teddy bears. (P/2)

MILLER, EDNA. *Mousekin's ABC*. Englewood Cliffs, N.J.: Prentice-Hall, Inc. (Treehouse Paperback), 1972. (P/2)

MUNARI, BRUNO. *Bruno Munari's ABC*. Cleveland: Collins-World, 1960. Striking illustrations on large pages. (P/2)

RUBEN, PATRICIA. *Apples to Zippers*. Garden City, N.Y.: Doubleday & Company, Inc., 1976. (P/2)

Adoption

BUNIN, CATHERINE and SHERRY BUNIN. *Is That Your Sister?* New York: Pantheon Books, 1976.

CAINES, JEANNETTE. *Abby*. New York: Harper and Row, 1973 (P/3)

HAYWOOD, CAROLYN. *Here's A Penny*. New York: Harcourt Brace Jovanovich, 1965. (1/5) Also by the same author: *Penny and Peter* (K/2), *Penny Goes to Camp* (1/5).

LAPSLEY, SUSAN. *I Am Adopted*. Scarsdale, N.Y.: Bradbury Press, 1975. (P/1)

Animals

BOND, MICHAEL. *A Bear Called Paddington*. New York: Dell, 1968. (1/5). Also by the same author: *Paddington Helps Out* (4/6), *More About Paddington* (3/7), and others.

DEREGNIERS, BEATRICE S. *May I Bring a Friend?* New York: Atheneum, 1974. (P/2)

DUVOISIN, ROGER. *Veronica.* New York: Knopf, 1961. (K/3)

DUVOISIN, ROGER. *Petunia.* New York: Knopf, 1950. (K/3) Also by the same author: *Petunia's Christmas* (K/3), *Petunia Takes a Trip* (K/3), *Petunia and the Song* (K/3), and others.

FATIO, LOUISE. *The Happy Lion.* New York: McGraw Hill, 1954. (K/3) Also by the same author: *The Happy Lion Roars* (K/3), *The Three Happy Lions* (K/3), and others.

GRETZ, SUSANNA. *Teddy Bears, One To Ten.* Chicago: Follet, 1968. (P/3) Also by the same author: *Bears Who Stayed Indoors* (P/3), *Bears Who Went To The Seaside* (K/2), and others.

MUNARI, BRUNO. *Bruno Munari's Zoo.* Cleveland: Collins-World, 1963. (P/3)

POLITI, LEO. *Song of the Swallows.* New York: Scribner, 1949. About the swallows of Capistrano. (K/3)

REY, HANS A. *Curious George.* New York: Sandpiper (Houghton Mifflin), 1973. (K/3) Also see: *Curious George Wins A Medal, Curious George Goes To The Hospital, Curious George Takes A Job, Curious George Rides A Bike*, and others. (All K/3)

WABER, BERNARD. *Lyle, Lyle, Crocodile.* New York: Houghton Mifflin, 1965. (K/3) Also by the same author: *Lyle Finds His Mother* (K/3), *Lyle and the Birthday Party* (K/3), and others

WHITE, E.B. *Charlotte's Web.* New York: Harper & Row, 1952. (P/3)

WILDSMITH, BRIAN. *Brian Wildsmith's Birds.* New York: Watts, 1967. (K/3) Also by the same author: *Brian Wildsmith's Fishes* (K/3), *Brian Wildsmith's Wild Animals* (K/3), and others.

Adventure, Suspense, Mystery

BENCHLEY, NATHANIEL. *A Ghost Named Fred.* New York: Harper, 1968. (K/3)

BONSALL, CROSBY. *The Case of the Hungry Stranger.* New York: Harper, 1963. An *I Can Read* mystery. (K/3) Also by the same author: *Case of the Scaredy Cats* (K/3), *Case of the Dumb Bells* (K/3), and others.

CORBETT, SCOTT. *The Hairy Horror Trick.* Boston: Little, Brown &

Co., 1969. (3/6) Also by the same author: *The Hangman's Ghost Trick* (3/6), *The Hateful Plateful Trick* (3/6), and others.

LIFTON, BETTY JEAN. *The One Legged Ghost*. New York: Atheneum, 1968. (P/3) Also by the same author: *Goodnight, Orange Monster* (1/3) and others.

SHARMAT, MARJORIE WEINMAN. *Nate the Great*. Illus. Marc Simot. New York: Coward, McCann & Geoghegan, 1972. (1/3) Also by the same author: *Nate The Great Goes Undercover* (1/3) and others.

SOBOL, DONALD J. *Encyclopedia Brown: Boy Detective*. Nashville, Tenn.: Nelson, 1963. (3/6) Also by the same author: *Encyclopedia Brown Shows The Way* (4/6), *Encyclopedia Brown Takes The Case* (3/6), and others.

American Indians

CLARK, ANN NOLAN. *Along Sandy Trails*. New York: Viking, 1969. A Papago Indian girl in the Arizona desert. (3/6)

D'AMATO, JANET and ALEX D'AMATO. *Indian Crafts*. New York: Lion Press, 1969. (1/4)

HOFF, SYD. *Little Chief*. New York: Harper, 1961. A lonesome Indian boy helps a buffalo. (K/3)

Anger

RICHLER, MORDECAI. *Jacob Two-Two Meets the Hooded Fang*. New York: Knopf, 1975. (3/7)

UDRY, JANICE. *Let's Be Enemies*. New York: Harper, 1961. (P/1)

VIORST, JUDITH. *Alexander and the Terrible, Horrible, No Good, Very Bad Day*. New York: Atheneum, 1976. (K/3)

WATSON, JANE W., et al. *Sometimes I Get Angry*. Racine, Wisc.: Western Publishing Co., 1971. (P/6) Also by the same authors: *Sometimes I'm Jealous*. (P/2)

Arts and Crafts

CHERNOFF, GOLDIE TAUB. *Just A Box?* Illus. Margaret A. Hartelius. New York: Walker & Co., 1973. (P/3)

CHERNOFF, GOLDIE TAUB. *Clay-Dough, Play Dough.* Illus. Margaret Hartelius. New York: Walker & Co., 1974. (P/3)

D'AMATO, JANET and ALEX D'AMATO. *Indian Crafts.* New York: Lion Press, 1968. (1/4) Instructions for Indian lodges, canoes, moccasins, necklaces. Also by the same authors: *Handicrafts for Holidays* (1/4), *Cardboard Carpentry* (2/5).

EMBERLY, ED. *The Wing on a Flea.* New York: Little, Brown & Co., 1961. (P/up) Also by the same author: *Ed Emberley's Drawing Book: Make A World* (2/up), *Ed Emberley's Drawing Book of Faces* (K/3), and others.

FIAROTTA, PHYLLIS. *Snips & Snails & Walnut Whales.* New York: Workman, 1975. (P/up)

HOLLAND, VICKI. *How to Photograph Your World.* New York: Scribner, 1974. (2/6)

HUGHES, LANGSTROM. *First Book of Rhythms.* New York: Franklin Watts, 1954.

LIONNI, LEO. *Little Blue and Little Yellow.* New York: Astor-Honor, 1959. (P/1)

PFLUG, BETSY. *You Can.* New York: Van Nostrand Reinhold Co., 1969. (P/3)

SPILKA, ARNOLD. *Paint All Kinds of Pictures.* New York: Walck, 1963. (K/3)

Baby in the Family

ALEXANDER, MARTHA. *Nobody Asked Me If I Wanted a Baby Sister.* New York: Dial (A Pied Piper Book), 1974.

GREENFIELD, ELOISE. *She Came Bringing Me That Little Baby Girl.* Illus. John Steptoe. Philadelphia: Lippincott, 1974. (K/3)

HOBAN, RUSSELL. *A Baby Sister For Frances.* New York: Harper, 1964. (P/3)

HOLLAND, VICKI. *We Are Having A Baby.* New York: Scribner, 1972. (K/1)

KEATS, EZRA JACK. *Peter's Chair.* New York: Harper and Row, 1967. (K/3)

KRASILOVSKY, PHYLLIS. *Very Little Girl*. New York: Doubleday, 1953. (K/3)

STEIN, SARA BONNETT. *That New Baby*. New York: Walker, 1974. Part of the "Open Family Series." Developed in cooperation with the Center for Preventive Psychiatry. These books have separate texts for adult and child. (1/6) Also by the same author: *Making Babies* (1/6).

Bible Stories and Prayers

BATCHELOR, MARY. *Prayers To Grow By*. Drawings by Gillian Gaze, photos by Jean-Luc Ray. Christian Herald Books, 40 Overlook Drive, Chappaqua, New York 10514. (P/3)

FIELD, RACHEL. *Prayer for a Child*. Illus. Elizabeth Orton Jones. New York: Macmillan Publishing Co., Inc., 1944. (P/1)

JONES, MARY ALICE. *Bible Stories for Children*. Illus. Manning de V. Lee. Chicago: Rand McNally & Co., 1952. (1/4)

SPIER, PETER. *Noah's Ark*. Garden City, N.Y.: Doubleday, 1977. Winner of the 1978 Caldecott Medal. (P/3)

TRESSELT, ALVIN. *Stories from the Bible*. New York: Coward, McCann, 1971. (1/up)

Black Children

FREEMAN, DON. *Corduroy*. New York: Viking, 1968. (P/3)

HILL, ELIZABETH S. *Evan's Corner*. New York: Holt Rinehart & Winston (K/3)

KEATS, EZRA JACK. *Snowy Day*. New York: Viking, 1962. (P/1) Also by the same author: *Whistle For Willie* (P/1), *Peter's Chair* (K/3), *Goggles* ((K/2), and others.

MCGOVERN, ANN. *Black is Beautiful*. Englewood Cliffs, N.J.: Scholastic Book Services, 1970. (K/3) Also by the same author: *Runaway Slave, The Story of Harriet Tubman* (Both 2/3)

SUTHERLAND, EFUA. *Playtime In Africa*. New York: Atheneum, 1962. (2/6)

UDRY, JANICE. *What Mary Jo Shared*. Chicago: Whitman, 1966. (K/2) Also by the same author: *What Mary Jo Wanted* (K/3), *Mary Jo's Grandmother* (K/3)

City Life

BINZEN, BILL. *Miguel's Mountain*. New York: Coward, McCann, 1968. Miguel appeals to the mayor to allow the children to keep their "mountain." (K/3)

BOURNE, MIRIAM A. *Emilio's Summer Day*. New York: Harper, 1966. (K/3)

BRENNER, BARBARA. *Barto Takes the Subway*. New York: Knopf, 1961. (2/5)

GRIFALCONI, ANN,. *City Rhythms*. Indianapolis, Ind.: Bobbs-Merrill, 1965. (K/3)

KEATS, EZRA JACK and PAT CHERR. *My Dog Is Lost*. New York: Crowell, 1960. (K/3)

LENSKI, LOIS. *We Live in the City: Short Stories*. Philadelphia: Lippincott, 1954. (K/3)

TRESSELT, ALVELT. *Wake Up City*. New York: Lothrop, 1956. (K/3)

Classics

Price for editions of children's classics vary widely. Some facsimiles of original editions are quite expensive, beautiful books. You can also find most classics in paperback.

BAUM, L. FRANK. *The Wizard of Oz*. New York: Macmillan, 1970. (3/6)

CARROLL, LEWIS. *Alice's Adventures in Wonderland*. New York: Delacorte, 1977. (2/6)

DALY, KATHLEEN N. *Raggedy Ann and Andy*. New York: Dell, 1977. (P/2)

DEBRUNHOFF, JEAN. *The Story of Babar*. New York: Random House, 1937. (P/3) Also by the same author: *Babar and Father Christmas* and others.

DuBois, William Pene. *The Three Little Pigs*. New York: Viking, 1962. (P/2)

Galdone, Paul. *The House That Jack Built*. New York: McGraw-Hill, 1961. (P/3) Also by the same author: *The Little Red Hen* (P/3), *Puss in Boots* (P/4) and others.

Greenaway, Kate. *Birthday Book for Children*. New York: Warne, 1880. (3/6) Also by the same author: *Under the Window* (2/5), *A-Apple Pie* (K/2), *Mother Goose* (1/4), and others.

Langstaff, John and Feodor Rojankovsky. *Frog Went A Courtin'*. New York: Harcourt Brace Jovanovich, 1955. (K/3) Also by the same author: *Over in the Meadow* (K/3).

Leaf, Monro. *The Story of Ferdinand*. New York: Penguin, 1977. (P/3)

Milne, A. A. *House At Pooh Corner*. New York: Dell, 1970. (P/up) Also by the same author: *Winnie the Pooh* (P/5), *When We Were Very Young* (2/5), *Now We Are Six* (P/4).

Potter, Beatrix. *Children's Favorites*. New York: Warne, 1975. (K/up) Four volumes, including *The Tale Of Peter Rabbit*.

Grahame, Kenneth. *The Wind in the Willows*. New York: Dell, 1969. (3/7)

Cookbooks

Ellison, Virginia H. *The Pooh Party and Cookbook Set*. New York: Dutton, 1972. (P/3)

Girl Scouts of the U.S.A. *Beginner's Cookbook*. New York: Dell, N.D. (1/6)

Cooperation

Bishop, Claire H. *Five Chinese Brothers*. New York: Coward, McCann, 1938. Five brothers work together to save the life of one brother. (K/3)

Courage

Lionni, Leo. *Swimmy*. New York: Pantheon, 1963. A small fish devises a plan for survival. (P/2)

Cowboys

LENSKI, LOIS. *Cowboy Small*. New York: Walck, 1949. (K/3)

SCOTT, ANN H. *Big Cowboy Western*. New York: Lothrop, 1956. (K/3)

Cultures

BEIM, LORRAINE and JERROLD BEIM. *The Little Igloo*. Illus. Howard Simon. New York: Harcourt Brace, 1941. Easy reader. (P/3)

BEMELMANS, LUDWIG. *Madeline*. New York: Penquin, 1977. (K/3) Also by the same author: *Madeline's Rescue* (K/3), *Madeline and the Bad Hat* (K/3), and others.

DEFOREST, CHARLOTTE B. *Prancing Pony: Nursery Rhymes from Japan*. New York: Walker, 1968. (1/7)

GLASGOW, ALINE. *Honschi*. New York: Parents, 1972. (K/3)

HALEY, GAIL E. *A Story, A Story*. New York: Atheneum, 1970. An African tale, beautifully illustrated. (K/3)

MACHETANZ, SARA and FRED MACHETANZ. *A Puppy Named Ghi*. New York: Scribner, 1957. (K/3)

POLITI, LEO. *Pedro, The Angel of Olvera Street*. New York: Scribner, 1946. (P/2) Also by the same author: *Moy Moy* (P/3).

YASHIMA, TARO. *Crow Boy*. New York: Viking, 1955. (K/3) Also by the same author: *Umbrella*. (P/1)

Death

BROWN, MARGARET WISE. *The Dead Bird*. Reading, Mass.: Addison-Wesley, 1958. (P/3)

LEE, VIRGINIA, *The Magic Moth*. Drawings by Richard Cuffari. New York: The Seabury Press, 1972. (2/3)

STEIN, SARA BONNETT. *About Dying*. New York: Walker, 1974. Developed in cooperation with the Center for Preventive Psychiatry, this book has separate texts for adults and children. (1/6)

VIORST, JUDITH. *The Tenth Good Thing About Barney*. New York: Atheneum, 1971. (K/4)

MORRIS, CHRISTOPHER G., ed. *The Magic World of Words*. New York: Macmillan Publishing Co., 1977. (1/3).

MORRIS, WILLIAM, ed. *Weekly Reader Beginning Dictionary*. New York: Grosset and Dunlap, 1974. (2/3)

PARKER, BERTHA M. *Golden Book Encyclopedia*. Racine, Wisc.: Western, 1969. (3/6)

SCARRY, RICHARD. *The Best Word Book Ever*. Racine, Wisc.: Western, 1963. (P/3)

SCHULZ, CHARLES M. *The Charlie Brown Dictionary*. New York: Random House, 1973. (1/3)

Dogs and Cats (See also Pets)

AVERILL, ESTHER. *Fire Cat*. New York: Harper, 1960. (K/3) Also by the same author *Hotel Cat*. (K/3)

BONSALL, CROSBY NEWELL, Photos by YLLA. *Listen! Listen!* New York: Harper and Row, 1964. (P/up)

FLACK, MARJORIE. *Angus and the Ducks*. New York: Doubleday, 1939. (K/2) Also by the same author: *Angus Lost* (K/2), *Angus and the Cat*. (P/1)

UDRY, JANICE M. *What Mary Jo Wanted*. Chicago: Whitman, 1968. (K/3)

ZION, GENE. *Harry the Dirty Dog*. New York: Harper, 1976. (P/3) Also by the same author: *No Roses for Harry* (K/3), *Harry by the Sea* (K/3), and others.

Family

FISHER, AILEEN. *My Mother & I*. New York: Crowell, 1967. A little girl finds that animal mothers are not as special as her mother. (P/3)

FLACK, MARJORIE. *Ask Mr. Bear*. New York: Macmillan, 1958. A little boy wants to find out what to give his mother for her birthday. (P/3)

LENSKI, LOIS. *Papa Small*. New York: Walck, 1961 (P/3). Also by the same author: *Let's Play House* (K/3), *The Little Family*. (P/1)

McCLOSKEY, ROBERT. *Blueberries for Sale*. New York: Penquin, 1976. A mother–daughter mix-up in Maine. (P/1) Also by the same author: *One Morning in Maine* (K/3), *Make Way for Ducklings* (K/3).

SONNEBORN, RUTH. *Friday Night is Papa Night*. New York: Viking, 1970. (P/3)

UDRY, JANICE. *What Mary Jo Shared*. Chicago: Whitman, 1966. (K/3)

WRIGHT, ETHEL. *Saturday Walk*. Reading, Mass.: Addison-Wesley, 1954. A little boy and his dad walk through the city. (P/2)

Fantasy

KEATS, EZRA JACK. *Jennie's Hat*. New York: Harper, 1966. What happened to a rather plain hat. (K/3)

LINDGREN, ASTRID. trans. FLORENCE LAMBORN. *Pippi Longstocking*. New York: Viking, 1950. A little girl performs great and marvelous feats. (3/6) Also by the same author: *Pippi Goes On Board, Tomten,* and others.

NORTON, MARY. *Bed-Knob & Broomstick*. New York: Harcourt Brace Jovanovich, 1957. (3/7) Three children, a witch, and a flying bed. Also by the same author: *The Borrowers* (3/up), *The Borrowers Aloft* (3/up), and others.

SCHWEITZER, BYRD B. *The Chinese Bug*. Boston: Houghton Mifflin Co., 1968. What small child has not dreamed of digging a hole to China once he finds out that the world is round? (K/3)

YASHIMA, TARO. *Seashore Story*. New York: Viking, 1957. A Japanese legend with unusual abstract illustrations. (K/3)

Farm Life

BROWN, MARGARET. *The Country Noisy Book*. New York: Harper and Row, 1940. (P/2)

KURELEK, WILLIAM. *A Prairie Boy's Winter*. Boston: Houghton Mifflin Co., 1973. (1/6)

LENSKI, LOIS. *Little Farm*. New York: Walck, 1942. (P/3)

MANNHEIM, GRETE. *Farm Animals*. New York: Knopf, 1964. (K/3)

TRESSELT, ALVIN. *Wake Up Farm*. New York: Lothrop, 1955. (K/3)

Fears

BROWN, MARGARET WISE. *Goodnight Moon*. New York: Harper, 1947. (P) Also by the same author: *The Little Fur Family* (P), *A Child's Goodnight Book* (P), and others.

FLACK, MARJORIE. *Angus Lost*. New York: Doubleday, 1941. (K/2)

LINDGREN, ASTRID. *Of Course Polly Can Ride a Bike*. Chicago: Follet, 1972. (K/3)

STOLZ, MARY. *The Bully of Barkham Street*. New York: Dell, 1968. Humorous story about a bully and why he is the way he is. (3/6)

WATSON, JANE WERNER, et. al. *Sometimes I'm Afraid*. Racine, Wisc.: Western, 1971. (P)

WILLIAMS, GWENEIRA. *Timid Timothy*. Reading, Mass.: Addison-Wesley, 1944. (P/3)

Friendship

COHEN, MIRIAM. *Will I Have A Friend?* New York: Macmillan, 1971. (K/1) Also by the same author: *Best Friends*. (K/3)

DEJONG, MEINDERT. *Along Came a Dog*. New York: Harper, 1958. A tender friendship between a dog and a hen. (3/6) Also by the same author: *Shadrach*. (P)

ETS, MARIE HALL. *Ghiberto and the Wind*. New York: Viking, 1963. (K/3) Also by the same author: *Play With Me*. (P/1)

FLACK, MARJORIE. *Ask Mr. Bear*. New York: Macmillan, 1971. About love and a birthday present (P/1)

FREEMAN, DON. *Corduroy*. New York: Viking, 1968. About a toy teddy bear that almost didn't get bought. (P/3)

LOBEL, ARNOLD. *Frog and Toad are Friends*. New York: Harper, 1970. (P/3) Also by the same author: *Frog and Toad Together* (P/3) and others.

MANNHEIM, GRETE. *Two Friends.* New York: Knopf, 1968. (K/3)

MINARIK, ELSE H. *Little Bear's Friend.* New York: Harper, 1960. (K/3)

Gardens and Plants

KRAUSS, RUTH. *The Carrot Seed.* New York: Harper, 1945. (K/3)

UDRY, JANICE. *Tree Is Nice.* New York: Harper, 1956. (P/1)

ZION, GENE. *The Plant Sitter.* New York: Harper, 1976. (P/3)

Growing Up

DUVOISIN, ROGER. *Veronica.* New York: Knopf, 1961. (P/3) Veronica learns from experience.

FLACK, MARJORIE. *Tim Tadpole and the Great Bullfrog.* New York: Doubleday, 1959. (P/3) Tim learns there are some things you just can't do till you grow up.

FREEMAN, DON. *Mop Top.* New York: Viking, 1955. (P/2) A little boy decides to get his hair cut after being mistaken for a mop.

GRAMATKY, HARDIE. *Little Toot.* New York: Putnam, 1939. (P/3) Beloved story of a playful tugboat that grows up to be a hero. Also by the same author: *Little Toot in London, Little Toot on the Mississippi* (P/3), and others.

KRAUSS, RUTH. *Backward Day.* New York: Harper, 1950. (P/3) After a day of being allowed to do everything backwards, it seems better to do things the way we already do them.

LIONNI, LEO. *Frederick.* New York: Pantheon, 1966. (1/3) Frederick just sits while everyone else works.

LITTLE, LESLIE JONES and ELOISE GREENFIELD. Ill., CAROLE BYARD, *I Can Do It Myself.* New York: Thomas Y. Crowell Co., 1978. (P/2)

VIORST, JUDITH. Ill., RAY CRUZ, *Alexander, Who Used to be Rich Last Sunday.* New York: Atheneum, 1978 (P/3)

ZION, GENE. *Harry the Dirty Dog.* New York: Harper, 1956. (P/3) Harry learns why baths are necessary.

BUCKLEY, HELEN E. *Grandmother and I*. New York: Lothrop, 1969. (K/3) A grandmother shares life's pleasures with her little grandson.

CLARK, ANN NOLAN. *Along Sandy Trails*. New York: Viking, 1969. A Papago Indian girl and her grandmother.

SKORPEN, LIESEL M. *Mandy's Grandmother*. New York: Deal Press, 1975. (P/3) About a little girl who took some time to get to like her grandmother.

UDRY, JANICE M. *Mary Jo's Grandmother*. Chicago: Whitman, 1970. (K/3)

WILLIAMS, BARBARA. Ill. KAY CHORAO, *Albert's Toothache*. New York: E.P. Dutton and Co., Inc., 1974. (P/2)

Holidays and Special Days

Birthday

AVERILL, ESTHER. *Jenny's Birthday Book*. New York: Harper and Row, 1954. (K/3)

FLACK, MARJORIE. *Ask Mr. Bear*. New York: Macmillan, 1971. (P/1) A small boy's birthday gift for his mother.

HOBAN, RUSSELL. *Birthday for Frances*. New York: Harper and Row, 1968. (P/3)

LENSKI, LOIS. *Surprise for Davy*. New York: Walck, 1947. (P) Davy's fourth birthday.

ZOLOTOW, CHARLOTTE. *Mr. Rabbit and the Lovely Present*. Ill. by Maurice Sendak. New York: Harper and Row (A Harper Trophy Picture Book), 1977. (P/2)

Christmas

BROWN, MICHAEL. *Santa Mouse*. Illus. Elfrieda DeWitt. New York: Grosset & Dunlap, 1966. (P/3) Also by the same author: *Santa Mouse Meets Mermaduke*. (P/3)

DUVOISIN, ROGER. *The Christmas Whale*. New York: Knopf, 1945. (P/S) A kindly whale helps Santa.

FRANCOISE, *Jeanne-Marie Counts Her Sheep*. New York: Macmillan, 1968. (P3)

KEATS, EZRA JACK. *Little Drummer Boy*. New York: Macmillan, 1968. (K/3) Old carol about the poor little boy's gift to Jesus.

LINDGREN, ASTRID. *Christmas in the Stable*. New York: Coward, McCann, 1962. (1/3) A little girl visualizes the Christmas story as happening on her farm.

MOORE, CLEMENT C. *A Visit from St. Nicholas: Twas the Night Before Christmas*. New York: McGraw-Hill, 1968. (P/3) An old favorite illustrated by Paul Goldone.

Easter

MILHOUS, KATHERINE. *The Egg Tree*. New York: Scribner, 1953. (K/3)

Jewish Holidays

CONE, MOLLY. *Purim*. New York: Crowell, 1967. (K/3) Also by the same author: *Jewish Sabbath* (K/3), *Jewish New Year* (K/3).

SIMON, NORMA. *Passover*. New York: Crowell, 1965. (K/3) Also by the same author: *My Family Seder* (P), *Our First Sukkah* (P), *Purim Party* (P), *Rosh Hashanah* (P), *Simhat Torah* (P), *Tu Bishvat* (P), *Yom Kippur* (P), and others. Festival Series of Picture Story Books published by United Synagog Book Service, 155 Fifth Avenue, New York, New York 10010.

Handicaps

FASSLER, JOAN. *Howie Helps Himself*. Chicago: Whitman, 1975. (1/3)

STEIN, SARA BONNETT. *About Handicaps*. New York: Walker, 1974. (1/6) Separate texts for parents and children.

FRITZ, JEAN. *George Washington's Breakfast.* New York: Coward, McCann, 1969. (2/6) Also by the same author: *And Then What Happened Paul Revere?* (2/6), *Why Don't You Get A Horse, Sam Adams?* (2/6), *Who's That Stepping on Plymouth Rock?* (2/6).

KEATS, EZRA JACK. *John Henry: An American Legend.* New York: Pantheon, 1965. (K/3) Legend of the great Black rail worker.

LAWSON, ROBERT, *Ben and Me.* New York: Dell, 1973. (3/6) Also by the same author: *Mr. Revere & I* (3/6)

LOBEL, ARNOLD. *On the Day Peter Stuyvesant Sailed Into Town.* New York: Harper, 1971. (P/3)

MCDERMOTT, GERALD. *The Voyage of Osiris.* New York: Windmill Books and E.P. Dutton, 1977. (3)

PARSONS, VIRGINIA. *Ring for Liberty.* New York: Golden Press, 1975. (P/2) Story of the Liberty Bell.

WILDER, LAURA INGALLS. *Little House on the Prairie.* New York: Harper, 1975. (1/6) Also by Wilder: *Little House* Books, 9 volumes. New York: Harper, 1973. (1/6) Includes *Little House in the Big Woods, Farmer Boy, On the Banks of Plum Creek, By the Shores of Silver Lake,* and others.

YATES, ELIZABETH. *Caroline's Courage.* New York: Dutton, 1964. (3/5) About a ten-year-old girl and her encounter with an American Indian girl.

Horses

ANDERSON, C. W. *Lonesome Little Colt.* New York: Macmillan, 1974. (P/3) Also by the same author: *Blaze and the Gypsies* (K/3) and others.

DENNIS, WESLEY. *Flip.* New York: Viking, 1941. (P/1) Also by the same author: *Flip in the Morning, Tumble: The Story of a Mustang.* (All P/1)

HENRY, MARGUERITE. *The Little Fellow.* Chicago: Rand McNally, 1975. (2/5) Also by the same author: *Justin Morgan Had a Horse.* (2/6), *Misty of Chincoteague* (2/6), and others.

KREMENTZ, JILL. *A Very Young Rider*. New York: Alfred A. Knopf, 1977. (2/up)

Hospitals, Doctors and Dentists

GREENE, CARLA. *Animal Doctors: What They Do*. New York: Harper, 1967. (K/3)

REY, MARGARET and H. A. REY. *Curious George Goes to the Hospital*. Boston: Houghton Mifflin, 1976. (P/3)

ROCKWELL, HARLOW. *My Dentist*. West Caldwell, N.J.: Greenwillow Books, 1975. (P/3) Also by the same author: *My Doctor*. (P/3)

STEIN, SARA BONNETT. *A Hospital Story*. New York: Walker, 1974. (1/6)

Humor

CARLE, ERIC. *The Very Hungry Caterpillar*. Cleveland: Collins-World, 1969. (P/2)

GAG, WANDA.. *Millions of Cats*. New York: Coward, 1928. (P/3) Also by the same author: *Snippy and Snappy* (1/3), *Nothing At All* (1/3), and others.

GEISEL, THEODOR (DR. SEUSS), *I Can Read With My Eyes Shut*. New York: Random House, 1978. (P/1)

KRAUSS, RUTH. *I Want To Paint My Bathroom Blue*. New York: Harper, 1956. (K/3)

MAYER, MERCER. *A Boy, A Dog and A Frog*. New York: Dial, 1967. (P/3)

McGREGOR, ELLEN. *Theodore Turtle*. New York: McGraw-Hill, 1955. (P/3)

REY, HANS A. *Curious George*. Boston: Houghton Mifflin, 1941. (P/3) Also see: *Curious George Wins a Medal, Curious George Goes To the Hospital, Curious George Takes a Job, Curious George Rides a Bike*, and others. (All P/3)

Manners

HOBAN, RUSSELL. *Dinner at Alberta's.* New York: Crowell, 1975. (1/3)

JOSLIN, SESYLE. *What Do You Say, Dear?* Englewood Cliffs, N.J.: Scholastic Book Services, 1977. (1/3) Also by the same author: *What Do You Do, Dear?*, *Dear Dragon: And Other Useful Letter Forms for Young Ladies and Gentlemen Engaged in Everyday Correspondence.* (K/up)

LEAF, MUNRO. *Manners Can Be Fun.* Philadelphia: Lippincott, 1958. (P/2) Also by the same author: *How to Behave and Why.*

SCARRY, RICHARD. *Richard Scarry's Please & Thank You Book.* New York: Random House, 1973. (P/1)

Math

EMBERLY, ED. *The Wing on a Flea: A Book About Shapes.* Boston: Little, Brown, 1961. (P/up)

GIRETZ, SUSANNA. *Teddy Bears One to Ten.* Chicago: Follett, 1968. (P/2)

LEAF, MUNRO. *Metric Can Be Fun.* Philadelphia: Lippincott, 1976. (1/3)

LIONNI, LEO. *Inch By Inch.* New York: Astor-Honor, 1962. (P/2)

SCARRY, RICHARD. *Richard Scarry's Best Counting Book Ever.* New York: Random House, 1975. (P/2)

SLOBODKINA, ESPHYR. *Caps For Sale.* Reading, Mass.: Addison-Wesley, 1947. (P/3)

STEINER, CHARLOTTE. *Ten In the Family.* New York: Knopf, 1960. (P/2)

Music, Song Books, Dancing

BALET, JAN. *What Makes An Orchestra?* New York: Walck, 1951. (3/7)

KREMENTZ, JILL. *A Very Young Dancer.* New York: Knopf, 1976. (K/3)

SEEGER, RUTH. *American Folk Songs for Children.* New York: Doubleday, 1948. (P/up) With simple piano music.

CONKLIN, GLADYS. *I Like Butterflies.* New York: Holiday House, 1960. (K/3) Also by the same author: *We Like Bugs, If I Were A Bird* (Both K/3), and others.

DALY, KATHLEEN. *A Child's Book of Birds.* New York: Doubleday, 1977. (K/4) Also by the same author: *A Child's Book of Flowers* (1/3), *A Child's Book of Insects* (1/3), and others.

FISHER, AILEEN. *Once We Went on a Picnic.* New York: Crowell, 1975. (K/3) A beautiful book, very rich in realistic pictures of birds, flowers, and insects; all are identified at the end of the book. Written in verse. Also by the same author: *Animal Houses* (K/6), *Do Bears Have Mothers, Too?* (P/2), and others.

GOLDIN, AUGUSTA. *Spider Silk.* New York: Crowell, 1976. (K/3) Also by the same author: *Bottom of the Sea* (P/3), *Sunlit Sea* (K/3), and others.

GRAHAM, MARGARET B. *Be Nice To Spiders.* New York: Harper, 1967. (P/3)

NATIONAL GEOGRAPHIC SOCIETY. *Books for Young Explorers.* Sets of four. Order from National Geographic Society, 17th and M Streets, Washington, D. C. 20036. (1/up)

RIDOUT, RONALD and MICHAEL HOLT. Ill., TONY PAYNE. *The Life Cycle Book of Butterflies.* New York: Grosset and Dunlap, 1974. (3)

SELSAM, MILLICENT. *How to be a Nature Detective.* Illus. by Ezra Jack Keats. New York: Harper and Row, 1963. (P/up) How to guess what animals have been around by their tracks and other clues they leave behind. Also by the same author: *Tony's Birds* (K/3), *Hidden Animals* (K/3), and others.

Pets (See also Dogs and Cats)

BIRNBAUM, A. *Green Eyes.* Racine, Wisc.: Western, 1973. (P/1)

BRONSON, WILFRID S. *Turtles.* New York: Harcourt Brace, 1945. (K/3)

UDRY, JANICE M. *What Mary Jo Wanted.* Chicago: Whitman, 1968. (K/3)

UNKELBACH, KURT. *Tiger Up a Tree: Knowing and Training Your Kitten.* Englewood Cliffs, N.J.: Prentice-Hall, Inc., 1973. (K/6) Also by the same author: *You're A Good Dog* (1/4) and others.

Poetry

BLISHER, EDWARD, ed. *Oxford Book of Poetry for Children.* New York: Watts, 1964. (K/3)

CARROLL, LEWIS. *Jabberwocky.* New York: Frederick Warne Company, Inc., 1977. (P/up)

LEAR, EDWARD. *The Jumblies.* Reading, Mass.: Addison-Wesley, 1968. (P/up) Also by the same author: *The Owl and the Pussycat* (P/4), *Nonsense Alphabets* (K/3), and others.

LEWIS, RICHARD, ed. *Miracles: Poems by Children of the English Speaking World.* New York: Bantam, 1977. (1/6)

O'NEILL, MARY. *Hailstones and Halibut Bones.* New York: Doubleday, 1961. (K/5)

STEVENSON, ROBERT LEWIS. *A Child's Garden of Verses.* New York: Penguin, 1950. (P/up)

Policemen

KEATS, EZRA JACK and PAT CHERR. *My Dog Is Lost.* New York: Crowell, 1960. (P/3)

LENSKI, LOIS. *Policeman Small.* New York: Walck, 1962. (P/3)

Science

ASIMOV, ISAAC, *ABC's of Ecology.* New York: Walker, 1972. (3/5) Also by the same author: *ABC's of Space* (3/5), *ABC's of the Earth* (3/5), *ABC's of the Ocean* (3/5), *Comets and Meteors* 2/5), and others.

ASIMOV, ISAAC, *The Heavenly Host.* New York: Walker, 1975. (2/6) Science fiction.

AMES, GERALD and ROSE WYLER. *Prove It!* New York: Harper, 1963. (K/3) Also by the same authors: *Magic Secrets* (K/3), *Spooky Tricks* (K/3), *Story of the Ice Age.* (3/7)

CHESTER, MICHAEL. *Let's Go To The Moon*. New York: Putnam, 1974. (3/6) Also by the same author: *Let's Go to Stop Water Pollution* (2/4), *Let's Go on a Space Shuttle* (3/5), and others.

FUCHS, ERICH. *Journey to the Moon*. New York: Delacorte, 1970. (P/3) Also by the same author: *Looking at Maps* (3), *What Makes a Nuclear Power Plant Work?* (3)

SCHNEIDER, HERMAN and NINA SCHNEIDER. *How Big is Big?* Reading, Mass.: Addison-Wesley. (K/4) Also by the same authors: *Let's Find Out About Heat, Water and Air* (2/6), *Let's Look Inside Your House* (2/6), *Got A Minute? Quick Science Experiments You Can Do* (K/3).

WYLER, ROSE and GERALD AMES. *Secrets in Stones*. Englewood Cliffs, N.J.: Scholastic Book Services, 1971. (K/3)

School

BREINBURG, PETRONELLA. *Shawn Goes To School*. New York: Crowell, 1974. (K/3)

CAUDILL, REBECCA. *A Pocketful of Cricket*. New York: Holt, Rinehart & Winston, 1964. (K/3)

HAYWOOD, CAROLYN. *B is for Betsy*. New York: Harcourt Brace, 1939. (1/5) Also by the same author: *Betsy and Billy* (1/5), *Back to School With Betsy* (1/5), and others.

UDRY, JANICE M. *What Mary Jo Shared*. Chicago: Whitman, 1966. (K/3)

Seasons and Weather

BURNINGHAM, JOHN. *Seasons*. Indianapolis, Ind.: Bobbs-Merrill, 1970. (1/4)

COLE, JOANNA. *Plants in Winter*. New York: Crowell, 1973. (P/3)

ETS, MARIE HALL. *Ghiberto and the Wind*. New York: Viking, 1963. (K/3)

KEATS, EZRA JACK. *The Snowy Day*. New York: Viking, 1962. (P/1)

TRESSELT, ALVIN. *White Snow, Bright Snow*. New York: Lothrop, 1947. (K/3) Also by the same author: *Rain Drop Splash (K/3)*, *Autumn Harvest* (K/3)

ZOLOTOW, CHARLOTTE. *Storm Book.* New York: Harper, 1962. (K/3) Also by the same author: *Summer Is* (P/up), *All That Sunlight* (2/5).

Self-Image

BURTON, VIRGINIA LEE. *Mike Mulligan and His Steam Shovel.* Boston: Houghton Mifflin, 1939. (K/3) The old steam shovel got the job done.

ETS, MARIE HALL. *Just Me.* New York: Viking, 1965. (K/3) A little boy decides to be himself.

GREEN, MARY M. *Is It Hard? Is It Easy?* Reading, Mass.: Addison-Wesley, 1960. (P/1) How different children can do different things at different times.

GUILFOILE, ELIZABETH. *Nobody Listens to Andrew.* Englewood Cliffs, N.J.: Scholastic Book Services, 1973. (1/3)

HOBAN, RUSSELL. *Bedtime for Frances.* New York: Harper, 1960. (P/3) Also by the same author: *Bread and Jam for Frances* (P/3), *A Baby Sister for Frances* (P/3), and others.

KRASILOVSKY, PHYLLIS. *The Very Little Girl.* New York: Doubleday, 1953. (1/3) Also by the same author: *The Very Little Boy* (1/3), *Shy Little Girl* (1/3), *Very Tall Little Girl.* (1/3)

LITTLE, LESSIE JONES and ELOISE GREENFIELD. *I Can Do It By Myself.* New York: Thomas Y. Crowell Company, 1978. (P/2).

YASHIMA, TARO. *Crow Boy.* New York: Viking, 1955. (1/3) Picture story about a shy boy who finds his own talent.

Sex Education

GRUENBERG, SIDONIE MATSNER. *The Wonderful Story of How You Were Born.* Illus. Symeon Shimin. Garden City, New York: Double-day & Co., Inc., 1970. (3)

NILSSON, LENNART. *How Was I Born?* New York: Delacorte Press/Seymour Lawrence, 1975. (3)

SHEFFIELD, MARGARET. *Where Do Babies Come From?* Illus. Sheila Bewley. New York: Knopf, 1977. (P/3)

STEIN, SARA BONNETT. *Making Babies*. New York: Walker, 1974. (1/up) Separate texts for parents and child.

Sports

KOLB, JONAH. *The Easy Hockey Book*. Boston: Houghton Mifflin, 1977. (3/6) Also by the same author: *Easy Baseball Book, The Goof That Won the Pennant*. (Both 3/6)

KESSLER, LEONARD. *Here Comes the Strikeout*. New York: Harper, 1965. (K/3) Also by the same author: *Kick, Pass & Run* (P/3), *Tale of Two Bicycles: Safety on Your Bike* (K/3), *Who Tossed That Bat? Safety on the Ballfield and Playground* (K/3), *On Your Marks, Get Set, Go*. (K/3)

SULLIVAN, GEORGE. *Better Ice Hockey for Boys*. New York: Dodd Mead & Co., 1976. (3/6) Also by the same author: *Better Ice Skating for Boys and Girls* (3/6), *Better Horseback Riding for Boys and Girls*. (3/6)

Time

HUTCHINS, PAT. *Clocks and More Clocks*. New York: Macmillan, 1973. (K/3)

TRESSELT, ALVIN. *Wake Up City*. New York: Lothrop, 1957. (K/3) Also by the same author: *Wake Up Farm* (K/3), *It's Time Now* (K/3)

ZOLOTOW, CHARLOTTE. *Sleepy Book*. New York: Lothrop, 1958. (K/3)

Children's Magazines

One of the celebrations of starting to school could be to help your child send for his own magazine subscription. In addition to bringing interesting reading material to him regularly, the subscription in his own name tells him that he is a person, just like a grown-up; and it teaches the purpose of printing legibly—so the publisher will know exactly who is to receive the magazine and where he lives.

The following list offers some suggestions.

Cricket. Edited by Clifton Fadiman. Stories, poems, drawings. Monthly. Walnut Lane, Boulder, Colorado 80301.

Highlights for Children. Activities, stories, poems, pictures. Includes a guide for parents showing what is emphasized in each issue. Published monthly, bi-monthly in summer and semi-monthly in December. 2300 West Fifth Avenue, P.O. Box 269, Columbus, Ohio 43216.

National Geographic World. About people, animals, places. Beautiful photos. Suitable for young and older children. Monthly. Dept. 00876, 17th and M Streets, Washington, D.C. 20036.

Ranger Rick. National Wildlife Federation nature magazine for children. Membership dues $7.00 U.S., $8.00 elsewhere. Monthly except June and September. Membership also includes: membership card, bike decal, books, camp and family vacation opportunities (additional fee). National Wildlife Federation, 1412 16th Street, N.W., Washington, D.C. 20036.

Ebony Jr. School age children. Published monthly except bi-monthly in June/July and August/September. 10 issues. 820 S. Michigan Avenue., Chicago, Illinois 60605.

My Weekly Reader. 1250 Fairwood Avenue, Columbus, Ohio 43216. Also, inquire about *I Can Read Book Club*, a service of *Weekly Reader*.

THE CHILD'S ROOM

Your baby will begin to learn from his surroundings from the moment he is born. The nursery does not have to be decorated with expensive ruffles and frills; although they are fun for the parents, they actually do little for the baby. Wherever the baby is (most of his waking hours will be spent wherever the rest of the family happens to be), he will be enriched by things he can see when he is lying on his back, by music and voices he can hear, food when he is hungry, safe colorful toys, clean comfortable clothing, and, of course, by people talking to him, picking him up, and playing with him.

The growing child's room (or, if he can't have his own room, his own little corner) is his little home within the family home. Having his own place with his own treasures teaches the child to think of himself as a person. It is best to avoid using this special place for punishment.

Furnishings for a growing child's room need not be fancy or even new—just sturdy, safe (no splinters or sharp corners), colorful, and easy to care for. Unless you have a large budget, it is better to paint up old furniture and then to put money into good quality play equipment, toys, books, and records. In spite of pink and blue being traditional baby colors, studies have shown that children love bright colors. When you choose paint for your child's room, be sure it is not lead based, because young children may pick at loose paint and eat it. Lead based paints may cause lead poisoning, so check all painted surfaces and make sure that there are no places where paint is chipping.

An excellent bed (for posture and practicality) is a foam mattress on a low plywood platform. Add colorful sheets, pillowslips, blankets, and a washable spread or quilt. A mattress pad over a rubber sheet provides comfort and protects the mattress from accidents.

Arrange your child's chest and closet with his small size in mind because you are going to want to teach him to put away his clothes. Give him a place for his toys, collections, pets, plants, records, and books. This space is his alone, and it is not to be violated by the rest of the family. It enhances a child's self-image to have things of his own which he and everyone else recognize as his. When he has a place to keep his own belongings, it is easier to teach him to take care of them.

Your child will make great use of a sturdy table and either small chairs that allow him to fit his knees under it or comfortable cushions. You can cut down an old table and paint it his favorite color (just make sure it isn't a two-hundred-dollar antique).

Make his walls and woodwork cheerful and hang his own work on the walls, along with educational material. Such material might include: a colorful map of the United States; art prints;

pictures from magazines; a big arrow pointing "up" and one pointing "down"; a big paper thermometer showing sweater weather, coat weather, and bathing suit weather; a paper clock with movable hands hung beside a real clock; educational posters; an easel; and, of course, his cork board. Consider his developmental stage and his interests when you add to his room and involve him in whatever you do. Wind chimes are pleasant and help him learn to listen, and a growing plant teaches him the concepts of nature and nurture. You may consider a tree outside his window so he can watch the seasonal changes—so he can see the leaves come in the spring, change color in the fall, and drop from the tree. You may want to put a bird feeder on his window sill; but if you do, be sure to keep a sturdy screen in the window for your child's safety. You may consider an easy to read thermometer (with Celsius readings) outside his window.

SEE ALSO: Children's Books; Toys, Games, Equipment; Self-Image; Collections; Gardening; Geography; History; Nature Study; Pets; Science; Arts and Crafts.

FILMSTRIPS
AND MOTION PICTURES

Films have the advantage of presenting appealing pictures accompanied by professionals speaking on selected subjects. It's almost like having a topnotch teacher presenting programs in your living room. However, you do have to have projection equipment, and film purchase is expensive.

If you have the equipment, you may want to consider renting films from time to time, or you may be fortunate enough to live near a library that lends films. One company to contact for buying or renting is: *Weston Woods, Weston, Connecticut 06880* (Phone: *203/226-3355*; they invite collect calls for catalogs and orders).

Most Weston Woods materials are related to well-known children's books. They offer a generous selection of sound filmstrips, tape cassettes, and booklets in combination; they also sell and rent motion pictures.

RECORDS AND TAPES

Some good children's records cannot be handled by children. Play some of them for your child on your record player. The following list of adult classics will not be hard to locate and they have child appeal, especially after repeated playing at appropriate times, such as mealtime, rest time, or bedtime. (See also: Music; Dance.)

Gentle Music

- Beethoven, *Moonlight Sonata*
- Brahms, *Little Sandman; Lullaby (Opus 49, #4)*
- Debussy, *Afternoon of a Fawn; Claire de Lune*
- Foster, *Swanee River; My Old Kentucky Home*
- Granger, *Country Gardens*
- Herbert, *Babes in Toyland*
- Liszt, *Liebestraume*
- Schubert, *Cradle Song*
- Sibelius, *Valse Triste*
- Strauss, *Artists' Life; Blue Danube; Tales from the Vienna Woods*

Marches

- Bizet, *Petite Suite: March Impromptu*
- Grieg, *March of the Dwarfs*
- Schubert, *March Militaire*
- Sousa, *Semper Fidelis, Stars and Stripes Forever*

Piano

- Chopin, *Polonaise; Minute Waltz; Concerto #5*
- Schumann, *Scenes from Childhood*
- Tchaikovsky, *Piano Concerto #1 in B Flat Minor*

Big Orchestra Excitement

- Beethoven, *Fifth Symphony*
- Brahms, *Hungarian Dances*
- Britten, *Young Person's Guide to the Orchestra*
- Copland, *Rodeo*

- Dvorak, *New World Symphony*
- Gershwin, *An American in Paris; Rhapsody in Blue*
- Mussorsky, *Night on Bald Mountain; Pictures at an Exhibition*
- Puccini, *Overture to Madame Butterfly*
- Ravel, *Bolero*
- Respighi, *The Pines; The Fountains of Rome*
- Rimsky-Korsakov, *Scheherazade*
- Rossini, *William Tell Overture*
- Sibelius, *Finlandia*
- Stravinski, *The Firebird Suite*
- Tchaikovsky, *Fifth Symphony; Nutcracker Suite; 1812 Overture*
- Wagner, *Ride of the Valkyries, Overture to Tannhauser*

Playing their own records gives children several learning experiences at once. *Choosing* is one exercise of value—deciding which record to play. *Working a machine* to make something of his choice happen will teach your child *purposeful self-direction*. Hearing all the different sounds and voices *sharpens discriminatory listening*. The only possible disadvantage to a child's having his own record player is the temptation, as with television, to let it substitute for parental attention.

Often it is difficult to find much of a selection of good children's records in general record outlets. Some communities have specialty record shops which advertise children's records. Also, many libraries lend records as well as books. It will be well worth your while to contact the following distributors, who will supply catalogs and sell directly to individuals: *Weston Woods, Weston, Connecticut 06880* (Phone: *203/226-3355*; they invite collect calls for catalogs and orders); *Folkway Records, 43 West 61st Street, New York, New York 10023* (Phone: *212/586-7260*). Here are a few representative selections available from these distributors:

Weston Woods

- *Really Rosie.* Sung by Carole King; scenario and lyrics by Maurice Sendak. #WW424
- *Why Mosquitoes Buzz in People's Ears.* African folk tale retold by Verna Aardema, ill. by Leo and Diane Dillon. Dial. Tape cassette and book package. #WW HBC199. Sound filmstrip. #WW SF199C

Folkway Records

- *American Games and Activity Songs,* Pete Seeger. #7601
- *American Folk Songs for Children,* Pete Seeger. #7674
- *Songs of Holidays* (Jewish). #7554
- *Afrikaans Children's Folk Songs.* #7201
- *Negro Folk Songs for Young People.* #7533
- *Israeli Songs for Children* (Hebrew). #7226
- *Children's Jamaican Songs and Games, Louise Bennett.* #7250
- *The Enchanted Spring, American Indian Tales:* #7753

Columbia Masterworks

You can order the following records through your local record shop:

- *Leonard Bernstein Plays for Young People* (three albums)
    Leonard Bernstein Conducts for Young People.
    Dukas: *The Sorcerer's Apprentice*
    Mussogrsky: *Night on Bald Mountain*
    Piston: Ballet suite from *The Incredible Flutist*
    Rossini: *William Tell Overture*
    Saint-Saëns: *The Carnival of Animals* (Bernstein narrates)
    Britten: *The Young Person's Guide to the Orchestra*
    Prokofiev: *Peter and the Wolf* (Bernstein narrates)
    Tchaikovsky: *Nutcracker Suite*

Arista Records

- *Free To Be Me,* Marlo Thomas (1976 Gold Recording Award), #AB4003

TELEVISION

Television can be a marvelous educational tool, but is a nonselective machine, presenting material to satisfy all interests and ages. You do not choose to clutter your life with everything in the public domain, so you do not choose to view everything that comes over the television. And you will likewise choose to avoid having this very effective learning tool clutter your child's mind with material you feel to be at best mediocre, at worst contrary to your life views.

Television Assets

- Most children enjoy it, and when children enjoy, they learn.
- It can bring a great deal of education into the home.
- It educates in pictures, action, and drama, all of which naturally have an impact on unskilled readers.
- It can afford to bring top talent into the home.
- It can stimulate reading.

Television Drawbacks

- It is hard to control because it is so very easy to turn the knobs.
- Some of the material shown is really objectionable, especially for young children.
- It does not develop muscles or finger skills. It does not encourage quiet thought. It does not develop personal relationships. It may or may not encourage action. It merely demonstrates life in ephemeral pictures.
- A child who is fearful of other children may use T.V. to avoid being with them.
- Without real life experiences, T.V. can lead to chronic fantasizing. Some people pretend all their lives that they can do things that they really can't do.
- T.V. can develop attitudes that are based on different values from yours, attitudes that can put a strain on teenage and adult family relationships.
- It can intrude on reading. Much poor reading is blamed on too much T.V. time and not enough reading time.

Using Television to Teach

First of all, limit viewing time, remembering that an hour a day for a week adds up to more than a school day in time spent. Make it *your* habit to select the programs your child will watch. Use newspapers or a television magazine such as *TV Guide* to find upcoming programs of interest. With your child, mark on his calendar the names of his shows and the times. When he is learning to tell time, draw a simple clock on his calendar to show the hour when his show will be on the television. You will be teaching about months, days, and hours in a way that relates to something of interest to him. Keep pencil and paper handy to jot down addresses to send for interesting material. Help your child address the envelope and get it to the mailbox. A colorful, simplified globe or map by the television encourages the family to locate places shown in the programs.

Let your child know why you disapprove of certain programs. Tell him your beliefs, speaking on a level that he can understand. If you watch programs with your child, you will be able to talk with him about any possible misconceptions he may have about what he has seen.

Television used thoughtfully can reinforce reading skills and enrich family activities. Follow up on programs your child has found interesting. For example, after a program about elephants in Africa, find Africa on the map and take him to see real elephants, if you can, at the zoo. Get books from the library and help him find pictures in magazines to hang on his corkboard. Help him paint and model elephants and teach him to recognize the word. If you can't take him to see live animals, describe the size of an elephant, perhaps in relation to a car. The next time he sees two-inch flat elephants on the screen, he will visualize real animals and will recall all the interesting things he learned about them.

Some of the current children's shows on television include *Sesame Street, Electric Company, Mr. Rogers,* and *Captain Kangaroo.* Also to be recommended are programs about travel and adventure, shows about animals and about things you and he are doing (sports, arts and crafts, cooking, gardening, puppets, pets, and so forth).

TOYS, GAMES, AND EQUIPMENT

When we observe the amount of time a young child spends playing, and when we consider how much is learned in the early years, we can see why parents will want to give considerable thought to the selection of toys. A variety of toys is needed to give the child the opportunity to develop a number of skills and concepts. A child does not need a lot of toys, but he does need ones of different types, to be used for different purposes. At the end of this chapter you will find a list of toys catalogued by developmental stage and type of activity.

It is impossible to avoid buying some toys on impulse, but most of the toy budget should be planned as carefully as the food and clothing budget. Some household items can double as toys and many toys can be made in little time and for little cost. The best way to stretch the toy budget is to make and improvise toys when you can, and then to set aside money regularly for toys which are both expensive and next to impossible to make—for example, a child's record player and records, bicycle, or calculator.

All through childhood, several educational objectives are accomplished with toys:

Large Muscle Development and Coordination. Proper toys and equipment encourage infants to develop their muscles in preparation for sitting, creeping, and walking; and they help the baby learn to focus his eyes and to reach for what he sees. Infant toys stimulate observation and movement. The creeper needs toys that roll on the floor, things to crawl into, and things to help him pull himself to a standing position. The toddler needs pull and push toys to encourage walking practice. The preschooler needs to run, jump, climb, dance, and swing in order to develop his large muscles for strong graceful movement. Some of the equipment he needs is much like that for the young school age child, though adjusted to his smaller size and lesser strength.

Hand and Finger Skill and Eye-Hand Coordination. In infancy, the child first reaches out to toys and then bats at them. He learns to take hold, first with his whole hand and then with his fingers. He needs to make his hands and his eyes work as a team.

Concepts. The infant learns, by playing with his toys, that things of the world have shape, weight, texture. He does not need "bought" toys to accomplish this task. When he begins to move about, he learns to conceptualize space, distance, direction, and locomotion. The preschooler's toys help him conceptualize direction (left and right), numbers and counting, representations of things (pictures and printing), living and nonliving things (plants and stones), and himself as a separate living person (self-image).

Perception.   There is more to seeing and hearing than just focusing the eyes and being able to hear. What is seen and heard must mean something to the child. Toys give the child the experience of seeing and hearing *and* understanding.

Concentration.   The infant takes in whatever happens to be nearby but, as the child gets older, he begins to choose what he pays attention to and develops the ability to concentrate. Some toys help to lengthen his attention span and to improve his concentration.

When buying or making toys, here are some considerations:

Safety.   In choosing toys for infants and toddlers, avoid very small toys and toys with small parts—objects that could be swallowed or put into the nose or ears. Make sure the edges of toys are rounded and that there are no sharp points. Wooden toys should be sanded smooth. Avoid toys that could be easily ignited. There should be no parts that can be broken off or bitten off and swallowed. Some plastic breaks easily and, when broken, is sharp. Avoid sharp-pointed toys, such as pencils and letter openers. Look for toys using nontoxic paints and materials because young children *do* put things in their mouths. Avoid plastic bags or wrappers which could smother the child. Make sure climbing equipment and swings are sturdy and well anchored and that the surface beneath is soft and uncluttered.

Suitability.   Your child should be physically and mentally ready for the toy. At the same time, get toys that are challenging—that are not too juvenile. In other words, be sensitive to your child's developmental stage. See Part I, *Understanding Young Children* and *Play.*

Variety.   Get toys that offer a variety of experiences and opportunities to fill all the necessary childhood developmental needs. See the lists at the end of this chapter.

Practicality.   When you buy a toy or a piece of equipment, pay what is necessary to have a sturdy piece. Some plastic toys are so flimsy that they cannot last for more than a few minutes. For example, there are some children's record players that would break under the weight of the child if he were to step on it or sit on it. See that there are not special care instructions that would require your constant supervision in order to avoid breakage. Be sure that the toy does not present a safety hazard.

Good quality toys are actually better values in the long run. They teach your child the very important concept of caring for possessions rather than buying, breaking, and discarding. Fewer and better toys also help the development of concentration.

The following list offers a variety of toys catalogued by age and by type of activity. Prices and sources are offered, though there can be economical substitutions if care is taken to observe safety factors and other important details. Send to the toy companies for catalogs and build your own collection of informative materials because much more is available than can be included here. Also, while discount toy stores generally offer lower prices, they often offer little guidance in selecting, so advance planning is advisable. Toy company addresses are listed following the toy lists. Do not count on the word "educational" printed on a box: It is quite the fashion now for manufacturers to call all toys "educational." Know the toy yourself. Build a balanced collection, making and using household items where you can and investing wisely when you must buy. In the following list, price ranges are coded as follows: A—under $5.00; B—$5.00 to $10.00; C—$10.00 to $20.00; D—$20.00 to $50.00; E—over $50.00.

Young Infants

Most infant toys you can improvise or make.

Cribs. Law now requires crib manufacturers to include certain safety features. However, if you buy a used crib, make sure the side posts are no more than 2⅜ inches apart. Avoid old paint, which could be toxic, brittle plastic parts that could break off, and rough splintered wood. If you plan to use the crib for more than one child, it will pay to invest in an innerspring mattress, otherwise a less expensive foam mattress will do. It is against the law to sell a used mattress for health reasons; for the same reasons you will not want to use a mattress unless you know where it came from.

Baby Seats and Carriers.   You can buy a plastic carrier with straps (not a carseat) for around $10.00, one without straps for less. Make sure there are places to add straps. Cloth carriers are available in which to carry the baby in front of you when he is an infant and needs to cuddle against and look at you. Some are convertible to back carriers when the child is old enough to hold his head up and sightsee. For comfort and ease of handling, try on different styles before you buy. When your baby is strong enough to hold his head up, you may want to consider the Delux Jolly Jumper, a doorway swing especially designed for infant support and safety. Installed carefully according to directions, it encourages the baby to reach his feet to the floor, strengthening and straightening his legs and feet. (C)

Car Seats.   Seat belts are unsatisfactory for children under four or for those who weigh under forty pounds. It is recommended that infant carriers face back, so the baby can look at whoever is driving. Car seats for children over seven months or so face forward. The Peterson 75 Safety Shell (D) can be converted from an infant carrier to a car seat. General Motors makes the *Infant Love Seat* (C) and the *Child Love Seat* (D). Both infant car carriers can be used outside the car as regular carriers.

Mobile.   Tie household items of interesting shapes and colors to a coat hanger which you can hang from the ceiling where breezes will make it move. You can change the items from time to time at absolutely no expense. You can buy a musical mobile from Eden Toys (C) that is perfectly charming. Unless the mobile is also a safe toy, hang it well out of reach.

Cradle Gym.   Stretch a piece of elastic across the crib. Hang safe, lightweight, colorful household items on the elastic near enough to hands and feet that contact is possible. Creative Playthings makes *The Baby Entertainer* (B) and the *The Baby Activator* (B).

Decorations.   You may decorate the walls and ceilings of your child's room with bright colored shapes, posters, and pictures. You can buy luminous stars, moon, and planets for the ceiling from

Childcraft (A). There are 37 pieces, so you might want to share with a neighbor. Childcraft also makes *Perky Prints* of animals (B).

Wind Chimes and Music Boxes.   You can make one with bits of bamboo, small tin cans, heavy nails, plastic discs, and so on. Explore your hobby shop. Or you can buy one at an import shop. Or you may like Childcraft's *Cradle Chimes* (B). The Eden *Musical Mobile* mentioned above is a windup music box. There are many music boxes available at reasonable prices. Hang wind chimes well out of reach because they are not necessarily safe toys.

Rattles.   Even though the infant cannot use his hands very much, you may want to make him a texture ball with a rattle or bells inside which he will enjoy with the help of others now and will grow into using by himself. Sew together scraps of different textured fabrics. Make a square "ball," stuff with newspaper or soft foam. You may want to attach a few floppy fabric envelopes into which you can place little bells. Be sure your sewing is firm and keep an eye on all rattle type toys to make sure your baby cannot get at the small bells and beads. You can buy Playskool's *Baby Bunny Ball* (B).

When the Baby Can Take Hold of Things

Shapes.   A baby needs things to be handled, chewed, examined, waved about, rattled, knocked together, pushed, and pulled. Try empty thread spools on a piece of heavy string or yarn, conventional clothespins, large buttons firmly attached to a piece of yarn, plastic measuring cups, or a bunch of old keys strung on heavy yarn or string. All these may be attached to the elastic cradle gym once in a while for variety. You may want to buy one or two toys, though it is not necessary. The following are suggestions:

- Creative Playthings: *Baby Clutch Ball,* (A) *Teething Jack* (A), *Three Teethers* (A)
- Childcraft's *Baby Beads* (B) can be used all through the early years.
- Playskool: *Baby Dressy* (B)—a small, soft, washable doll with a flippy bib and easily unfastened diaper
- Fisher Price: *Fun Flower* (A)

Toys that Make Noise. You can make rattles out of sturdy plastic or tin containers if you are very careful to enclose the beans or whatever rattles very securely. Babies can choke on such small items and they do pick at toys—so be very careful. Glue the lids on with very strong non-toxic glue; be sure there are no sharp edges or toxic materials. Check on *all* toys, whether made or bought, regularly for safety. Playskool makes *Baby Flower Chime Roly Poly*, for bath, for rolling on the floor, and for making music (A). Childcraft makes *Rattle Pals* (A).

When the Baby Is Able to Sit Up

Playpens. Playpens range in price from $20 to $50. You may as well invest in a sturdy one so it won't fall apart; unlike a mattress, you can sell it when you are finished with it.

Some child development authorities are adamant against the use of playpens, claiming that confining a creeping child denies him proper exercise and intellectual stimulation. A playpen should have only limited use for this reason; but since mothers and fathers do have many responsibilities, you may find it helpful to provide stimulating quiet play for your child in the play pen for a small part of the day. Also, learning to play alone and quietly for some part of the day may well be developmentally beneficial. A good time to use the playpen regularly is in the morning after breakfast because your child will be more likely to explore toys independently when he is fresh and has not started the more active part of his day. Put the playpen where he can see you, stimulate him with a change of toys (unless he objects), and, for his sake, do not take advantage of his good nature by keeping him confined too long. Invest enough in a playpen to get a safe, sturdy one, such as the Hedstrom playpen. You will be able to pass it on to your second child or sell it if it is well made. Usually, though not always, well-made equipment is safer, so examine the pen carefully for safety features.

Stroller. Fold-up strollers make it possible to take your little one anywhere with you. There are different types, one being the "umbrella" stroller, which folds up to an umbrella shape that can be carried over your arm. When you shop for a stroller, make sure of the safety features connected with the folding mechanism and look toward your baby's comfort in the seat. The stroller should have harness latches, and you will want to buy a good harness.

High Chairs. The following features are of interest for safety, practicality, and later use:

- Folding chairs are easier to store, but they should have a double lock to ensure against accidental collapse.
- A comfortable crotch strap and harness keep the child from sliding down or standing up.
- A removable tray and arms low enough to fit under your dining table extends the use of the chair.
- A large wraparound tray with a good rim keeps spills confined.

You may want to compare the Cosco (D), the Hedstrom (D), and Penney's high chair, catalogue #5898 (D). The latter is considered by *Consumer Reports* to be a good value.

Baby Seats. There are bouncy baby seats made from fabric and metal, some of which sit on the floor and some of which hang from a door lintel. The baby enjoys watching what is going on around him as he gently bounces. Childcraft makes the *Doorway Swing* (C).

A washable soft cuddly toy is a must for now and for the next couple of years. There are many on the market and there are patterns for making them.

Toys. You do not have to buy toys for your child to experiment with at this age because, with imagination, you can find safe household items and put together safe toys to fulfill the baby's need to explore shapes, sizes, weights, textures, *bitability*, and *bobability* in the bath. You probably have more of a variety of potential toys in your cupboards and drawers than you could possibly want to buy. However, for gifts and for a little something special, you may be interested in one or more of the following:

- Playskool: *Baby Blocks* (B); *Baby Play Mirror* (A); *Baby Touch and Stack* (A)

- Childcraft; *Shapes and Sounds* (A); *Action Blocks* (A); *Soft Rubber Blocks* (B); *Unbreakable Mirror* (A); *Rainbow Pile-Ups* (A)
- Fisher Price, *Flower Mirror and Rattle* (A)

When the Baby Creeps

The cuddly toy will still be a favorite, though you probably won't need to buy one—the old familiar one becomes more beloved as time goes on.

Large Cloth Blocks for Stacking and Pushing Over. You can make these with foot square fabric remnants, sewn together and stuffed with newspaper. Childcraft makes six cloth blocks with bells and rattles inside (B).

Push-pull Toys without handles, with or without Music Maker; Safe Wheeled Toys, such· as Creative Playthings Crawligator *(C).* Childcraft makes a *Spool Cart* (B) which combines the skill of fitting and shape recognition with a push toy. Playskool's *ABC Block Express* (A) is a little advanced, but it can be pushed and the blocks may be fitted and stacked: it should last a long time.

Cartons and Overturned Chairs to Crawl In and Out of. You may think of some other safe piece of furniture or equipment around the house that would make a good crawl-through or a nook to crawl into. You may be able to improvise better equipment than what you could buy for a considerable amount of money. This kind of equipment is excellent for developing muscles and coordination, but the baby must be supervised so he doesn't get hurt.

Bath Toys. Any safe thing that floats and that the baby can get a hold of is a good bath toy. You can make small balsa boats or you can seal empty plastic containers. A ball will serve as a bath toy now; then a little later, the toddler will use it for rolling and throwing. Here are some good bath toys:

- Childcraft: *Baby Boat* (A); *Baby Bobbers* (B)
- Playskool: *Baby Water Friends* (B); *Tubby Turtle* (B); *Sailor Mouse and His Floating Raft* (B)

Shapes, Colors and Textures.   You can make pillows using fabrics of different textures; you can get wood scraps (free at most lumberyards) to sand smooth. These wood scraps make interesting shapes to handle. Keep safety in mind whenever you make toys. Childcraft makes a *Shape Sorting Box* (A).

Toddler

Large Muscle Development
and Coordination

Unobtrusive supervision is required to avoid injury to the inexperienced toddler.

- A low slide; climbing and crawling equipment
    Childcraft: *Toddler's Gym* (E); *First Step Gym* (E)
    Creative Playthings: *Indoor Gym House* (D)
    Community Playthings: *Toddler Tower* (E)—a part or a whole set may be purchased.
- Untippable straddling and riding toys; a hobby horse; a kiddie car
    Childcraft: *Bucky the Wonder Horse* (C); *First Pony* (C)
    Creative Playthings: *Riding Truck* (D); *Climb Aboard Exerciser* (D)
    Playskool: *Walker Chair* (B); *Tyke Bike* (C); *Toddler Truck* (C)
    Community Playthings: *Kiddie Car* (C)
- A low wagon; push and pull toys with handles
    Childcraft: *Didimobile* (B); *First Wagon* (D); *Kiddie Wagon* (C)
    Fisher Price: *Popcorn Popper* (A)
    Playskool: *Wagon of Blocks* (B); *Toddler Taxi* (C)
- Wading pool
- Large cartons
- Large stuffed animals or dolls to wrestle with and hug
    Playskool: *Dapper Dan* or *Dressy Bessy* (B)

Hand and Finger Skill,
Eye-Hand Coordination

- Nesting and stacking toys; simple put-together toys
    Playskool: *Hide and Seek Nesting Cars* (A); *Mini Take Apart As-*

sortment (B); *Puzzles* (Sesame Street, Peanuts, Disney, Storybook, First) (A); *Bristle Blocks* (B)

Creative Playthings: *Log Boat* (A); *Peg Bus* (B)

- Blocks and shape-sorting toys. You may want to look into good quality block sets that you can add to as the child grows.

  Childcraft: *Wooden Blocks*, available in sets or by the piece—32 pieces (C); 104 pieces, 23 shapes (E)

  Playskool: *Basic Kindergarten Wood Blocks* (B); *Colored Wood Blocks* (B); *Vending Machine* (B); *Take Apart Jeep*

  Creative Playthings: *Hardwood Blocks*, varying sets—52 pieces (D); 105 pieces (E); 152 pieces (E)

- Toys for playing in sand, dirt, and water. Collect these from your own plastic bottles, plastic funnels, straws, plastic dishes and cups, buckets, plastic jars with lids, old pots and pans, and so forth.

  Playskool, *Bath and Beach Set* (B)

- Hammer and peg bench

  Childcraft: *Hammer and Bench* (B)

  Creative Playthings: *Pound a Ball* (B)

  Playskool: *Cobbler's Bench* (B); *Nok-Out-Bench* (B)

- Wooden train, car, and other wooden play objects

  Childcraft: *Down at the Station* (D); *Magnetic Train* (B)

  Creative Playthings: *Steam Roller* (A); *Auto* (A); *Airplane* (A)

- Fingerpaints and plasticine—both used with adult supervision

Self-Image

- Low table and chair set; small rocking chair

  Childcraft: *Plastic Top Tables* (E)

  Community Playthings: *Child's Rocking Chair* (C)

- Doll

  Community Playthings: *Community Dolls*, each (D)

  Childcraft: *Brother and Sister Dolls*, each (B)

- Toy phone

  Community Playthings: *Princess Phone* (B)

  Fisher Price: *Chatterphone* (A); *Pop-Up Operator* (A)

- Toys that make music, such as a drum, bells, a baby xylophone, and push-pull toys with chimes.

  Childcraft: *Tam Tam* (B); *Bell Tree Xylophone* (A); *Xylo Bells* (A)

  Playskool: *Baby Drum* (A)

  Fisher Price: *Pull Xylophone* (A)

- Colored blocks, shape sorting games, very simple wooden puzzles, stacking and nesting toys; toys with different shapes, colors, textures, and weights.

  Playskool: *Nesting Eggs* (A); *Nesting Nuts and Bolts* (A); *Nesting Bowls* (A); *Stacking Barrels* (A)

- Fingerpaints and plasticine—with adult supervision

Preschooler

Animals

- Toy animal sets
- Posters and pictures of animals
- Animal games
- Blocks with animal pictures
- Miniature zoos and farms
- Colorful pictures of local birds and animals
- Bird feeder
- Shelf pets, such as hamsters and gerbils, and equipment for their housing and care

Art and Crafts

Arts and crafts develop creativity and concepts of texture, shapes, colors, and space. They also develop finger skills and eye-hand coordination that make printing and writing easier to learn.

- Easel, paints, and paper

  Childcraft: *Double Adjustable Chalkboard Easel* (D); *Art Workshop* (B)

- Fingerpaints, crayons, clay, plasticine
- Materials for collages

- Shapes

    Childcraft: *Felt Board with Cutouts* (A); *Intarsio* (C); *Colorshapes* (B)

- Printing materials
- Kaleidoscope

    Childcraft (A)

- color, match, build

    Edu-Cards (A)

- Colored construction paper

Building and Carpentry

- Blocks
- Wooden workbench
- Building sets

    Lego: *Preschool Building Sets* (A-B); *Legoville* (C)

- Odds and ends from the lumber yard
- Tools

Finger Skills,
Eye-Hand Coordination

You can make or scrounge many of the items on the following list.

- Put-together tool box

    Creative Playthings (C)

- Spools and shoelaces
- Simple jigsaw puzzles; put-together puzzles
- Shaped blocks

    Childcraft: *Intermediate set* (D)

- Sand and water toys for pouring, levering, and so forth
- Wooden workbench

    Childcraft (B)

    Community Playthings: *Workbench and Vise* (E); *Workhorse* (D)

- Felt board and felt shapes
- Building bricks

    Lego: *Preschool Building Sets* (A-B); *Legoville* (C)

    Playskool: *Bristle Blocks*

- Lacing boards
- Blunt scissors, old magazines, paste, and paper
- Doll with easy to manage doll clothes
- Doll house with easy to handle, sturdy furniture
- Shape-sorting toys
- Finger puppets
- Picture dominoes
- Printing toys
- Crayons
- Toy villages
- Ring toss game

Geography

- Toy villages
- Board games with steps, like Parchesi, teach a child directionality, which later helps with map reading.

History; Time

- Height measure on the wall
- Clock
- Calendar
- Pictures of historical storybook characters

*Large Muscle Development
and Coordination*

Unobtrusive supervision is still required.

- Outdoor play equipment: Low horizontal bars; a balancing board (a 2″ x 4″ x 8″ board on 2″ blocks); a sand pit and/or an old mattress for tumbling; a low ladder; a low rubber tire swing; a seesaw and a slide.
  Community Playthings: *Balance Beam* (C); *Seesaw* (D)
  Creative Playthings: *Ladder Exerciser* (E)
- Low-slung, nontipping tricycle, child skis, double runner ice skates.
  AMF: *Tricycle*, varying heights (C–D)
  Childcraft: *Trike Racer* (D); *Snow Skates* (A)

- A small wheelbarrow.

  Community Playthings: *Child Size Wheelbarrow* (D)
- Combination objects to make several play toys.

  Community Playthings: *Variplay Triangle Set* (E). The set includes: 4 wheels, a long and a short board, a set of wooden triangles which the child can combine in many ways to make a two-child riding toy, a seesaw, a slide, a push toy, and other imaginative arrangements.

Mechanics

- Sand toys with cranes, trailers, levers, dumping mechanisms, Ertl and Buddy L; (A–C)
- Take-apart and put-together toys
- Transportation toys
- Wooden workbench
- Old locks and keys, hinges, clocks, and so forth
- *Pinwheel sparkler*

  Childcraft (A)
- Blunt scissors
- Mechanical top
- Child's record player and records

Music

Musical toys help your child become a discriminating listener and learn to enjoy rhythm. Many musical instrument stores carry good toy instruments for children.

- Musical instruments

  Childcraft: *Rhythm Band Set* (C); *Xylo-Bells* (C); *Rikki-tikki* (C); *Colormonica* (B); *Tom-tom* (B); *Zither* (C)

  Creative Playthings: *See Through Music Box* (A); *Rhythm Band Set* (C); *Xylopipes* (C)
- Toy piano
- Child's record player and records

Premath

Toys that encourage counting, sorting, estimating, weighing, measuring, and the identification of shapes and numerals deepen a child's understanding of number concepts and number uses. Here are a few of many math toys available for preschool children.

- Balance scale

     Ohaus: *Primer Balance* (C)

- Learning Games, Inc.: *Cuisenaire Rods*, which are colored rods in a set to be used for sorting, counting, playing games and, later, for solving math problems. They are used in schools all over the world. Write Learning Games, Inc. for information on their Home Mathematics Kit. (C) (See Figure 5–1.)

- Ideal: Abacus (C)
- Childcraft: *Skill shapes* (B); *Numberland* (A)
- Calendar

     Childcraft: *Night-Lite Calendar* (A); *Day By Day Calendar* (B)

- Clock
- Numbered blocks
- Height measurer to hang on the wall

     Childcraft: *So Big Ruler*, which has metric measures too (B)

- Cash register and play money

Prereading and Writing

Toys on the following list develop concepts of shapes, letters, and directionality; some encourage practice in speaking.

- Shapes

     Childcraft: *Felt Board with Cutouts* (A)

     Creative Playthings: *Jigsaw Puzzles*, varying sets—7 piece, large and simple (A); 10 pieces for color-matching (A); 36 pieces (A)

     Playskool: *Alphabet Blocks* (A)

- Crayons and paper
- Games

     Creative Playthings: *Dominoes* (pictures and shapes), each (A)

     Childcraft: *Lottino* (B); various sorting games

     Edu-Cards: *Jumbo Lotto* (A); *Animal Dominoes* (A); *Picture Dominoes* (A)

- Play equipment for playing store, school, and so forth.

     Childcraft: *Real Play Telephone* (C); *Interphone* (C)

Figure 5–1.

- Toy sets to put together
  Questor: *Train and Track Set* (A) or (B), depending on number of parts
  Playskool: *Richard Scarry's Puzzletown Sets* (C)

Pretending, Role-Playing

Children do not have to have completely realistic toys for pretending and role playing. A doll house made from a carton or a playhouse made with a sheet over a card table can be more fun than an expensive detailed layout.

- Doll house with family
- Toy village with people
- Box of discarded adult clothes and accessories
- Toy kitchen equipment and utensils, or real ones

66

- Toy housekeeping equipment
- Doctor, nurse, policeman, cowboy outfits
- Dolls and doll furniture
- Puppets and puppet stage
- Equipment for playing store, gas station, school, and so forth
- Play house
- Toy trucks, cars, and so forth

Science

- Sand and water toys
- Collection material, boxes, and shelves
- Water toys
  Childcraft: *Water Pump* (A)
- Pulley
- Prism
  Childcraft (A)
- Garden tools and supplies
- Ant farm
  Childcraft (B)
  Uncle Milton (B)
- Large magnifying glass
  Childcraft: *Stool Magnifying Glass* (C)
- Back-packing equipment
- Flashlight
- Magnet
- Garden pinwheel
- Soap bubbles
- Shelf pets, such as hamsters and gerbils, and equipment for their housing and care

Self-Image

His very own things make your child feel like a real person.

- Table and chair
- His own corkboard
- His own bedding

- His own books and book shelf
- His own collections
- His own toys and a safe place for their storage

Young School Age Child

Arts and Crafts

You and your growing child will be fascinated with your local hobby shop.

- "Junk box" containing all kinds of odds and ends for use in craft projects
- Easel, paints, paper
- Clay
- Beadcraft sets
- Mosaic sets
- Coloring sticks, colored pencils, wick pens
- Plastic craft
- Water color markers, washable
    Childcraft (A)
- Stamp pad kit
    Childcraft (B)
- Camera
- *Crayola Crayon Color Lotto*
    Edu-cards (A)

Finger Skills,
Eye-Hand Coordination

- Building blocks
- Beads to string
- Simple weaving
- Small tools, wood, large screws, nuts, bolts, and so forth
- Jigsaw puzzles
- *Crystal mosaics*
    Childcraft (B)

- Simple construction sets
- Ice-hockey game, with players controlled by twisting rods
- Craft materials
- Chinese checkers
- Suction cup dartboard game
- Follow-the-dot book
- Tracing book
- String or rubber design board
- Sewing boards
- Beginning erector set

Gardening

These items are available from garden centers, hardware, or department stores.

- Wheel barrow or wagon
- Tools—small enough for a child to manage, but of sturdy quality
- Gro-light—a light made by several bulb manufacturers specifically for indoor gardening
- Timer for gro-light
- Little Greenthumb Window Garden—a six foot panoramic fold-out, game board, and growing instructions. (National Wildlife Federation) (B)

Geography

- *U.S. Color 'n Stick Map*
  Childcraft (B)
- *Pedometer*
  Childcraft (B)
- *Wood Train and Track*
  Childcraft (C)
- *Richard Scarry's Puzzletown Sets*
  Playskool (C)
- *U.S. Map Puzzle*
  Playskool (B)

- *Game of the States*
      Milton Bradley (A)
- *Walk Along Sesame Street*
      Milton Bradley (A)
- *U.A. Map Puzzle*
      Milton Bradley (B)
- *Worlds Unlimited*—three six-inch globes of earth, moon, and the heavens
      Childcraft (C)

Large Muscle Development and Coordination

- Outdoor gym equipment
- Jumping rope
- Bicycle
- Scooter
- Low basketball net
- Punching bag
- Stilts
- *Rope trolley*
      Childcraft (B)
- Balancing board
- Beginners' roller skates
- Ice skates
- Doorway gym bar
- *Jumping shoes,* with springs
      Childcraft (B)
- Skis
- Climbing rope
- Frisbee
- Pogo stick

Math, Numbers Concepts

As with reading and writing, just as with baseball and tennis, the right practice equipment generates understanding and skill.

- Blocks
- Felt board with geometric shapes
- Dominoes
- Easy card games
- *"Sum stick"*
    Childcraft (A)
- *"Fun sets"* math game
    Childcraft (B)
- Abacus
- Calculators

> *Little Professor*, Texas Instruments (C). Programmed problems for the child to solve. Informs dramatically whether or not solutions are correct. Addition, subtraction, multiplication, division, and games. The degree of difficulty can be adjusted to the child's math capability.
>
> *Dataman* Texas Instruments (D). A more sophisticated version of the *Little Professor*. The child can introduce problems. Additional games.

- Calendar
- Cash register and play money
- Height measurer to hang on the wall
- Ruler, compass (for drawing circles), triangle
- String board
- Simple calculator
- *Straw Mill Factory*
    Centsable Toys (B)
- *Arithmetic Flash Cards*
    Edu-Cards, each (A)
- New math addition and subtraction flash cards
    Edu-Cards (A)
- Metric flash cards assortment
    Edu-Cards (B)

Music
See also preschool toys.

- Harmonica

- Calliope
    Childcraft (A)
- Tuned xylophone or glockenspiel is appropriate for about the third grade level.
- Recorder
    Childcraft (B)

Nature Study
See also science toys.

- Wildlife conservation stamps and album, wildlife "Old Maid" and "Concentration" card games, singbird dominoes, wildlife "Lotto," wildlife puzzles. (National Wildlife Federation)

Pretending, Role-Playing
See also preschool toys.

Problem-solving

- Simple model kits—airplanes, cars, trains—available from hobby shops
- Young children's crossword puzzle book
- Board games requiring decision-making (e.g., checkers)
    Learning Games, Inc.: *Quick Master Chess* (C)
- Old appliances to take apart and put together
- *Straw Mill Factory*
    Centsable Toys (B)

Reading and Writing

Toys and games make the practice of reading fun, and reading practice is necessary for the development of reading skill. Activities that make writing useful and fun for the child will encourage him to write.

- Games requiring easy reading
- Writing paper and post cards for correspondence
- Word-building games
- Games requiring some concentration
- *Ends 'n Blends*
    Childcraft (B)
- Old typewriter

- Printing set
- *Alpha Worm*, a self-correcting alphabet puzzle
    Childcraft (B)
- Calendar with holidays
- Homemade calendar with large enough blocks for pictures and printing, making a diary
- *Alphabet game*
    Childcraft (A)
- *Scrabble Sentence Game for Juniors*
    Childcraft (A)
- Homemade blank books, bound blank books
- Follow-the-dot books
- Felt board with felt letters
- Tape recorder

Science

See also preschool toys.

- Collection materials from nature walks; boxes and shelves for arranging and storing collection
- Gardening equipment and plants
- Child's microscope
- Compass
- Binoculars
- Kits for making simple pumps, motors
    Childcraft: MiniLab Kit, a set of two kits, appropriate for third grade and up (B)
- Outdoor thermometer outside his window
- Camera—The *Diana* is an inexpensive one available from The Workshop for Learning Things and from Sax Arts and Crafts. (A) You may want to consider the Polaroid One Step. (D)

Self-Image

- Desk, chair, lamp for studying
- Hats with emblems of local sports teams
- His own flashlight·
- A real watch
- Sleeping bag with washable liner
- Tent

RESOURCES

Children's Books

Books

LARRICK, NANCY. *A Parent's Guide To Children's Reading.* New York: Bantam, 1975.

Catalogs, Book Lists, and Magazines

The New York Public Library. Office of Children's Services, 8 E. 40th Street, New York, New York 10016.

The Children's Book Shop. 5705 Ogden Road, Washington, D.C. 20016. A list of hardcover and paperback books available by mail order. Catalog, 25 cents.

Gryphon House. 3706 Otis Street, Mt. Ranier, Maryland 20822. Any children's book in print may be ordered from this distributor. Catalog free upon request.

The Calendar. Children's Book Council, 67 Irving Place, New York, New York 10003. Published three times every two years. Lists of children's books and of free and inexpensive materials. A one-time handling charge of $5.00 puts you on their mailing list.

The Horn Book Magazine. The Horn Book, Inc., Park Square Building, Boston, Massachusetts 02116. New books for children; articles on authors, stories, and characters; reviews of records, films, and filmstrips. Most libraries have this magazine. Six issues a year at $12; single copy, $3.00.

Children's Rooms

Books

BROWNING, SARAH. *Children's Rooms: How to Decorate Them to Grow with Your Child.* Indianapolis, Ind.: Bobbs-Merrill, 1976.

STODDARD, ALEXANDRA. *A Child's Place.* New York: Doubleday, 1977.

SUNSET EDITORS. *Things to Make for Children.* Menlo Park, Cal.: Lane Books, 1967. Also in the same series, "Children's Rooms and Play Yards," 10th Printing, 1976.

Materials

Animal Welfare. Posters, 17 x 22, two color. Washington, D.C. 20037: Humane Society.

Ranger Rick's Animal Parade. Posters, 21 x 28, color, one for each of thirty-two different animals; other wildlife decorative items are also available. Washington, D.C. 20036: National Wildlife Federation.

Toys, Games,
and Equipment

Books

CANEY, STEVEN. *Steve Caney's Toy Book.* New York: Workman Publishing, 1972.

HARTLEY, RUTH E. and ROBERT M. GOLDENSON. *The Complete Book of Children's Play.* New York: Thomas Y. Crowell, 1963.

"Things to Make for Children," *Sunset Book.* Menlo Park, Ca.: Lane Books, 1967.

Government Publications

Order from the Assistant Public Printer (Superintendent of Documents), U.S. Government Printing Office, Washington, D.C. 20402.

Toys in the Making (from household items). 1790–00011. The same in Spanish: *Es Devertido Constrair.* 1790–00017.

Toy Safety and Banned Toy List. U. S. Bureau of Product Safety. 1712–00165.

Toy Company Addresses

Buddy L Corporation
Customer Service Department
200 Fifth Avenue
New York, New York 10010

Childcraft Education Corp.
20 Kilmer Road
Edison, N.J. 08817

Creative Playthings
CBS, Inc.
Princeton, N.J. 08540

Community Playthings
Rifton, N.Y. 12471
(914) 658-3142

Cuisenaire
See, Learning Games, Inc.

Ertl Toys
Dyersville, Ia. 52040

Educational Design Associates
Box 712
Waldorf, Md. 20601

Ideal School Supply Co.
Oak Lawn, Ill. 60453

Instructo Corp.
Paolii, Pa. 19301

Jolly Jumper, Inc.
144 Water Street,
South Cambridge,
Ontario, Canada

Learning Games Inc.
10 Cove Lee Drive
Westport, Conn. 06880

Milton Bradley
Springfield, Mass. 01101

National Wildlife Federation
1412 16th Street, N.W.
Washington, D.C. 20036

Natural Sciences Industries
Far Rockaway, N.Y. 11691

Ohaus Scale Corporation
29 Hanover Road
Florham Park, N.J. 07932

Playskool
(see Milton Bradley)

Questor Educational Products
Bronx, N.Y. 10472

Richards Teaching Aids
12315 Wilkins Avenue
Rockville, Md. 20852

Sax Arts and Crafts
207 N. Milwaukee Street
Milwaukee, Wis. 53202

Structo
(See Ertl)

Texas Instruments, Inc.
2305 University Avenue
Lubbock, Tx. 79415

Trend Enterprises, Inc.
New Brighton, Minn. 55165

Uncle Milton Industries, Inc.
Culver City, Ca. 90230

The Workshop for
  Learning Things, Inc.
5 Bridge Street
Watertown, Mass. 02172

6

settings

CAMPS

Although camp is not necessary and does not fit with every family's way of vacationing, it does fill a need for many families and it is an excellent way to teach children independence and responsibility.

If you decide to use camping opportunities for your child, the best way to introduce him to camp life is to start him off in a day camp. Very young children are usually apprehensive about an overnight stay away from home. You may want to introduce your child to staying away overnight by letting him "sleep over" with a neighbor's child from time to time once you know your child won't panic and want to come home. (This could be a cooperative baby-sitting arrangement).

There are camps which offer general camping experience, and there are those which specialize. When your child is older and his interests are becoming more identifiable, he may be interested in a specialized camp. There are sports camps (hockey, swimming, sailing, horseback riding, tennis), backpacking and canoeing camps, foreign language camps, arts and music camps, camps with religious emphasis. There are camps for blind or deaf children, for emotionally or mentally handicapped children, for diabetics, and for children with other physical handicaps.

For most young school age children, the initial camp experience will primarily be learning to work and play with peers and developing independence from parents, all the while benefiting physically from nourishing food, regular hours, exercise, and supervised activities in the fresh air.

Because camps are often located some distance from home, it can be difficult to make a personal inspection; yet you will certainly want to know as much as possible about the campsite and personnel. You can start your exploration by going to the library and asking for books on camps. Go early because as the season approaches, you may have to put your book on order and wait. One well-known book is Porter Sargent's *Guide to Summer Camps and Summer Schools* (available also in paperback from *Porter Sargent Publishing, Inc., 11 Beacon Street, Boston, Massachusetts 02108.* Phone *(617) 523-1670).* If you write to *The American Camping Association, ACA Publications Department, Bradford Woods, Martinsville, Indiana 46151,* or call them—*(317) 342-8456*—they will supply you with lists of accredited camps in your area. The list is divided into four regions—Northeastern, Southern, Midwestern, and Western—and it gives you information on the charges, the type of camp, its accreditation, how long the camp has been operating, and the name and address of camp director.

When you follow up your research by writing the camp director, you may want to make the following specific inquiries:

- What is the ratio of counselors to campers?
- What will be the total cost? Are there extra fees?
- What about doctors and medical facilities?
- What first aid training have the counselors had?
- Ask for sample menus and inquire about whether the children are allowed second helpings of the basic foods.
- What clothes are needed?
- What arrangements are there, financial and otherwise, if the child must leave camp and return home early?

You will notice that the American Camping Association approves some camps for their sites only, which means that they approve the facilities, but that, in some cases, different groups use the site, so the Association cannot approve the personnel and programs.

As you and your child prepare for him to go to camp:

- Talk about specific things you know he will be doing so he will have some idea what to expect.

- Avoid talking about how much you will miss him, but if he asks, tell him you certainly will. Tell him everybody feels that way sometimes.

- Don't start talking about his going away far in advance of his going for the first time.

- Buy plain, sensible clothes like all the other kids are wearing and don't send any more than the camp director suggests. Your child will want to fit in with the other kids and will not want to have to worry about a lot of stuff.

- Attach name tags to EVERYTHING you hope to see again.

- Don't panic and rush off to camp when the first homesick letter arrives. Homesickness is common in the first few days, but counselors know how to deal with it, and very soon you will get a more upbeat letter. If you visit in spite of having been advised against it by a qualified camp director, you are apt to find that, by the time you get there, your child is happily engaged and doesn't need you at all.

COMMUNITY

A sense of the family's belonging to and contributing to the community gives children security and self-confidence. Growing up feeling friendly and responsible toward the community of which he is a part not only orients a child's thinking toward his own existence, but also toward common goals. Social concern and patriotism are rooted in such a way of thinking.

The very young child's *community* is very close by. He learns to be at home in a *community* when he learns to be a viable part of the family and a concerned friend to close neighbors. The advantages of close neighbors' acceptance of young children cannot be overestimated. If at all possible, acceptance should be encouraged by considerate friendliness on the part of parents.

When your child is still a preschooler, you and he can begin to participate in community activities—story hour at the library, church activities, sporting events, swimming lessons, park service nature walks, fairs and carnivals, nursery school, and so on. The nature of the activities will depend on your interests and where you live as well as on the age and interests of your child. It isn't hard to find out what is going on. Try your local library, school, town hall, or county office. Read the local newspaper (published just for your town or county) and talk with people around town.

Throughout elementary school, your child should be gradually moving *away* from home. You will want him to be acquainted so he can move *into* the community. Church groups, Scouts, and 4H are organized for just this purpose. If the child moves into a void without positive connections in the community, he may grow up knowing and caring little about his community relationships and responsibilities.

All through the school years, your help will be vital in assuring your child's adjustment to good community activities. Be understanding and gentle. Don't force. Your child may well choose what he wants to do by what his friends are doing, which is all right as long as the activity is constructive. Your objective in this case is to teach him how to enjoy friends in a positive community environment. His wanting to be with peer friends is the first step, so all you need to do is to make sure opportunities and transportation are available.

SEE ALSO: Field Trips; Friendship; Human Ecology; Independence; Geography.

DAY CARE

The idea of "day care" for young children used to relate to babysitting services for children whose mothers *had* to work outside the home. Today there are many families in which both parents *choose* to work outside the home at least part-time, often full time. An increasing number of single-parent families also need day care assistance. As a result of these needs, several different kinds of day care facilities and arrangements are becoming available.

Your primary consideration, when looking for child care, will be the person who will be spending many hours with your child in his formative years. Recognizing the tremendous influence he will have on your child, you will want to make sure this person looks at things the way you do. Also a very important consideration is the day care facility, for it is the environment in which your child will be living part of his young life. You want it to be safe, clean, and enriching.

There are different kinds of day care facilities to be explored. You may find, by talking with your neighbors or by looking through classified ads in local papers or on supermarket bulletin boards, that there is a mother nearby who is providing day care for a small number of children in her home. Some home care facilities are licensed by the state or county and some are not. The ones that are licensed are usually a little more expensive, but, unless you know the responsible person, licensing can provide you with a way of knowing that minimum standards are being met. Often unlicensed home care facilities are of good quality but fail to fulfill one or another minor requirement. Whichever you find available, you will want to check on the following aspects of the facility:

- Is there enough space for each child to move about freely?
- Is there a safe place for children to play outside?
- Are the kitchen, washroom, and toilet clean?
- Do you approve of the menus?
- Do you approve of the toys, games, and books?
- How many other children are there? One adult should not try to care for more than three or four infants and toddlers.
- What are the arrangements for a child who becomes sick?
- Do you notice any unsafe features?
- Do you and the person in charge agree on values and discipline?

The above criteria apply to any kind of day care you choose for your child. The following are some avenues you may want to

explore: Your local public school, the department of human resources or health, or a university department of human ecology
may provide facilities; or they should be able to advise you. Some
churches and synagogues provide day care, as do some YMCA,
YWCA and YMHA groups. These same organizations also may
offer Mothers' Day Out programs, which provide care for children
while parents participate in classes and other adult activities. The
U.S. Department of Health, Education, and Welfare (Office of
Human Development, Office of Child Development, Washington
D.C. 20013) provides helpful material on day care.

Still another way of handling day care, especially for parents
who are not employed full time, is the playgroup. If you can get
together with a small group of parents who have the same values as
you, you may find that organizing into a *playgroup* will be a creative
and economical solution to child care problems. Parents take turns
planning and caring for a small number of children in their homes,
sharing time and the cost of quality toys and equipment and giving
the children a variety of enriching experiences.

SEE ALSO: School.

FAMILY

Long before a young child starts school, he learns how to cope with
life by imitating the members of his family. And the impressions of
himself he gets from his family are an integral part of what he
thinks of himself all his life. Also, each individual family passes on
its cultural heritage to its children; culture being the sum total of
the ways of living that develops in families over generations. So a
child not only learns who he is and how to do things from his
family, he should also learn that he belongs, that he has roots and a
heritage. Since public schools, especially in America, teach children
from any number of cultural backgrounds, they cannot hope to
develop each child's cultural identity with any refinement. So the
responsibility for orienting a child as an individual and for teaching
him his cultural heritage must remain with the family.

Family storytelling is one natural and enjoyable way to keep family history alive. It is good that grandparents love to talk about "the old days." Family traditions in the arts and crafts, in cooking, and in ways of celebrating special events become focal points in childhood memories which, in turn, are passed on to the next generation. Keep special pictures and objects (labeled and dated) to enjoy from time to time with your children. When planning a vacation with and for older children, consider visiting the places where your family lived in past generations; you might also make a family project of tracing lost connections. All of this does not mean that you must live in the past—far from it. Children are the future. Family culture is simply an important part of their total existence.

The Child

The newborn is not aware of parents as such. He accepts any warm and loving person who gives him good care. Within a few weeks, however, the baby begins to recognize the individual who cares for him. How this caretaker handles the infant is important to the child's early impressions about people. Some authorities claim that a child benefits from getting used to many caretakers; others say that the child needs the security of having a single primary caretaker. In modern families, where often both parents work, it is not likely that a young child will have one caretaker all through his early years. His time will be divided at least between his father and mother, and very likely he will spend part of his time with another person or persons. Practically speaking, it would seem best to accustom your child to whatever arrangement you will need to fit your circumstances, keeping in mind that your child needs the security of consistency and remembering that whoever cares for him is going to influence him. And unless parents give their children quality attention when they *are* with them, they will lose *their* influence. As the child grows, it is vital for him to feel that he means a lot to his family. Shared experiences and responsibilities deepen devotion, and, in so doing, keep children close and make them feel wanted.

Mothers and Fathers

There is a difference between the ways in which mothers and fathers relate to and influence children. The very young child gravitates toward his primary caregiver, who has traditionally been his mother. She bears the child, nurses him, and is so close to him in the early years that she is bound to be the focal point of his existence. She is so attuned to him that he can communicate his needs to her in his nonverbal ways. His devotion to her is legendary. However, even though the young child does not understand sex differences, he absorbs feelings about the difference between mother and father which are an important part of the development of his sexual identity. As early as three, children, without any instruction, recognize their fathers as either the same or the opposite sex as themselves and respond accordingly. Without both male and female adults to relate to, even at this early age, children miss opportunities to absorb the nuances of their own sexual identity. During the school years, the attitudes of each parent toward the males and females in the family will have a profound effect on how well the children, as adolescents and adults, respond to members of their own and the opposite sex.

Sexual and cultural identity combines with the child's feelings about himself as a personality. A child's mental health and intellectual progress depends heavily on his feeling of being considered worthy by his parents and on his building confidence daily at home under their tutelage.

Siblings

Extended families—that is, families in which several generations, aunts, uncles, and cousins, live close to one another and share responsibility for one another—usually develop devotion among siblings. Also, children of parents who are close to their own brothers and sisters will be more apt to be close to theirs. We suspect that part of the loneliness we experience in contemporary society results from parents, brothers, and sisters being separated from one another. With travel so much easier now than it once was, one wonders whether the separation is so much a matter of distance due to mobility as it is a matter of attitudes that cause people to lose contact with their families. It is possible for brothers and sisters to lead strong independent lives and still be devoted and supporting of one another. Many families, obscure and prominent, are devoted to and supportive of each other regardless of circumstances. In other words, the strength of the family cannot be realized by schools or by society—only by parents and children in the family setting.

Grandparents

There is a kind of learning about life that only grandparents can give children. The whole family is fortunate if grandparents live nearby and can spend a lot of time with their grandchildren. If they live far away, close contact should be kept through letters, pictures, phone calls, homemade gifts, samples of the children's accomplishments, and visits.

Grandparents have a special devotion to their grandchildren and so have no difficulty at all in making them feel loved. Yet they are bound to have expectations of their grandchildren which differ from those of the children's parents. Your child will learn from them that different people have different ideas about what is or isn't acceptable. Also, from his grandparents, your child will learn about older people. He will learn to understand how they look at things and how to be kind to and appreciative of them.

Grandparents exemplify the concepts of generations, of family continuity, of cultural identity, of the passage of time, of history. They love to talk about their own childhood, and about the days when Mommy and Daddy were little.

Grandparents have skills and interests to bring to children; and, since they are relieved of the day-to-day responsibility for their care, may enjoy planning special activities if they are encouraged to do so. They are usually patient with children; having raised a family themselves, they have gained perspective. Just about all the activities in this book are enhanced by their participation. If grandparents are kept up to date on their grandchildren's interests, they love to buy and make appropriate gifts.

Sometimes there is a tendency on the part of the grandparents to be shy of in-laws. They hesitate for fear of being "in the way," so parents need to take the initiative in involving them in the family. When enough time is spent together, an open, easy, loving relationship can develop that is beautiful for the grandchildren.

SEE ALSO: Children's Books (family, holidays, grandparents); Holidays; Everyday Teaching; Sibling Rivalry; Housekeeping, Duties and Chores; Talking with Children.

SCHOOL

The word *school*, for most of us, brings back memories which can influence how we feel about our children's education. Some of us were afraid of school, some of us were bored, and many of us did not understand the purpose of school until later in life. Some of us liked school for the social life, some for the teachers and the work, some for both of these, and some of us generally hated it for all sorts of reasons. Because schools have changed and because our children are different from us, they will have their own feelings about school, hopefully positive, arising from their own interests and inclinations.

The fact that schools have changed pleases some people and displeases others. In the past ten years, more knowledge has been accumulated than in all previous history, a fact which must cause a reordering of educational priorities. Since one can't possibly learn about everything, the question becomes, "What should be taught?" Besides having to make judicial changes because of the knowledge explosion, educators are also aware of and want to use what has been learned in the last century about child development and the psychology of learning.

In the last several years, some school systems have instituted a more informal approach to elementary education, based on what has been done in British early childhood education. In informal education, children are not forced to learn what adults think they should learn, but rather what they themselves find interesting. The teacher then weaves the skills to be learned around the child's chosen activity, expecting that the child will learn better when motivated by his own interest. Such teaching methods have come to be labeled *open* or *informal education* and have become the center of a great public controversy. Actually, most schools use a combination of self-motivation and a teacher-directed curriculum. Some schools are more informal than others and some parents, more than others, like them that way, so there is now a movement toward providing, within the public system, schools of different types. Since parents are supposed to bear the ultimate responsibility for their children's education (because we live in a free society), it seems right that they have the opportunity to make knowledgeable choices between different kinds of schools.

Educators are becoming more and more interested in parents as the essential ingredient in a child's success in school. They want to encourage parents to participate without reservation in bringing home and school closer together. You will want to take advantage of this cooperative attitude (there was a time when teachers were encouraged to keep parents out of the classroom). There is no question about the value of having good communication between home and school. Learn all you can about what is being taught and how, beginning at the beginning with your young child, so you can follow through with him on his new methods and materials. It takes reorganizing some parts of your brain a little, even with very elementary work, but you will gain new insights and will be better able to help your child succeed.

Preparing your child for school begins at birth, though in very informal, pleasant ways. All the preschool activities in this book are meant not only as preparation for school, but also simply for pleasure. Teaching your child to feel comfortable with other people, adults and peers alike, is more something to plan and arrange than to talk about. A child will be most successful if he has learned to be independent, how to take care of himself. He needs you to care about his food, his sleep, his exercise, his eye and ear exams. Toys, games, books, and even chores teach skills and concepts that will be useful in school. There are books, television programs, and adult education courses which will help parents learn how to relate the preschool child's informal everyday activities to the learning of skills and concepts which prepare him for school.

Nursery Schools

Nursery schools are usually half-day and serve children from age three to five. They are generally privately run and they charge a fee. Some are church or university related, and some are run with the cooperation of parents as part-time teachers. A good nursery school is a transition between home and kindergarten. It can get at any little problems early; it helps children who do not have other children to play with; it is good for shy children; and it encourages creativity and skills that will be used later.

To find a good nursery school, contact:

- Your local public school
- The local YWCA, YMCA, or YMHA
- Your local city or county social service department, health department, or department of human resources
- Your state licensing agency for nursery schools (You will want to choose a licensed school unless you are closely involved with the school yourself.)
- Your local university department of education
- Local churches and synagogues
- Friends and neighbors

You will want to discuss licensing, location, transportation, hours, how much you can pay, the age and sex of your child, any handicaps and special attention required, what arrangements you need for the times when your child is sick, and whether or not you are expected to serve as volunteer staff. Look at more than one school, so you can make comparisons. Plan to visit without your child, but when school is in session, so you can see not only the physical appearance of the place but also how the children are handled and how they react to the adults in charge. You will want to check the following:

- Is there enough space for each child to move about freely?

- Is there enough light and air; is it clean?
- Is there a safe place for the children to play outside?
- Is there indoor and outdoor equipment for large muscle development?
- Are there educational materials, toys, and games; what books does the school have?
- Ask for sample menus for meals and snacks to note the nutritional value of what is offered.
- Ask to see the kitchen; is it clean, well organized?
- When and how are the children fed?
- How many adults are there per child? Two adults for every six to ten infants and toddlers, two adults for every twelve to fifteen three- and four-year-olds; for five-year-olds, one adult to every fifteen to twenty, an additional adult on call at all times (these ratios are recommended in the *Child Care Handbook*, published by the American Home Economics Association).
- Are there any safety hazards?
- What are the first aid facilities; are there places to accommodate a sick child?
- Does someone know first aid procedures?
- Are there arrangements for rest periods?
- Is there a time and place for quiet activities like painting and reading?
- If you are a single parent, will your child have the opportunity to be with an adult of the opposite sex?

Special Nursery Schools

Head Start

Head Start is a federally financed program which requires that 90% of the children participating in the program come from families that are below the poverty level. It involves nutrition, health, social opportunities, educational play, counseling, and parent involvement—all aimed at helping children succeed upon entering public school. Your city or county social service agencies will be able to advise you about this educational opportunity in your area; or you may contact any one of the following regional offices of the U.S. Department of Health, Education and Welfare:

Office of Child Development, HEW
John Fitzgerald Kennedy
  Federal Building
Government Center
Boston, Massachusetts 02203
(617) 223-6450

Office of Child Development, HEW
Federal Building
26 Federal Plaza—Room 3900
New York, New York 10007
(212) 264-2974

Office of Child Development, HEW
Post Office Box 13716
3535 Market Street
Philadelphia, Pennsylvania 19101
(215) 596-6763

Office of Child Development, HEW
Peachtree-Seventh Building
50 Seventh Street, N.E.—Room 358
Atlanta, Georgia 30323
(404) 526-3966

Office of Child Development, HEW
300 South Wacker Drive
15th Floor
Chicago, Illinois 60606
(312) 353-1781

Office of Child Development, HEW
Fidelity Union Tower—Rm. 500
1507 Pacific Avenue
Dallas, Texas 75201
(214) 729-2492

Office of Child Development, HEW
Federal Building
601 East 12th Street, 3rd Floor
Kansas City, Missouri 64106
(816) 374-5401

Office of Child Development, HEW
1961 Stout Street—Rm. 7426
Denver, Colorado 80202
(303) 837-3106

Office of Child Development, HEW
Federal Office Building
50 Fulton Street—Rm. 143
San Francisco, California 94102
(415) 556-6153

Office of Child Development, HEW
Dexter Horton Building
710 Second Avenue
Seattle, Washington 98101
(206) 442-0482

Indian and Migrant
  Programs Division
Office of Child Development, HEW
Post Office Box 1182
Room 2014
Washington, D.C. 20013
(202) 755-7715

Montessori Schools

In the early 1900s, Dr. Maria Montessori devised a structured program for the development of children from age three to twelve. Her methods have been used and copied all over the world, and in the 1960s, they became well known in the United States. Most of the Montessori schools in this country serve preschool children. They are *not inexpensive*.

Maria Montessori believed that children developed best when allowed to learn at their own pace in a well-structured atmosphere. All Montessori schools use the same type of program and equipment and are supervised by teachers who have one year of post baccalaureate training in the Montessori method.

For further information, contact a Montessori school in your area or write to *Washington Montessori Institute, 2119 S Street, Washington, D.C. 20008.*

Waldorf Schools

The Waldorf schools were originated by Rudolph Steiner, who was also the originator of a spiritual philosophy called anthroposophy, the central belief of which is that, through reincarnation, human evolution is perfected. The aim of education, therefore, in the schools established by Rudolph Steiner and his followers, is to develop the soul and spirit of the child as well as his body and his intellect. Within the concept of this philosophy and purpose, Waldorf schools present a unique art oriented curriculum. The schools are informal and it is considered important that each child be treated with respect. There is no proselytyzing in the classroom, so you need not subscribe to Rudolph Steiner's philosophy to consider a Waldorf school. At the elementary level, Waldorf schools are day schools only, so, if you are interested in the above educational approach and you live near a Waldorf school, you may want to phone for brochures and make an appointment for an interview.

Kindergarten

A child is ready for kindergarten if he knows how to wash his own hands and button his own coat. He knows that books are for reading. He can paint, model, jump, swing, climb; maybe he can do little puzzles, sing, print his name, and get along pretty well without his mother—sometimes. He is five, the age at which parents consider whether their child is ready for kindergarten. If he is ready, he should take this giant step into the school system; if not, he should wait a year. Starting your child at the right time gets him situated in his school career so that he is, from the beginning, developmentally in tune with the progression of class years. If you are unsure, seek an outside opinion from a teacher or counselor.

The kindergarten curriculum, although similar to that of a nursery school, is developmentally geared to the five-year-old; and, in an informal way, it anticipates first grade. There will be art work, music, experimenting, show and tell, conversation, stories, indoor and outdoor play, dancing, and a few field trips. The children will learn how to do things for themselves, how to be proud of and share their capabilities, and how to be considerate of others in a group.

Kindergarten teachers usually encourage parent participation. Let it be known if you can play an instrument or sing, if you use interesting tools in your hobbies or occupation, and if you can make or do anything that may be of interest to kindergarten children. The teacher will be grateful; and your child will be proud and pleased. The class will be enriched and will, through observing your participation in the school world, begin to build concepts of relevancy between school and real life.

Elementary School

Is your child ready for first grade? Because timing children's experiences to their stage of development rather than to their years is so very important for learning, you will want to observe your child carefully when he is moving toward the age of six. Your child should not only be physically ready—with properly developed vision and the motor skills he will need to carry out first grade activities—but he also needs to be emotionally ready to function without excessive strain. Here are a few clues to readiness for first grade:

- Is he near the age of the other children in his class? Younger children often have social problems all through school.

- Does he choose his friends from among his own age group or from younger children? There is a rate at which each individual develops emotionally as well as in every other way—and that rate is often inherited—so it is best to allow the child to be in class with children who share his own emotional age.

- Can he concentrate, at least for a short while, on a game or project?

- Are his teeth well developed for his age? At five-and-a-half- to six, are his two front lower teeth coming through? The six-year-molars at about six? A delay in teething has nothing to do with intelligence or with ultimate success, but it has been found that it may accompany slower maturing in other physical and emotional ways.

- Are his eyes ready for reading? A five-year-old can focus on fixed objects but has trouble moving his eyes along a line of printing (tracking). At five-and-a-half he begins to track, but he is easily disoriented. If your child shows little interest in reading, it may be that he is slow in developing the physical ability to track; if he is moved into first grade, he may have trouble keeping up with the reading program.

- Between the ages of five and six, a child should be able to draw a circle, beginning at the top and moving around counterclockwise to complete the circle. Delayed ability here, if accompanied by other manifestations, may tell you that your child is not ready for first grade.

- If you do not feel that your own observations are adequate and if you feel that advice you have from your child's school is prejudiced, you may get a valuable third opinion from your local child guidance clinic. It is easier to hold back a year at the start than to make the adjustment later.

Once your child has entered school, if you find him *consistently* floundering in his school work and unahppy with his classmates, you may consider it very likely that he will so continue throughout school. The earlier he is properly adjusted within a school program which meets the needs of his developmental age, the better. Remedial work is recommended only if the child is emotionally and mentally with his age group, and for some reason, such as a diagnosed and relievable problem or illness, has fallen behind his class. Once your child is in school, watch for any one or more of these following symptoms:

Consistent tension, physical complaints, unhappiness, or rebellion

Inability to keep up with work or with the other children

Lack of interest in class work

Lack of interest in classmates

If you observe any of these trends, you may want to discuss the possibility of your child's re-entering an earlier graded class. One of the benefits of more informal school arrangements is that their flexibility allows the slower maturing child to find his own proper place without the stigma of demotion.

Classroom Behavior

Much poor classroom behavior results from the child's being out of phase with what is going on. Either he cannot keep up with the group or he is ahead of them and bored. If a child has a distorted self-image (he thinks too little—or too much—of himself), he may fail to apply himself and resort to unpopular behavior. A good teacher will work hard at helping each child work up to his capability and will work at the self-image problem too, but without parent cooperation, he will find it almost impossible to be of much help.

Naturally, some teachers are going to be better for your child than others. You cannot rely completely on your child's criticism of his teacher. It is best not to criticize his teacher in front of him. Develop in your child the attitude that, no matter how he feels about his teacher, his education is basically his own responsibility and that you stand ready to help him make up for whatever he can't get from any one teacher. You don't have to condone the teacher's methods or behavior, but you want to avoid encouraging your child to be disrespectful.

All children have some classroom crises, and these should be discussed sympathetically; but it is advisable to not rush off to school immediately. Overanxious parents are not popular with busy teachers, and the children of overanxious parents are not always popular with other children.

However, if a problem persists, it is necessary to act decisively. You do not want your child to develop an aversion to school. Allowing him to suffer for any length of time in school, for whatever reason, is seriously destructive.

Start by talking with his teacher. Do not be too ready either to take issue with him or to accept his diagnosis of your child's problem. Listen with an open mind; and then, if you do not understand or agree with what the teacher said, read books and/or seek follow-up advice. You and the teacher should be able to identify the problem and work out a solution. If you and the teacher cannot solve the problem, go to a school counselor; then, if necessary, go to the principal, and then to an outside consultant. It is best not to discuss all this with your child. Just let him know that you are concerned and that you are trying to find out how to help him. Express your confidence that he will not let this temporary situation get him down.

Private Schools

There are no private schools in Russia because the state, under the guise of maintaining a classless society, can conveniently, at the same time, prevent unorthodox educational ideas from developing outside the system. Only a relatively few people in the United States send their children to private schools (many cannot afford them, many choose public schools on principle), yet the existence of such schools offers a richness to the fiber of American education that would otherwise be missing. Were we not permitted to have private schools, we would not have Choate, Exeter, or Montessori schools, nor would we have such valuable innovative schools as the "Schools without Walls" in Philadelphia and the storefront schools like the very successful Harlem Prep.

If, for whatever reason, you are interested in a private school for your child, pursue the project in detail, beginning with consulting directories such as Porter Sargent's *Handbook of Private Schools* or *Lovejoy's Prep School Guide*. Both are found in most libraries. Then you will want to pursue the subject in detail through visits, interviews, and references from parents of students and other reliable sources. For the very young child, it is usually advisable (and happiest for the family) for the child to attend a nearby day school, although this is a choice that must be made by each family, given its knowledge of the surrounding circumstances.

SEE ALSO: Children's Books (school).

RESOURCES

Books and Pamphlets

Guide to Selecting a Private Camp. Published annually at the beginning of each year. Association of Private Camps, 55 W. 42nd Street, New York, N.Y. 10036

Guide to Summer Camps and Schools. 1977. Porter Sargent Publishers, Inc., Boston, Mass. 02108

Parents Guide to Accredited Camps. Published annually in four parts (Northeastern, Southern, Mid-Western, Western). American Camping Association Publications Department, Bradford Woods, Martinsville, Ind. 46151

YMCA Resident Camp Directory. 1977. National Board, YMCA, 291 Broadway, New York, N.Y. 10007

YWCA Resident Camps. 1978. National Board, YWCA, Data Center, 600 Lexington Avenue, New York, N.Y. 10002

Community

Organizations

Boy Scouts of America, North Brunswick, New Jersey, 08902.

4-H National Foundation, 7100 Connecticut Avenue, Chevy Chase, Md. 20015.

National Future Farmers of America, Alexandria, Va., 22309.

YMCA. A modest membership fee makes swimming and other sports and exercise programs available. There are also arts and crafts and "Mother's Day Out" programs. Different Ys have different special programs. Inquire about Indian Guide and Afro-Guide programs for parents and young school age children. Call the Y in your community.

Books and Pamphlets

BROAD, LAURA PEABODY and NANCY TOWNER BUTTERWORTH. *The Playgroup Handbook*. New York: St. Martin's Press, 1974.

GOAD, MARCINE H. *Every Parent's Guide to Day Care Centers*. Chatsworth, Cal.: Books for Better Living, 1975.

American Home Economics Association. *Child Care Handbook*. 2010 Massachusetts Avenue, N.W., Washington, D.C. 20036, 1975.

McCARTHY, JAN and CHARLES H. MAY. *Providing the Best for Young Children*. Washington: National Association for the Education of Young Children, 1974.

Government Publications

Order from the Assistant Public Printer (Superintendent of Documents), U.S. Government Printing Office, Washington, D.C., 20402.

Day Care Facts. 1973. L 36.112:16, 029–016–00011-9.

Day Care, Family Day Care, ed. by Carol Seefeldt, Ph.D. and Laura L. Dittman, Ph.D. U.S. Dept. of Health, Education, and Welfare, Office of Child Development. 1791–00188.

Day Care for Your Child. 1974 HE 1.452:D33. 017–091–00194–4.

Day Care Serving Preschool Children. 1974. HE 21.11:3. 017–091–00196–1.

Family Day Care. 1973. HE 21.11:9. 017–091–001880–0.

Serving School Age Children. 1972. HE 21.11:4. 071–091–00165–1.

Magazines

Day Care and Early Education. 72 Fifth Avenue, New York, New York 10011. The magazine of the child-growth movement. It concerns itself with the needs of day care administrators and personnel, concerned parents, and educators. Emphasis is preschool education. Five issues a year, $9.95.

Books

CROSS, ALEENE A. *Enjoying Family Living*. Philadelphia: Lippincott, 1967.

CURTIS, JEAN. *A Guide To Working Mothers*. New York: Doubleday, 1977.

DODSON, DR. FITZHUGH. *How to Father*. Los Angeles: Nash Publishing Company, 1974.

DODSON, DR. FITZHUGH. *How to Parent*. Los Angeles: Nash Publishing Company, 1970.

School

Books—Preschool

AMES, LOUISE BATES, Ph.D. and JOAN AMES. *Don't Push Your Preschooler*. New York: Harper & Row, 1974.

HODGEN, LAUREL and JUDITH KOETTER, et. al. *School Before Six*. St. Louis: Cemrel Institute, 3120 59th St., 63139.

Government Publications

Head Start, A Child Development Program. DHEW(OHD) 76–31092. Order from U.S. Dept. of H.E.W., Office of Human Development, Office of Child Development, Washington, D.C. 20201.

Books and Pamphlets—School

BERSON, MINNIE PERRIN. *Kindergarten, Your Child's Big Step*. New York: Dutton, 1959.

BLOCK, N.J. AND GERALD DWORKIN. *The IQ Controversy*. New York: Pantheon, 1976.

FINE, BENJAMIN. *The Stranglehold of the IQ.* New York: Doubleday, 1976.

GLASSER, WILLIAM. *Schools Without Failure.* New York: Harper & Row, 1975.

GOWAN, JOHN CURTIS and E. PAUL TORRANCE, eds. *Educating the Ablest: A Book of Readings on the Education of Gifted Children.* Itasca, Ill.: F.E. Peacock Pubs. Inc., 1971.

HOUTS, PAUL L., ed. *The Myth of Measurability.* New York: Hart Publishing Co., 1977.

Individually Guided Education. Wisconsin Research and Development Center for Cognitive Learning, 1025 West Johnson Street, Madison, Wisc. 53706.

LOVEJOY, CLARENCE EARLE. *Lovejoy's Prep School Guide* (4th ed.). New York: Simon and Schuster, 1974.

MURROW, CASEY and LIZA MURROW. *Children Come First.* New York: American Heritage Press, 1971. Informal education in British primary schools.

PROVUS, MALCUM, Ph.D. and DOUGLAS E. STONE, Ph.D. *Programmed Instruction in the Classroom.* Chicago: Curriculum Advisory Service, Inc., 833 S. Wabash Ave., Chicago, Ill. 60605.

SARGENT, PORTER. *Handbook of Private Schools.* Boston: Porter Sargent Publishing, Inc. Yearly publication.

Organizations

Council for Exceptional Children. 1920 Association Drive, Reston, Va. An information source which can supply prepared bibliographies and individualized computer bibliographies with abstracts on exceptional children. The Council also has its own publications.

III

teaching

You do not need to be a professional teacher in order to teach your child. Many of life's values cannot be taught anywhere but at home. Many skills that are used in school are developed at home, and motivation to learn in school grows out of parental attitudes and interest.

Teachers talk about "learning skills"—those which make it easier for a person to think, understand, and remember. The skills discussed in Chapter 7 (Learning How To Learn) are not expected of a preschool child, but their beginnings can be encouraged if parents know what activities induce their development.

Every child finds learning easier and more fun if what is to be learned is a relevant current "happening." Everyday living at home presents many opportunities for successful teaching, if parents recognize the possibilities and understand how to maximize them. That is the rationale underlying Chapter 8 (Everyday Teaching). The more a child enjoys, experiences, and practices at his own level at each developmental stage, the more he will enjoy school and the greater will be his chances for success. Parents need to order their own priorities to allow time to stop and teach whenever opportunities arise.

What makes a good teacher of young children is patience and understanding as well as the ability to motivate and to take pleasure in seeing children grow up happy, healthy, and able to maximize their capabilities. Whatever your background, you can be a good teacher. Whether you are teaching your own child or working with other people's children, your personal interest and help can make all the difference in the world to a child's accomplishment.

7

learning how
to learn

THE ART OF TEACHING
A YOUNG CHILD

A private teaching session once or twice a week helps the child
immensely with his school work. If the child builds misconception
on top of misconception in the beginning, his entire education will
be built on a shaky foundation. It is important that he thoroughly
understand and master each step as he progresses. Your individual
attention continually clarifies elements of subject matter and reinforces skills in a way that is impossible in the classroom.

Here are some miscellaneous tips for successful teaching of
young children:

- Get close and let the child touch you. Children are very sensitive—it
  hurts them when they want to touch and people draw away.
- Don't make assumptions about a child's intelligence—you may be all
  wrong and do him a great injustice.
- Some children are better at using their hands and feet than
  others—remember that this is not necessarily connected with intelligence.

- The starting point for teaching is the child's interests. First find out what he really enjoys, then use that in your teaching as much as possible.

- Hungry children are grouchy and listless and can't learn well. If you suspect your child is hungry, provide an energizing snack at the beginning of a lesson.

- Motivating a child to want to learn is the greatest thing you can do for him. He will learn to the best of his ability if he wants to.

- Read through each lesson ahead of time and gather books, games, and materials to help the child enjoy and understand.

- Be thorough, but not boring. Have many things to do—games to play, books, and puzzles—all giving the child familiarity with the same bit of learning. He will then move comfortably into new material.

- Observe how manuscript is taught in school in order to avoid confusing the child when you print with and for him (Figures 15–2 and 15–3 in Chapter 15).

- Healthy young children have a short attention span. Change activities when they get bored or itchy. They need some physical movement from time to time, so for a change of pace, suggest playing some physical games. One such game calls for the teacher or other children to give directions, such as, "Touch the top of your head with your left hand and your left foot with your right hand" or "Jump up and down five times, then turn a summersault, then pat your tummy four times." These silly activities cause laughter and effect relaxation.

- When correcting, correct one thing at a time in order to avoid confusion.

- Children like to work if they can see what they have accomplished in a short time. Help them say, "I worked and look what I learned to do."

- When teaching letters and numbers, teach the same facts in many ways until the skill is thoroughly mastered. Use games, toys, sandpaper, crayons, clay, pictures, and so forth.

- There are many ways to teach the same concepts and facts. Different children have different learning styles. If a child does not understand something, stop and think about another way to get through to him.

- Help the child learn that he is not stupid because he makes mistakes. If a child is laughed at or scolded when he tries and fails, he may stop trying. "Everyone makes mistakes."

- If you find yourself on a collision course with a child, change the subject. Do something else.

- Humor makes learning fun. Children love comic situations.
- A child likes to try things for himself. Let him try, but understand that he will get discouraged quickly if he is not up to his task. Don't let him get bogged down—help him succeed.
- Give the child limited choices of what he would like to do—within the context of what you want to teach him. Choosing motivates participation.
- Make sure the child understands before you move on to the next step. Each advance is built on a knowledge of what went before.
- Have a good time. You want the child to connect learning with good times.
- Teach games that children can play with each other.
- Use large print for young children.
- Do not try to move the child ahead of his class. If his work is up with the class, use your teaching time for enrichment.

SEE ALSO: Talking with Children; Reading with Children.

CONCENTRATION

The very young mind absorbs bits and pieces of information at random, which is why distraction works well as a way of discouraging undesirable behavior in young children. As a child begins to discover that he is an individual, he begins to make decisions about what he wants to pursue and what, at any given moment, he will ignore. It is a gradual process. At first, directed attention occurs for very short amounts of time; then, as the child becomes more and more self-directed, he learns to zero in on his interests and maintain longer periods of concentration.

You cannot exactly *teach* a child to concentrate, but you can attend to the conditions under which concentration will develop and you can help him to understand the concept so he can direct himself to use it. Here are some ways to help your child develop his ability to concentrate:

- Encourage your child to be self-directed and independent.
- Do not overwhelm him with too many assorted toys. Keep some toys put away in order to encourage attentive rather than casual play.

- Encourage your child's strong points and special interests, because it is natural to pay serious attention to what is interesting.

- The anticipation of something pleasant awaiting the completion of chores and homework discourages dawdling and daydreaming and encourages the habit of attending to the job at hand for the purpose of getting to a goal or closure point.

- Break assignments requiring overly long periods of concentration into short segments so that the child has two or three short-term goals (closure points) to meet.

- Occasionally, make a game out of doing bits of homework or out of reinforcing skills by timing your child with an egg timer. "Get ready to turn on your concentration; get set, *go*." You might even push an imaginary button on top of his head, or suggest that he "rev up" an imaginary crank beside his ear in order to get across the idea of turning his mind to a task. This is just one trick for getting across the concept of deliberately concentrating; you may think of better ideas.

- As your child matures, gradually increase the complexity of games and puzzles.

SEE ALSO: Games; Math; Reading; Spelling.

CREATIVITY

The ability to assimilate information and impressions and then to come up with a new approach is creativity, whether it is in the arts, math, science, government, teaching, or any other discipline. Most people, for whatever reason, are more creative in certain areas than others. Usually, original thinking is present in areas of interest, so the habit of thinking creatively can be encouraged especially well by paying attention to your child's own inclinations. Fabricating with blocks, clay, sand and other materials, making pictures and other creative pieces, making up songs, poems and stories, and acting out grown-up roles are some activities in which a child can be creative. Out of all the available creative activities, your child will zero in on certain ones. In pursuing those activities, he will naturally develop the skills and pursue the knowledge he needs to enhance his creativity. Even a preschooler, whose ability to concentrate is limited, will indicate what he likes by spending more time with it. Don't expect anything out of the creative efforts of your preschooler. Expectations channel effort into preconceived formats. You want your child to do original thinking. Just follow his interest, give him materials and tools, and encourage him with appreciation, models, and ideas. The richer his inventive experience before school, the better motivated he will be to continue his creative approach throughout his formal education.

Educators are always trying to find ways to balance the teaching of skills with the encouragement of creative thinking. In a classroom full of children, it is difficult to strike the proper balance for each child. Parents deal with only one or two children at a time and they know their children well. Home is a freer and more relaxed environment than any school can ever be. For all these reasons, parents can provide the best balance between skill and development and creativity.

SEE ALSO: Creative Arts.

CURIOSITY

All normal infants and young children are born with curiosity. Without experience, children can get hurt or damage property because of their urges to poke, push, pull, and chew. Sometimes adults can see only the danger to the child and the property; in their concern they seem blind to the marvelous gift of curiosity. Because curiosity is a basic motivation for learning, parents need to find ways to keep their child safe without frustrating his natural desire to probe and experiment.

Children who are always other directed—always told what to do and taught exactly how to do it—have no opportunity to ask themselves questions and figure out answers. They don't have a chance to learn how to discuss interesting possibilities with other people. They may accumulate skills and knowledge in school, but they will not have learned what it takes to go beyond what someone expects.

So encourage your child to follow his curiosity. Even though you must deny some experiences, do so as unobtrusively as possible so your child won't get a "no" complex about his desire to "find out what happens when. . . ."

SEE ALSO: Discipline; Fear; Independence; Collections; Science; Nature Study.

DISCIPLINE AND THE DEVELOPMENT OF SELF-DISCIPLINE

There are several factors involved in good discipline; and all of them have to work together for success. First, the child must know that his parents love him and that when they make requirements of him, it is *because they love him.* Discipline must be *consistent* so the child can learn what is expected of him. The child should *not be made to feel guilty* for indiscretions. You must understand your child's *developmental age, his physical condition, his problems,* and *his needs* in order to make discipline both reasonable and educational. The child should begin early to learn to make decisions and to *take responsibility for his own behavior, building his capability under your guidance.* The environment surrounding the child should give him an *opportunity to learn and expand himself* without hurting himself or getting into trouble.

Infants

No one would say that an infant is "bad" if he sleeps all day and is raring to go at night, in spite of the fact that it is awfully hard on exhausted parents. If he is given attention during the day, a healthy baby will learn (in time) to sleep at night. An infant will learn to cry a lot if he finds that he can only get attention by crying. If he is given attention when he is happy and contented, he will persist in being happy and contented. This is positive discipline and habit formation—and it makes sense. When an infant's behavior is reasonable and satisfying, loving attention has been proven to encourage the continuation of such behavior.

Toddlers

With toddlers, parents have to be gentle, consistent, and careful in their requirements. They must recognize that the child is small and vulnerable, that he has needs he cannot express, and that unjust punishment will live with him all his life. In order to minimize the number of "no's," childproof your house for the toddler. For the time being put away your fragile valuables, cover wall sockets, install gates at the top and bottom of stairs, and remove assorted dangerous temptations. He has enough problems trying to carry out his natural desire to learn without unnecessary frustration. Also, it is easier to teach "no's" when there are not too many of them. Give your toddler plenty of safe, interesting things to do and opportunities to run about for exercise. The more things he can do legitimately, the fewer confrontations you will have. It is unreasonable to expect a young child to behave well when he is tired, so plan feeding, bathing, visiting, shopping, and so on at times when the child is not overtired. When a bad situation does occur and distraction with an interesting toy won't work, it becomes necessary to simply remove the child from the situation. If the situation is dangerous, you will want to speak a sharp "NO." At this point, some authorities suggest a paddywhack on the bottom as a deterrent. Others hold the view that spanking is a violent act and should be avoided. Whatever your views, the spank, if used, should be used immediately following the dangerous behavior; it should be rarely used and it should be gently administered. Keep in mind that you are much bigger and stronger than the baby. Spanking alone does not teach the child; gentle firmness and consistency do.

The toddler, in his rebellion against authority, is showing you that he is a normal child with a desire to be responsible for his own behavior. But, of course, he doesn't know how. This is your cue to start teaching him how by giving him opportunities to make choices. By giving him a couple of choices (such as, "Do you want to walk or ride in your stroller?"), both of which are acceptable, you give him the opportunity to carry out his natural desire to be in charge of himself. At this tender age, he will be starting the long process of learning how to choose to behave—while you are there to teach him self-discipline through the choices you offer.

Preschool Child

As the child moves out of toddlerhood toward school age, he seems to reach a new level of understanding and is easier to get along with. This is a good time to encourage him to play with other children. You can't possibly discipline your child in social behavior as well as his peers can, and they are the generation he will be dealing with all his life. You will then become the sympathetic advisor instead of the disciplinarian. This also is a good age to turn over a few health and grooming habits to your child. And you can give him the responsibility for a chore or two. Be pleasantly matter-of-fact about whatever you expect your child to do, as though you assume that all children are expected to do these things. With your preschool child, you have the advantage of being the undisputed authority, so whatever you insist upon consistently—and gently—is law in your child's eyes. He may not like what you require and may fuss, but he hasn't yet the resources with which to confront you and confuse issues.

School Age Child

As your child grows older, you and he will benefit from your earlier consistent guidance. Within the framework of each developmental stage, your child will be able, with your help and understanding, to take over more and more control of his own life. To discipline an eight-year-old as you would a four-year-old would be insulting and would invite rebellion.

As a rewarding part of your child's growing up, you should consult him on family expectations before making rules for him to follow. Encourage him to express his needs and desires, and you express yours. If you and he both want the bathroom at the same time every morning, discuss the problem together. Look for ways to accommodate both of you whenever possible. You will accomplish a great deal if you approach disciplinary matters this way—from the age of five or six to adulthood. Show your child that you respect him as a person and give him the self-esteem necessary for personal responsibility. As the family learns how to work out ways of living together, the child is learning how to participate in solving problems, not only with his family, but with everyone. When he shares in problem-solving, he learns the *need for self-discipline* and the *need for rules*; and he becomes committed to helping maintain that which he feels he had a part in designing.

SEE ALSO: Feelings and Behaviors to Understand; Feelings and Behaviors to Encourage.

HABIT FORMATION

A habit is an almost unconscious inclination to perform certain activities in certain ways. Much of a person's lifelong behavior develops out of habits formed in early childhood. Of course, there are "good" habits and "bad" habits, and there are habits that seem to be good until we learn better ways of doing things. You will want to help your child to develop habits that are currently considered beneficial; but you will also want to pay close attention to your child's sense of self-direction so that he will later be able to take matters in his own hands and change his habits when the need arises. You will not try to "*break*" your child's objectionable habits, such as sucking his thumb or biting his nails; rather, you will want to relieve tension and *teach him how* to break habits and *motivate him to want* to break his own destructive habits. Concurrently, however, time spent developing beneficial habits in early childhood is time and worry saved later for both children and parents.

An infant begins to form habits out of the pleasure and sense of security that are connected with eating, sleeping, waking, being cuddled, and bathed. He forms the habit of being pleasant with people as they respond lovingly to him when he is warm and smiling. If he gets attention only when he cries, he will form the habit of crying for attention. In other words, habits are formed as a response to that which brings pleasure. As the baby grows, make happy and regular rituals out of eating, bathing, reading, and so on.

During the "terrible twos," when your child is often a bit hard to get along with, you and he will both benefit from having started habit-forming rituals early. Your efforts will be reinforced by your acquiesing to his adamant demands to follow the established rituals in every detail day in and day out. He will find comfort in his familiar expectations. You will be well on your way when your child wants to take over part of the ritual himself. If you encourage him and if you are not too fussy about how he does things—he may not be as quick or as thorough as you would be—he will be taking charge of his own good habit, which is what you are aiming toward. Keep the activity as unobtrusive as possible after it becomes old hat, but carry on, day in and day out, loving and praising all the while.

Sometime between two-and-a-half and three-a-half, your child, acting surprisingly grown-up all of a sudden, will be in the mood to do a lot of things for himself. During this period, you will need a combination of trust, diplomatic suspicion, and gentle inspection. You should not expect too much of your child and you will need to help him from time to time so he doesn't get bogged down. At this point, repetition and the reward of your approval are more important than quality workmanship. Start with activities he can do successfully without too much effort such as putting on his own hat and hanging his coat on a hook; then gradually add to his repertoire as he gains speed and skill.

There is a difference of opinion on rewarding children for performing activities adults want them to do. If you do use rewards, keep them simple and relevant (do not, for example, give candy for brushing teeth). Do not expect the child to wait for his reward for a time longer than that reasonable for his stage of development. Never fail to produce his reward once it is promised, because to renege on a promised reward will destroy your credibility and will ruin your habit formation program. Rewards can get complicated and they really are not necessary in most cases. You don't want your child to get hooked on material rewards for doing things that are in his best interest. As he grows older, he should be encouraged to take a grown-up view of continuing the habits you have taught him, to see their value for himself, and, having practiced for so many years, to be responsible without much conscious effort.

SEE ALSO: Everyday Teaching; Feelings and Behaviors to Encourage; Learning How to Learn; The Art of Teaching a Young Child.

MEMORY

Some people think that the retention of facts is immaterial to the educated person—that all one needs to remember is where to go for facts. Others believe that an educated person, by definition, is a person who knows—remembers—a lot.

Both views are only partially correct. It would be just as much of a mistake for a child to spend long hours having a lot of half-understood facts drilled into his head as it would be to neglect to pass on to him what we have learned about the development of memory. In the first instance, adults assume too much responsibility, thus creating a passive learner who remembers only because someone else forced him to memorize. Passive learners drop out of the educational process at the first opportunity, which may be as early as first grade (a child can be physically present in the classroom and turned off mentally). Sometimes, on the other hand, adults take the line of least resistance and fail to help the child at all, thus leaving him to reinvent the wheel, which he may be able to do; but some thoughtful guidance will make a world of difference in how he learns to develop his ability to recall.

To set the emotional stage, a child who spends at least a good part of his day working independently on his own projects will learn how to develop his memory all by himself. Self-directed people do not learn to remember because someone told them to but because they find it to their advantage to do so. What the child learns today in one project will be remembered for use tomorrow in a new and perhaps more advanced activity.

Educators have learned a lot about how the young child's learning style is manipulative rather than abstract. Abstract concepts mean relatively little to him, so why should he be motivated to remember words and numbers that are not connected to anything he can identify and use? Educational toys make use of this important information about early childhood.

There is no doubt that memory is enhanced by repetition and positive reinforcement. There are both repetition and positive reinforcement in recognizing the familiar in new situations. When one hears a familiar theme in the middle of a symphony one has never heard in its entirety, the symphony will be remembered. The pleasure of recognition is positive reinforcement. On the other hand, fear hampers memory. School tests can be frightening for conscientious children. When he is doing his homework, help your child learn to test himself so that when he has to take tests in school, fear will be less likely to interfere with his ability to recall. Treat school tests casually and avoid making too much of an issue of grades. Rather, use school tests as indications to you and your child of what facts and skills need further reinforcement.

As a child comes upon the same or related facts in a variety of situations, he begins to develop concepts. Having conceptual understanding makes it possible for him to remember still more facts because he can plug them into an organized framework, the general idea of which he understands. A variety of toys, games, and experiences with some overlapping commonalities will allow a child to absorb concepts which will help him to remember what he learns at home and in school.

SEE ALSO: Self-Image; Independence; Habit Formation; Concentration.

PERCEPTION

When a person takes the messages he receives through his senses and incorporates them into his understanding, he is perceiving. In other words, perception is not just seeing and hearing, it is the generation of mental images based on a combination of sensory intake and experience. Very young children perceive through mental images that are disconnected and nonverbal. They absorb all kinds of physical and emotional impressions, which become deep seated and long lasting.

As they grow, their perceptions become better defined through experience and through mental and physical maturity. What had been flat and two dimensional takes on depth as the child begins to move about and explore. Were a child never to move about or feel, his eyes might have 20/20 vision but he would have no depth perception.

So far, we have been talking about simple perception—absorbing isolated impressions. But there is also organizational perception, which develops as the child begins to sort out relationships. His early reasoning is very simple and direct. These early efforts to reason cause and effect often amuse adults because, although one can see a certain naïve logic, the conclusions are often absurd. "That smoke is making a lot of fire."

The more a child is encouraged to perceive accurately and in depth, the better defined his simple perceptions will become. In turn, then, his perceptual organization will become richer and more accurate. In other words, simple perceptions are the raw material for the perceptions he builds in his own mind. You can help him learn accuracy and depth; you can develop the habit of careful observation. Give him a variety of experiences in looking, listening, feeling, smelling, and tasting, and encourage his physical activity. Talk with him about his observations, calling special attention to qualities you observe and responding to his ideas.

A child also perceives attitudes. He registers the treatment he receives, but it won't be until later that he concerns himself with why he receives a certain kind of treatment. As he matures, he begins to connect the treatment he receives with his own behavior. Because his world is circumscribed, his notion of proper behavior depends entirely on what his parents say it is. He begins to connect his ability to do what his parents want him to do with the treatment he receives. If conditions are such that he can't measure up to what they expect, he combines his apparent inability to succeed with all his memories, building a perception of himself as a failure. To the young child, parents are always right, so his perceptions are built on what they say and do, regardless of reality. For example, if a parent consistently points out to a child that his brother always remembers to do the right thing and asks why he can't, the child will accept the parent's view that he seems unable to do the right thing. No matter how distorted the parent's view may be, he grows up perceiving himself as a failure. Generally, such tragedies as addiction and suicide do not grow out of reality, but out of distorted perception.

Each child has his own unique way of seeing the world and of organizing what he sees. His perceptions change as he matures. No one can fully fathom anyone else's perceptions, but parents need to recognize the fact that their child's perceptions are gradually developing. Parents will want to be seriously concerned about how their child is perceiving himself and the world.

SEE ALSO: Self-Image; Reading.

RESOURCES

The Art of Teaching
a Young Child

Books

AMES, LOUISE BATES, Ph.D. and JOAN AMES CHASE, Ph.D. *Don't Push Your Pre-Schooler*. New York: Harper and Row, 1974.

AVERY, MARIE L. and ALICE HIGGINS. *Help Your Child Learn How to Learn*. Englewood Cliffs, N.J.: Prentice-Hall, Inc., 1962. Covers preschool through early school.

COHEN, DOROTHY H. *The Learning Child*. New York: Pantheon, 1972.

FOX, LORENE K., PEGGY BROGAN, and ANNIE LOUISE BUTTER. *All Children Want to Learn*. New York: The Grolier Society, 1954.

FRAIBERG, SELMA. *The Magic Years*. New York: Scribner, 1959.

GORDON, IRA. *Baby Learning Through Baby Play: A Parents' Guide for the First Two Years.* New York: St. Martin's Press, 1970.

GORDON, IRA, et al. *Child Learning Through Child Play.* New York: St. Martin's Press, 1972.

LEHANE, STEPHEN. *Help Your Baby Learn.* Englewood Cliffs, N.J.: Prentice-Hall, Inc., 1976.

WARREN, VIRGINIA BURGESS. *Tested Ways to Help Your Child Learn.* Englewood Cliffs, N.J.: Prentice-Hall Inc., 1961. Covers preschool to college.

Government Publications

Bibliography, Home-Based Child Development Program Resources. Order from U.S. Dept of H.E.W., Office of Human Development, Office of Child Development, Head Start Bureau, P.O. Box 1182, Washington, D.C. 20013.

Low Income Teaching Kit, Child Development Teaching Material. 1972. Order from Assistant Public Printer (Superintendent of Documents), U.S. Government Printing Office, Washington, D.C., 20402. Al.2:P 12A. 001–00004–7. Sixteen publications plus an order blank.

Magazines

Early Years. P.O. Box 1223, Darien, Conn., 06820. Oriented around children from preschool through third grade.

Learning–The Magazine of Creative Teaching. 1255 Portland Place, Boulder, Colo., 80302. Preschool to eighth grade. Curriculum trends, TV suggestions, book reviews, learning materials.

Creativity

Books

MAYNARD FREDELLE, Ph.D. *Guiding Your Child to a More Creative Life.* New York: Doubleday, 1973.

Books

BARUCH, DOROTHY. *How to Discipline Your Children*. New York: Public Affairs Pamphlet #154, 381 Park Avenue, South, New York, 10016.

BARUCH, DOROTHY. *New Ways in Discipline*. New York: McGraw-Hill, 1949.

BRIGGS, DOROTHY CORKVILLE. *Your Child's Self-Esteem*. New York: Dolphin Books, 1975. See especially Part V, "Discipline and Self-Esteem," pages 223–60.

DREIKURS, RUDOLPH and PEARL CASSEL. *Discipline Without Tears, What To Do With Children Who Misbehave*. New York: Hawthorn Books, Inc., 1972. Revised edition.

DREIKURS, RUDOLPH. *Logical Consequences: A New Approach to Discipline*. New York: Hawthorn Books, Inc., 1968.

DREIKURS, RUDOLPH and LOREN GREY. *Parent's Guide to Child Discipline*. New York: Hawthorn Books, Inc., 1970.

GORDON, DR. THOMAS. *Parent Effectiveness Training*. New York: New American Library, 1975.

MAZLISH, ELAINE and ADELE FAVER. *Liberated Parents, Liberated Children*. New York: Avon, 1975.

SPOCK, DR. BENJAMIN. *Raising Children in a Difficult Time*. New York: Pocket Books, 1976.

8

everyday
teaching

COLLECTIONS

School age children love to collect. How enriching their collecting becomes depends on how well parents work with the child's interests. Every kind of collection can lead to fascinating areas of study, though parents must be careful not to overdo their enthusiasms or force them on their children. The child must take the initiative for his collection. Grownups can be interested and helpful, but never interfering. If you keep your antennae attuned, you will know when your participation is appreciated and when you have stayed too long or interfered too much.

Within the foregoing parameters, there are things you can do to encourage and enrich your child's collecting. Try to find books about his current interest, help him print labels, take him to see museum collections of similar objects, go with him to help search for additions to his collection, talk about it, proudly show it to other people, and encourage the child to talk about it. When you are away, keep your eyes open for additions to bring home to him. Encourage collections that tie in with school studies.

- stamps
- rocks
- pictures—art
- pressed flowers
- bird pictures
- animal pictures
- small animals (also pets)
- shells
- books
- records
- pressed leaves
- carved and pottery animals
- costume dolls
- miniatures
- pictures of friends and family
- souvenirs
- seeds, acorns, pine cones
- coins

SEE ALSO: Child's Room; Creativity; Curiosity; Field Trips; Arts and Crafts; Nature Study.

DEMOCRACY

The best way to introduce your child to the concept of democracy is to implement democratic procedures in groups of children and in the family. When your child is old enough to play and talk with other children (at five or six), introduce the ideas of group discussion and rule of the majority. When a difference of opinion arises in a group, take time to encourage each child to state his opinion and then show them all how to "take a vote." You will be surprised how quickly they will begin to use "voting" as a defense against a strong-willed compatriot. Discussions will be noisy and the losers may pack up and go home, but learning will be taking place. Of course this is an oversimplification of the democratic process, but it is a starting point for children to learn, through actual experience, the rationale behind democratic procedures.

A family cannot be a truly democratic unit, yet it is at home that children learn most of the attributes needed for democratic participation. A young child wants and needs his parents to be authority figures. As he grows older, however, parents can successfully democratize the family, gradually giving children more of a voice in family matters, encouraging both independent and cooperative decision-making.

SEE ALSO: Talking with Children; Community; Cooperation; Conflicts; Decision-making; Morality.

FIELD TRIPS

A field trip for a very young child should be short and geared to his level of interest. It need be no more than a walk around the block or through the park. Preschool children are not ready to learn much from sightseeing, yet they do like to get out and they enjoy building up a mental collection of familiar sights. They love to take houseguests on a guided tour around the neighborhood, pointing out all the interesting things to them.

In school, teachers begin educating children about the world by talking about the local community. You can enrich your child's school experience by taking him to see the places his teacher is discussing. We become so familiar with our own communities that we sometimes forget all the places and things that are nearby. If you are new in the community, you may not have become acquainted with local places of interest. Some newspapers list events, particularly those happening on weekends. Your librarian and the Chamber of Commerce should be able to guide you, and, in cities, hotels usually have booklets of suggestions for visitors available at the reservation desk.

Besides the places of interest that are usually listed, there are more possibilities than can be mentioned. Don't be shy about asking whether you can bring your child for a visit. Depending on where you live, you and your school age child may enjoy learning more about the following:

- Different kinds of farms
- Fire and police stations
- Newspaper plants
- Small and large airports
- Train stations and short train rides
- Radio and television stations, local shows
- Factories and mills
- Specialty stores (hardware, sporting goods, art supplies, etc.)
- Reservoirs, dams, water purification plants
- Restaurant kitchens
- Repair shops (auto, welding, shoe repair, etc.)
- Arts and crafts establishments, shows, museums
- School and community musical presentations and sporting events
- Cultural festivals, bazaars, suppers, and so on
- Sightseeing bus tours, boat excursions
- Docks, beaches, boats, and ships

SEE ALSO: Community; Travel; Knowledge and Skills; Manners.

GROOMING HABITS

Clothes

Little children get their clothes dirty all the time, but at least you can have your way in dressing them in practical clothes of happy colors and flattering styles. Not so when they get older and become peer conscious, when they become adamant about wearing "what the other kids are wearing." They have no conception of cost or practicality: They only know that they don't want to be different. You begin to wonder whether all this development of self-image and peer friendships was such a good idea after all. Don't be discouraged. One of the benefits of understanding child development is recognizing the positive nature of what looks, on the surface, like a problem. Actually, wanting to dress like the rest of the kids is a good sign.

Clothes for the infant need to be soft, roomy, and easy to launder. It is best if they do not have to be pulled over his head. They need to allow freedom of movement so he can enjoy all of his developmental exercises in comfort.

Since you have to deal with clothes constantly as your children are growing up, you can use them to teach about colors and textures, about seasons and temperatures, and about how to get fingers to do what you want them to—all in addition to teaching them the basics about clothes selection. The preschooler needs rough and ready clothes, ones that are easy for him to learn to put on and take off himself. By the time your child starts school, you will want him to be able to do as much for himself as is possible for his age—both for the sake of his teacher and for his own self-image as an able member of the class.

As soon as your child shows an interest in any part of getting dressed, talk to him about it and guide his hands in whatever job he wants to tackle. As he learns each part, let him do it and tell him how pleased you are with what he can do. You have to keep the ball rolling by doing for him (or with him) what he cannot do for himself with reasonable success. When he takes the responsibility for doing the whole job, be patient. He will be slow and awkward, so give him plenty of time to work on his muscle coordination and finger skills. You can gradually speed him up by having something interesting waiting for him when he finishes his task.

If you try to keep your child clean all the time, you will both miss out on a lot of fun. It is best to *expect* spills and grubby knees. Let him wear easy-to-wash clothes, even for dress-up affairs. Fortunately, with wash and wear fabric, you can, without being a slave, start him out—whether to play, school, or to a wedding—clean and combed. He needs to learn this, because when he grows up, such grooming will be expected.

Take your preschooler with you when you shop for his

clothes. Talk to him about selections in order to educate him a little before the time comes when he will become terribly peer conscious.

"You'll need a sweater for fall because the days will be getting cool."

"We have to find a coat for you because the cold winter days are coming."

"I know you like the shirt, but it has long sleeves and will be too warm for summer. It's spring now and summer will be hot."

"That is a pretty red jacket, but we can't wash it. It won't be that pretty red very long unless we can wash it."

"I'd rather read stories with you than iron, so let's find clothes that I won't have to iron."

When your child becomes very conscious of what his friends are wearing, he may be more reasonable about the practicalities of clothes selection if you have discussed his clothes with him earlier. It helps, too, if you observe what his friends and classmates are wearing and take into account that he needs to be acceptable to them. Your budget *is* important, and if you are helping him in other ways to be a cooperative member of the family, it will be easier to discuss budget with him. You don't want to talk about how poor you are to get his cooperation; neither do you want him to feel that you can afford to spend unwisely.

As your child grows older, let him, within reason, select his own clothes as much as possible, even if you may prefer other choices. He will feel better in his clothes if he likes them, and he will be learning by experience the process of selection.

The Bath

Here are a few simple comfort-oriented suggestions to help your child enjoy this very necessary daily ritual:

- Make sure the room is warm enough. If the house is cool, perhaps a safe electric heater can be used to take the chill off the bathroom.
- Make sure the bath water is just right—not too hot and not too cold. Test it with your wrist, and show your child how to test the water before he jumps in.

- Do not put too much water in the tub until your child has learned not to panic when his head is submerged. If he slips down or falls in deep water, he may fear the bath for quite a while. If he does develop a fear of the bathtub for any reason, give him sponge baths until you can entice him into a very shallow bath.

- Wash your child's face with a soft cloth which has been fairly well wrung out to avoid having soap run into his eyes. Rinse carefully and thoroughly, avoiding too much water until he has become accustomed to having his face under water.

- Wash his hair with a shampoo that will not sting his eyes.

- Be gentle. Recall the old-fashioned picture of a child squirming under the iron grip of an adult. Make a conscious effort to keep your grip relaxed and your rubbing gentle

- Be pleasant and relaxed. Avoid bathtime when you or your child are tired, irritable, or in a hurry or when it interrupts a special activity like being with Daddy or Mommy after a day away.

- Be careful but quick. Face washing, specifically, is not too pleasant for children, so the less time spent on it the better.

To Teach

Daily.   When your child takes hold of the cloth and wants to wash himself, encourage him. Do not be critical of his efforts; do not insult and annoy him by rewashing. If he is still terribly dirty, you might say that he did just fine, but how about this one spot? He'll probably be quite pleased with himself after he removes it, and he will have learned the purpose of washing.

Make an enjoyable ritual out of grooming sessions because a comfort in rituals develops from them. A toddler will be apt to tell a baby sitter exactly when to do what and how to do it—which is fine.

As you wash each part of his body, talk or sing about it. "This is the way we wash our feet," "knees," "genitals," "neck," or "ears."

Keep a nail brush handy and use it on fingernails and toenails as part of the routine. *Be gentle.*

Teach him how to rinse thoroughly so soap curds won't irritate his skin.

Teach him how you are drying all the parts of his body thoroughly—between toes, around the genital area.

Have baby powder and lotion handy for the parts that tend to become irritated or chafed. To avoid clogged pores, however, do not use both powder and lotion on the same parts.

Weekly.   Choose a time when nothing else interesting is going on to spend a few minutes on fingernails and toenails. The schedule need not be rigid, but the activity should take place regularly so your child will get used to the idea. To prevent painful hangnails, right after his bath, gently push back the cuticle around the nails with an orange stick. It is surprising how little time all this takes if it is done regularly. At the same time, you can check to see whether a haircut is needed, or perhaps you might trim a few straggles.

SEE ALSO: Habit Formation; Health Habits; Self-Image; Discipline.

HEALTH HABITS

When parents teach their young child health care they are dealing in an area in which habit formation is more important than the child's understanding and execution of those habits. A young child should be too natural and too active to be concerned about his health. Your task is to teach, gently and consistently, by means of short experiences inserted regularly into your child's busy days and weeks. Erratic demands and evaluations of his performance only cause resentment without developing beneficial routines. With the help of your gentle and consistent routines, your child should approach his teens with the ability and the know-how to carry on by himself with little conscious effort. He will begin to appreciate the value of what you have taught him when he and his peers become conscious of health, skin, hair, clothes, and overall appearance.

General Cleanliness

The old saying that *everybody has to eat a peck of dirt to grow up healthy* is some comfort to parents since, if they are going to allow their children enough freedom from nagging to grow up happy, they will cringe at the amount of dirt ingested between handwashings. Routine times for handwashing—before and after eating, after using the toilet, and after messy play—is about all parents can demand. But regular attention to those times sets the habit adequately, does a passing fair job of keeping germs and chemicals from being ingested, and keeps some smears off the furniture. Have a cloth handy and do the handwashing job for your very young child; then gradually teach him how to do it himself. Teach your child to avoid using a hankie, a drinking glass, a toothbrush, or eating utensils that have been used by someone else. In order to do this, you will have to see that clean items are always easily available.

It is distressing to adults to see a child licking his lips because his nose is running. Young children, however, are oblivious to the condition. Parents will want to make it *their* habit to see that their child always has a clean tissue in his pocket, so that anyone can help him with his runny nose. After the tissue is used, hand it to the child to put in the wastebasket while you get a clean replacement for his pocket. As he matures and can take better care of himself, continue to insist on his carrying a clean tissue and on his properly disposing of used ones.

A child should develop the habit of washing fruits and vegetables before eating them. Farmers often use chemical insecticides which should not be ingested; also, unless food is cooked, the child might pick up infections from food handlers. Again, do it for your child until he matures enough to do it for himself without too much effort. Teach him, too, to avoid eating things that are not food. If he seems to crave eating such things as paint or paste, talk with the doctor about the possibility of his need for an adjustment in his diet.

Exercise

Little children exercise most of the time they are awake. There are some books on formal exercises for infants and young children; though if they are given good indoor and outdoor play equipment, children will naturally make good use of it for exercise. Sometimes television intrudes on physical exercise. If this happens, parents may well point out the benefits of developing and maintaining muscle tone through regular exercise and insist on it. It helps if parents have a regular exercise program of their own.

Sleep and Rest

Adequate rest is necessary for children to stay healthy and to be alert enough to learn. However, the development of the habit of relaxing and resting is more important than hard and fast "lights out" rules. Some children need less sleep than others, so forcing them to lie in a dark room when they can't sleep only turns them against bedtime and creates a situation where you have a fight on your hands every night. It is better to set a time for retiring to bed (except for special TV programs or other nonrecurring events), with the option of reading or playing quietly until sleepy. When you set the stage for relaxing but leave the sleeping up to your child, you show him that you respect him and that you expect him to be capable of deciding when he is sleepy. By setting the time for retiring to bed, you help him to settle down and to avoid running on nervous energy. When your child wakens during the night, go to him to take care of his needs; then, unless he is sick, leave him to go back to sleep by himself. Sometimes, when he has matured into a new period of awareness, he will be excited and more apt to be wakeful and must learn to go back to sleep. You don't want him to continue to rely on you. Perhaps a night light will comfort him; and certainly your quiet but firm approach and not turning on a bright light will help. Having had your attention at bedtime and a period of settling down will also help him to sleep better.

Eyes

Poor eyesight and partial blindness, in most cases correctable, puts an extra burden on a child's learning capability. Because children are not aware of poor vision, it is the parents' responsibility to care for their children's eyes. Do not wait for your child to enter school to take him for an eye examination. If his eyes wander or are crossed when he reaches six months of age, take him immediately to an ophthalmologist (an M.D. who is an eye specialist) because the earlier his condition is corrected the better. When a child's eyes don't focus, his brain tells him to see with one eye in order to avoid a confused image, so the unused eye fails to develop. The resulting condition, ambliopia or *lazy eye, can be corrected but only if it is caught early.* By age six it is more difficult to correct, and by nine, little can be done to restore proper vision in the unused eye.

Every child should have his eyes examined by an ophthalmologist by the time he is four. Symptoms of lazy eye are not always apparent. Near-sightedness and far-sightedness cannot be corrected, but enabling a child to obtain 20/20 vision with glasses will add to his comfort and his ability to learn. He will not be able to tell you that he can't see well because he has no way of knowing what good vision is, hence the need for the examination.

If you notice any of the following symptoms, take your child, no matter how old he is, to an ophthalmologist:

- Red and watery eyes
- One eye turns in or out or wanders
- Persisting sties
- Drooping, red, or swollen eyelids
- Frowning, squinting, rubbing his eyes
- Looking at things sideways with the head tilted
- Double vision
- Headaches, dizziness, nausea
- Inability to see things at a distance

Mouth and Teeth

Parents will be interested in (1) the development of the child's teeth, jaw, and tongue; (2) avoiding cavities in baby teeth as well as in permanent teeth; and (3) teaching the child to do what is necessary to keep teeth and gums healthy.

The breast-fed baby suckles in an upright position, giving the tongue and jaw proper exercise, so the bottle-fed baby should be held in the same position. The breast-fed baby is not as susceptible as the bottle-fed baby to what dentists call "nursing bottle caries" (cavities) because he never goes to sleep with a nipple in his mouth.

Giving the baby a clean pacifier is better than letting him play with his bottle, although a pacifier is no substitution for parental attention (which is better in every way and cannot possibly cause mouth problems). Clean the baby's gums every day with a clean piece of gauze. The stimulation is good for them. When the teeth erupt, clean them by adding a tiny bit of fluoridated toothpaste to the gauze. (Dentists recommend fluoridated toothpaste even if the water supply is fluoridated.) Teething is harder for some children than others. Teething rings and zwieback help—and so does love and distraction. If the pain is upsetting the baby, consult your doctor before giving medication.

Take good care of baby teeth because they are very important to the development of the jaw and the permanent teeth. If anything happens to a baby tooth, see a dentist so he can make sure that the space for the permanent tooth is preserved. As the baby goes onto solid foods, begin right away to develop *eating habits which will contribute to healthy teeth*, that is, help your child to develop a taste for other than sugared foods (see Eating and Nutrition). When several teeth have come in, get a small, soft, multitufted toothbrush and fine unwaxed dental floss. *Floss between the teeth once each day and brush at least twice a day.* Daily flossing has been proven important in preventing cavities between the teeth, in keeping gums healthy by removing particles of food that become wedged at the gumline, in removing plaque, and in preventing bad breath. When you are brushing and flossing, let your child hold a mirror so he can see what you are doing. Talk to him about the procedure: Tell him how helpful he is and how pretty his teeth look when you are finished.

At around three, when your child enters a more cooperative stage and when his coordination is improving, take him shopping for a new toothbrush (let him choose the color, but be sure that you choose one that is as soft as possible) and get him his own tube of toothpaste. He will be very proud to take over the morning brushing, though you should continue the evening brushing and flossing until you are satisfied that he can do a thorough job. At about this same age, take him to the dentist with you when you go for a checkup, so he can become familiar with the office, the people, and the procedures. Then, at about four, take him for his own checkup. If your dentist does not work well with children, find one who does, because this early experience in the dentist's office will color his attitude toward dentists for a long time. Dental work is no longer the painful experience it was some years ago. Let your child take along his little mirror, so he can watch what the dentist is doing in his mouth. Ask the dentist to give your child a lesson in brushing and flossing and ask his advice on everything that has to do with daily care and special needs, such as braces.

From three on, pay close attention to habit formation in dental care—brushing at least twice a day, flossing once a day, good nutrition, and twice yearly visits to the dentist. As your child reaches school age, let him take over all the responsibility for daily care, but don't let him break the habits you have been nurturing so carefully. Get him some plaque-staining material at the druggist so he can see the places he misses.

Skin and Hair

It takes gentle persistence to take regular care of a child's skin and hair. Children are traditionally impatient with the whole business. But it is necessary to keep them free of rashes and other skin problems. It is necessary, too, to teach children how to care for themselves properly before the "acne years" of puberty. Young children's skin problems usually come from allergies; from contagious diseases; and from chafing due to improper drying, weather, and irritants such as perspiration, urine, and feces. Parents will want to teach their children to pay special attention to the parts of their bodies where skin problems and/or odors may occur: neck and ears, around the hairline, nose and chin, in the genital and anal areas, between the toes, under the arms—all areas that children tend to give the once-over lightly in washing, rinsing, and drying. School age children are beginning to be socially aware, so they tend to be a little more amenable to the rituals necessary to maintain the social advantages of cleanliness and clear skin. As a child approaches puberty, he should know, too, that keeping the hair clean, in addition to keeping hair and scalp healthy, helps keep the skin on the face and neck free of the oil which contributes to acne.

Nutrition

The foods your child learns to enjoy will be a prime factor in his continuing good health and appearance throughout his life. Since the brain and nervous system, just as well as the rest of the body, respond to proper eating habits, good nutrition contributes immeasurably to a child's ability to learn. You will find a full discussion of nutrition and eating in this chapter.

Illness

When your child is feeling miserable, your problem is mainly that of comforting him and getting him better. Because this book is not dealing with the medical care of children but with teaching your children, it will recommend, for the serious stage of illness, only comfort and love *and* good medical attention. The period of recuperation, however, which offers a trying time for child and parent, is also a real learning time.

When your child is recuperating from an illness, he will find that his position in the household is enhanced by the drama of what he has been through. He will have a tendency to be rather demanding. During this time, the parents will need to continue loving care and a reasonable amount of extra attention, but they will want to avoid making the recovery period so pleasant that the child prefers it to other activities. You want your child to want to be well, to find life more pleasant when he is well than when he is sick. Plan some activities such as a field trip to look forward to.

Because your child will be lonely and bored during this quiet period, the time you spend with him can be used to introduce some of the quiet activities in this book. Look in the chapters on books and toys at the lists for your child's developmental stage for play ideas that can be amusing and educational yet sedentary. Supply him with materials, get him started, then leave him to amuse himself. And of course, at this time, he will be especially amenable to hearing stories, poems, and songs. Play some appealing music on your record player; his own record player will also be "company" for him. See The Fertile Environment, Part II.

While you are medicating your child, you have the opportunity to teach him how to handle drugs and medicines. Do not tell your child that medicine is candy. He will find out soon enough that it doesn't taste like candy and he won't believe you next time. Also, you want him to be wary of medicine and drugs all his life. Talk about how the doctor, who has learned all about sickness, decides what medicine will make him better; and tell him how the doctor tells the druggist what to write on the bottle so you know just how much to give and how often. You can make a paper clock with medicine times marked on it; but make a point of throwing it away when the sickness is gone. Always, every time you use it, read the label on the bottle so your child will learn this safety procedure. Have a favorite juice handy to get rid of the bad taste of the medicine as soon as possible. Compliment your child on his courage when he takes his medicine and remind him that he will soon be well and won't have to take it anymore. If he puts up a fuss, calm him and soothe him while you make it clear that he cannot get out of taking it. Perhaps the juice and a story will help him decide to get the ordeal over with.

When your child has to go to the hospital, let him know that you will be right there with him. Tell him what to expect. Most large hospitals have orientation programs for children and materials to send you upon request. Be sympathetic but matter of fact about the situation, as though this is just one of those things we all have to face now and then. When you go to the doctor's office or hospital, take along a toy or two and a book for distraction during waiting times. Do not shame your child if he panics. Help him to regain his composure by being calm and understanding.

TABLE 8-1
Immunizations, Doctor Visits, and Laboratory Tests*

Age	Appointment	Purpose
2 weeks	Office Visit	Check for growth, development, and feeding
6 weeks	Office Visit	Check for growth, development, and feeding
2 months	Office Visit	Diphtheria, Pertussis, Tetanus (injection#1)
3 months	Office Visit	Oral Polio Vaccine (#1)
4 months	Office Visit	Diphtheria, Pertussis, Tetanus (injection #2)
5 months	Office Visit	Oral Polio Vaccine (#2)
6 months	Office Visit	Hematocrit (blood test for anemia) Diphtheria, Pertussis, Tetanus (injection #3)
7 months	Office Visit	Oral Polio Vaccine (#3)
9 months	Office Visit	Tuberculin Test (Tine) Urinalysis Urine Culture
12 months	Office Visit	Cholesterol (fasting early morning)
15 months	Office Visit	Measles, Mumps, Rubella (injection)
18 months	Office Visit	Diphtheria, Pertussis, Tetanus Booster (injection) Oral Polio Vaccine Booster Hematocrit
24 months	Office Visit	Tuberculin Test (Tine) Urinalysis Urine Culture (for females) Diphtheria, Pertussis Tetanus Booster Oral Polio Vaccine Booster
4–6 years	Office Visit	
After 6 years	(and for life)	Yearly Physical Examination Tuberculin Test every two years Tetanus Booster every ten years (If the child sustains a dirty wound, a bite, or a puncture wound, he should be given a tetanus injection if he has not had one for five years.)

*This is a tentative schedule and will vary with each baby and with each pediatrician.
This schedule is included with the kind permission of Robert B. Shearin, M.D. and Thomas G. Tanton, M.D., who based the following generally on recommendations by the American Association of Pediatrics.

SEE ALSO: Habit Formation; Grooming Habits; Discipline.

HOLIDAYS

Children are enthusiastic about holidays; and when children are enthusiastic, they are ready to learn. No one has to ask a child to *pay attention* to Christmas or Halloween. We have to ask ourselves, then, whether we are taking advantage of good teaching opportunities for enriching our children's cultural heritage, or whether we are letting them learn only the shallow commercial aspects of each celebration.

Because of limited space, this book must treat holidays in a general way, since, in America, we have too many national, ethnic, and religious celebrations to describe. Each has its own origin and its particular traditional activities. At the end of this section, we refer to books on all our holidays.

From family celebrations, children learn the pleasure of companionship—those times when everyone in the family joins in preparation and celebration. Older folks in the family can teach the traditional ways of celebrating special days. The seasonal aspects of the festivities give children a way to remember summer, winter, fall, and spring. A feeling of time—past and future—grows out of holiday memories and anticipation each year. You can teach the calendar by looking forward with your child to special days.

Holidays inspire creativity as well as conviviality. They are associated with dance and music, arts and crafts, special foods, parties, parades, and dramatic presentations. Build your child's creative efforts into your family traditions. Keep homemade decorations from year to year—they become more precious as the years go by. Remember and talk about the origin of the celebration and the memories of past family festivities. Take pictures and date them; bring them out each year for years and years. Since we spend most of our lives in the present and future, holiday time is a time to relax and enjoy ourselves, to remember the past and how much we mean to each other.

SEE ALSO: Family; Community; History; Creative Arts.

HOUSEKEEPING HABITS, DUTIES, AND CHORES

Being able to keep some semblance of order and reasonable clean-liness requires skills that parents can begin to teach early, as long as they set the stage with the child's level of ability and size in mind and maintain a balanced view of the inevitable degree of mess that always goes with creative activity.

Children need to feel that they are a vital part of the family, which can only happen when they participate in all aspects of fam-ily life. "Housekeeping" is a part of every family's life. Children need to learn *how to do* the things we all must do to keep ourselves in working order. They need to grow up expecting to take their fair share of communal responsibility, regardless of the number of people around who might do things for them.

When children are small, you won't gain time immediately by teaching and working with them. You could do the job more quickly yourself. But time spent teaching all along the way will be well spent. As your child matures in know-how, self-discipline, and his sense of responsibility, he will release time for you to do more interesting things with him.

Your child will probably not be amenable to doing routine chores like making his bed, hanging up his clothes, and putting away his belongings, but you will nevertheless have to require these chores of him. Use a quilt on his bed, low hooks and hangers for his clothes, a hamper for soiled laundry, a wastebasket for trash, boxes and shelves for his toys and books; anything you can think of to make the job easy and understandable. Set a routine time that precedes an anticipated daily event, such as a story or snack, when everything not in use is put where it belongs. Anticipation of what is to come will tend to discourage dawdling. If you arrange storage space well and if you maintain a routine, the job should take only a few minutes. In habit formation, it is important that a requirement take very little time out of the day's activities. If it becomes too much of a chore, as when things get into a vast disarray, the child feels swamped and rebels, and your habit formation efforts fall by the wayside. Don't expect too much neatness in the beginning. Just getting things where they belong and the bed covered up is a step in the right direction—even if things are askew. Help when help is needed for encouragement and be pleased with his efforts. Hug him when he surprises you with his initiative and good intentions.

When your child reaches three or so, he will relish not only imitating you in his play, but he will also feel proud and grown-up if he is allowed to do real jobs. Take advantage of his enthusiasm. As you do your housework, think about the many little jobs that match his capabilities. It is best to assign one well-thought-out chore and to follow through with teaching. Thinking up chores on the spur of the moment without attention to teaching and habit formation may be fun for the child, but it does not take advantage of a motivation for learning. Your child's attention span is short and his skills are only developing, so don't let him get bogged down before his job is done. If necessary, help him to achieve his goal.

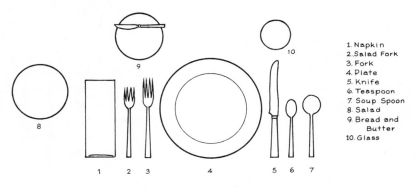

1. Napkin
2. Salad Fork
3. Fork
4. Plate
5. Knife
6. Teaspoon
7. Soup Spoon
8. Salad
9. Bread and Butter
10. Glass

Figure 8-1. Place Setting

Children love to mess around with water, so tackle watery jobs gladly (where spots and spills won't matter). Show your child how you scrub off spots, then wash, dry, and polish (do not let him use harsh soaps). Show him how to use brushes, sponges, and clean clothes; how to measure soap; how to conserve water and still do a good job. Encourage him to be thinking of better ways to do things and show him tricks you have learned. Let him run the vacuum and teach him how to vacuum thoroughly without a lot of wasted effort and without collisions with furniture. Point out procedures that save time and work. A preschool child won't do too well, but he will be learning because he loves to talk and do things with you.

For messy activities, set up a place and a procedure that will allow for maximum learning and creativity while also keeping the living quarters decent. The place, or places, may be in your child's room, in the basement, or in any corner where it won't matter if there is a mess—even if you expect company when he is in the middle of an important project. The learning value of children's projects is enhanced by their being completed and appreciated. In the "project area," arrange everything your child will need nearby: old newspapers, a smock, a dustpan and brush on hooks, tools, a wastebasket, and a variety of creative materials in boxes. Teach him a procedure that will allow him freedom to enjoy himself yet will make cleaning up easy. It may be to (1) put on his smock, (2) put newspapers on the floor, (3) get out the materials and tools. When the project is finished, (1) put his creation in a safe place, (2) wrap trash in the newspapers and throw it in the wastebasket, (3) put the tools away, (4) wash his hands, (5) hang up his smock and (6), if necessary, use the dustpan and brush.

At eight or nine, children can learn how to do things requiring more care. They can, and should, be taught how to do laundry, clean windows, polish furniture, scrub floors, clean closets and drawers—in fact, to handle just about any household job that is not too delicate or dangerous. With school and play, they do not have time to do very much housekeeping; nevertheless, they should be taught how and given practice in various skills by rotating responsibilities.

When he is old enough, the child can be paid for special, out of the ordinary, jobs. It is better to pay by the job than by the hour in order to avoid a hassle over dawdling. Don't put your child down by paying him less than you would someone else for the same work and don't overpay him out of kindness. Pay a reasonable amount so he will acquire a realistic view of the value of money and of work.

Your child would be mighty unusual if he did not offer resistance to doing chores. One way to reduce resistance (and to teach reading at the same time) is to list the chores that need to be done, and then to let the children decide who will do what and when—as long as each job is done when needed. Have a family conference to hear everybody's ideas. You will also get more cooperation if the whole family "turns to," perhaps early on Saturday morning, to get quick results in a joint operation.

In teaching housekeeping habits, you go beyond the subject itself. Care for our total environment is an extension of good housekeeping practices. Learning to organize thoughts is a form of achieving mental order. These activities present no great problem, regardless of interests and careers, if skills and habits are acquired early in a loving and cooperative household.

SEE ALSO: Cooperation; Dawdling; Habit Formation.

LEARNING HOW TO EAT

Table manners used to be the main thrust of teaching children how to eat. Now we know that there is much more involved in the development of eating habits and social amenities. We know that too many expectations and too much nagging at the table are apt to cause a child to develop a negative attitude toward eating at mealtime and persuade him to like the kinds of food he can enjoy anywhere but at the family table.

The enjoyment of eating begins in infancy when nursing is accompanied by a relaxed, attentive, loving attitude on the part of the mother. Good feelings and good food enhance each other. Sustain the same feelings when you introduce solid foods to your baby's diet. Let him suck a little off a blank nipple or the end of a small spoon. Gently let him take the initiative whenever he seems so inclined. When he reaches the stage at which he delights in picking up bits and pieces of things to put in his mouth, take advantage of his enthusiasm. Let him explore with his hands and mouth as many foods as his diet accommodates. Needless to say this is messy, so everything involved has to be easy to clean. Be sociable, relaxed, and loving during this rather trying period so your child will learn about good food in a very positive way.

Learning to drink from a cup requires the development of swallowing muscles which are separate from sucking muscles. There is no need to start the cup before that development takes place because it is unpleasant for both of you to have your baby choking, gulping air, and sputtering milk all over the place. When you do introduce the cup, put a tiny bit—just a mouthful—of milk from his bottle in a small plastic cup so that, if he can't make his tongue work right for swallowing, you won't have too much of a mess. The game of "you put the milk in the cup" after every swallow turns out to be a social event. It gives you the opportunity to gradually increase the amount you put in the cup as he becomes more skillful.

As your child grows to toddlerhood, eat with him quite often in order to maintain the connection between good company and good food. This is also important because in this way you can be a model for him to imitate—and this is the first step in teaching table manners. Keep the ball rolling by paying attention to the colors, textures, temperatures, flavors, and arrangement of the food on his plate. To a reasonable extent, let him help with planning his meals, but do make an effort to limit his choices to nourishing foods.

Allow plenty of time for his meal. A young child has little sense of time, so when his appetite becomes satiated, he quite naturally slows down. When he says he is finished, remove his plate. It doesn't improve the appetite to look at food when you have had enough, and the tension created by pushing him to eat more does not enhance the mealtime attitudes you have been trying to develop. If he has not eaten his meal, however, do not allow snacks right after the meal. Because children grow in spurts, they will be hungrier at some times than at others. Be considerate of his likes and dislikes during toddlerhood, a time when he finds security in the familiar. He will become more adventuresome in a few months.

Young children have notoriously poor table manners, which is understandable. They are wiggly; they are intensely interested in handling things; and their attempts to coordinate are not always successful, causing frequent spills. When your child is in a bad humor, when things have been going wrong for him, he will be even more wiggly and accident-prone. An uptight family will just make matters worse. Some adults are used to dining with children, but others find it tiresome after a long work day. Sometimes work hours and baby hours don't coincide. If you do not have your young child with you at dinner every night, invite him as often as possible so he will be encouraged to practice the skills needed for good table behavior and so he will look forward to family dinner as a happy time.

Start taking your child to a restaurant occasionally when he reaches the preschool age. It doesn't have to be very often in order to be a valuable learning experience. Point out that, when one is in a restaurant, one must stay at the table for the comfort and safety of everyone around. In the beginning, you may want to carry a small toy and a celery stick or something similar with you in case you run into an unexpected delay in service. Parents usually find that, if they don't sit at the table too long, their children can be encouraged to feel proud, to act grown up, and to be amazingly well behaved in a restaurant.

Assume that your child wants to please. Compliment his good behavior, do not make an issue of accidents, do not talk about table manners ad infinitum, and *do* direct some of the conversation into subjects in which he can participate. Table manners depend on skills *and* on a child's feeling that he is a viable part of the group.

NUTRITION

Good nutrition builds every part of the body, making a child strong, attractive, and capable. You will be giving your child a precious gift if you help him learn to enjoy the right foods, because eating habits are acquired in childhood and last a lifetime. Current studies in preventive medicine are laying more and more stress on proper eating habits.

Some foods are nourishing *and* taste good. Others taste good but do not nourish; they only spoil a healthy appetite. Good nutrition builds the child's brain as well as the rest of his body, making him better able to learn.

It isn't really a matter of "teaching" nutrition to young children because they are too immature to understand. In fact, continually talking about foods that are "good for them" can turn them against the foods you want them to learn to like. What is required is that *you know what foods are nutritious and which are not and that you introduce a variety of good foods, avoiding the non-nutritious ones.*

During your baby's first year, his diet is under the doctor's supervision, so the addition of new foods is by his recommendation. You can prepare infant foods yourself and explore the many prepared foods and juices at your market. When you prepare the foods yourself, you know exactly what you are feeding your child. When you buy prepared foods, read labels carefully for nutritional information. Do not hesitate to introduce as many new foods as your doctor suggests, no matter what your own tastes are. If your baby turns up his nose at certain foods, don't force them on him. Wait a couple of weeks and try again, perhaps in a different way— for example, serve banana slices as finger food rather than as mashed banana.

Starches and Sweets

Avoid feeding your child much starch and sugar (carbohydrates), because excess carbohydrates are stored in the body as fat. Sugar has little nutritive value, it is hard on teeth, and it spoils the appetite for more nourishing foods. Of course, it is impossible to deny children cookies, but it is possible to make cookies nourishing by including nourishing ingredients. Oatmeal, peanut butter, and whole grain cookies, perhaps with raisins or other fruits, are more nutritious than sugar cookies or chocolate cookies. Because sweets are more filling than nonsweet foods, it is best to reserve them for the end of a meal, though they should not be used as a reward for eating more nourishing foods. It is very easy to fall into the habit of offering favorite foods as a reward for "good behavior," but doing so sets up an artificial desire—a mental connection between food and doing something worthwhile. Later the child may reward himself with food for doing worthwhile things, which can lead to obesity. It is best to keep food in the context of nutrition and socializing.

When your child begins to visit on his own and when he starts school, he will be introduced to tantalizing foods that have little or no nutritive value. Everyone runs into situations in which, to be sociable, he eats foods that are not very beneficial. Don't embarrass your child by making an issue of it in front of others, but explain the situation in the privacy of your home. A consistent, low-keyed effort to provide your child with the right foods, and with little bits of nutrition information as the occasion presents itself, will set the proper patterns in spite of unavoidable deviations.

Snacks

Young children need to eat more often than adults simply because they have small stomachs and because they expend a lot of energy. Keep nourishing snacks handy for mid-morning and mid-afternoon snacks. In fact, if you are going to be away from home, carry a nourishing snack with you so that you won't have to satisfy his need for food with sweets from a vending machine. At home, have several snack choices on hand, because he will enjoy and benefit from making his own selection. Here are a few suggestions:

- Apple wedges
- Banana slices
- Berries
- Cabbage wedges
- Carrot sticks
- Cauliflowerets
- Celery sticks
- Cheese cubes
- Dried peaches
- Dried pears
- Fresh peach wedges
- Fresh pineapple sticks
- Grapefruit sections
- Green pepper sticks
- Melon cubes
- Orange sections
- Pitted plums
- Pitted prunes
- Raisins
- Tangerine sections

- Tomato wedges
- Turnip sticks

Note: Some of the above can be stuffed with cheese or peanut butter or can be dipped in softened cheese or sour cream.

Miscellaneous Food Tips

- Fruits and vegetables that have just been picked are appealing and generally the most nutritious, which is one reason why people enjoy growing their own or buying from farm markets.
- Keep perishable foods in the refrigerator. Do not let them stand on the kitchen counter any longer than absolutely necessary.
- Because fast food restaurants usually serve a limited menu, whenever you patronize them, make up for missing nutrients at other meals and at snack time.
- Do not keep frozen foods longer than the recommended time and do not thaw them ahead of when you expect to use them.
- Some packaged foods have little nourishment. Read nutritional information on the label, so you will know what you are serving your family.
- Steamed vegetables retain more nutrients than those cooked immersed in water. A steamer is a good investment.
- Many nutrients are in or just beneath the skin of fruits and vegetables. If it is necessary to remove the skin, leave as much of the highly nutritive layer as possible.
- Broiled meats are easier to digest than fried meats.

Young Child's Daily Nutrient Needs

In the following list, some vitamins and trace elements and some of the B complex vitamins are not mentioned. If you serve a well-balanced variety of foods, you will not need to worry about providing special foods for these nutritional elements. If your child is offered certain foods but does not eat them, do nor force him to do so. Try alternate foods containing the same elements. Remember: It is the long haul and habit formation that you are concerned with as well as day-to-day nutrition. If your child seems to crave eating paint or some other nonedible material, talk with the doctor; perhaps some element is missing from his diet.

The items printed in bold face in the following list are the best sources of each element.

- Protein—necessary for body tissue growth and maintenance

    Meat, cheese, fish, poultry, nuts, dried beans and peas, eggs, milk, and whole grain products

- Calcium—for the development of bones and teeth, for the regulation of muscular and nervous responses, of heart rhythm, of blood clotting

    Milk, cheese, dried beans and peas, nuts, whole grain products, spinach, broccoli, clams, oranges, carrots, and kale

- Iron—for blood hemoglobin, which transports oxygen to the cells

    Molasses, meat, liver, fish, poultry, raisins, dried beans, nuts, spinach (and other vegetables), eggs, fruits, potatoes, and whole grain products

- Iodine—necessary to maintain normal thyroid functioning for the regulation of metabolism and body growth

    Iodized salt (look for notation on salt box)

- Vitamin A—for growth; for resistance to infections, especially eye, ear, nose, throat infections; for skin and dental health

    Spinach, sweet potatoes, watercress, kale, the outer leaves of lettuce and cabbage, carrots, tomatoes, apricots peaches, red cherries, whole milk, eggs, liver, butter, asparagus, broccoli, pumpkin, squash, plums, and prunes

- Vitamin B₁ (Thiamin)—for digestion, elimination, metabolism, vitality, and a feeling of well-being

    Milk, cheese, meat, beans, whole grain products, sweet potatoes, pototoes, wheat germ, peanuts, eggs, oranges, pineapple, tomatoe, grapefruit, and unpolished rice

- Vitamin B₂ (Riboflavin)—for general health and vigor, skin health

    Milk, cheese, meat, eggs, beans, dried beans and peas, nuts, whole grain products, carrots, spinach, and other dark leafy vegetables

- Vitamin B (Niacin)—for body growth, for the proper use of oxygen

    Meat, dried beans and peas, nuts, whole grain products, tomatoes, sweet potatoes, and potatoes

- Vitamin C—for gums and teeth, capillary walls, resistance to colds and other infections, bone health

  Oranges, tangerines, grapefruit, tomatoes, raw vegetables (vitamin C deteriorates in cooking and storage), bananas, strawberries, watermelon, canteloupe, raspberries, and lettuce

- Vitamin D—for proper depositing of calcium and phosphorous in bones and teeth

  The body manufactures this vitamin from sunshine. It is available in vitamin supplements, but is not found in any appreciable amount in most foods.

TABLE 8–2
Young Child's Daily Food Needs

The following foods can be served at mealtime or snack time. Do not overlook snack time to fulfill requirements (see Snack Suggestions, page 143). The following information is offered as a general guide. You will need to adjust it for age and individual appetite.

AGES ONE TO THREE

Food	Daily Amount
Milk (or equivalent substitute)+	2½ to 3 cups
Meat, fish, liver, poultry (or equivalent substitute)+	2 servings, each 1 ounce
Vegetables, fruits, vegetable and fruit juices (serve a variety)	½ to 1 cup
Whole grain bread and cereals (or equivalent substitute)+	¼ cup oatmeal and 2 slices bread or ½ cup oatmeal and 1½ slices bread

AGES THREE TO SIX

Food	Daily Amount
Milk (or equivalent substitute)	4 cups
Meat, fish, liver, poultry (or equivalent substitute)	3 ounces
Fruit, vegetable, fruit or vegetable juice (serve a variety)	1½ to 2 cups

AGES THREE TO SIX

Food	Daily Amount
Whole grain bread, cereal (or equivalent substitute)+	⅓ cup oatmeal and 3 slices bread
	or
	⅔ cups oatmeal and 2½ slices bread

AGES SIX TO NINE

Food	Daily Amount
Milk (or equivalent substitute)+	6 cups
Meat, fish, liver, poultry (or equivalent substitute)+	4 to 6 ounces
Vegetable, fruits, fruit or vegetable juices (serve a variety)	2 or more cups
Whole grain bread, cereal (or equivalent substitute)+	½ cup oatmeal and 4 slices bread
	or
	1 cup oatmeal and 3 slices bread

+SUBSTITUTES

Note: Where you use cheese as a substitute for milk, it cannot, at the same time, also be considered as a meat substitute.

MEAT

1 egg = 1 ounce meat, fish, liver, poultry
½ cup dried beans or peas = 1 ounce meat, and so on
2 tablespoons peanut butter = 1 ounce meat, and so on
1 ounce cheese (1) = 1 ounce meat, and so on

MILK

1 ounce cheese = ⅔ cup milk
½ cup ice cream = ⅓ cup milk
½ cup cottage cheese = ⅓ cup milk

WHOLE GRAIN CEREAL AND BREAD

½ slice bagel
½ bun
1 square cornbread

1½ graham cracker = ½ slice bread   = ½ slice bread
2½ pieces melba toast
4 saltines
½ waffle
½ biscuit
1 cup fortified flaked or puffed cereal = ¼ cup granola
1 cup fortified flaked or puffed cereal = ½ cup bran or ½ cup oatmeal

Overweight
and Underweight

When we talk about being overweight or underweight as problems, we are talking about more than an inherited tendency toward a stocky or slim build—more, too, than the normal preteen pudginess. Parents can create a problem by fussing and ridiculing whether or not a real problem exists.

Overweight

Authorities say that, if a child's height is in the normal range for his age, overweight problems more often arise from improper eating and/or emotional problems than from a physical cause. Whatever the cause, it is the parent's responsibility to get at it immediately—even for infants—because the problem will persist and possibly accelerate once it gets going.

As the first step in gaining control of the situation, see the doctor to make sure there is no physical abnormality or illness. For infants, follow his advice on diet. From toddlerhood on, when the child is eating family food, look at the family diet. If it is heavy on starches and sugars, it will be to everyone's advantage to create a better balance. It would be too much to expect your young child to understand being denied food that he sees the rest of the family eating. Because fatness is a severe handicap for children, family cooperation in proper diet would be a loving act on the behalf of a very important human being.

A child can be underweight, in spite of having a balanced diet presented to him, if he is sick, if he associates food with unpleasantness, or if he is emotionally upset: all of these take away the appetite. If your child shows a sudden weight loss, see the doctor immediately, because weight loss can be a symptom of diabetes, TB, a tumor, or extreme emotional stress—all of which you want to have diagnosed at the earliest possible moment.

Chronic overweight or underweight conditions caused by emotional problems are treated similarly. When some people are unhappy, they eat more; others eat less. An unhappy fat child is on a merry-go-round. He feels worthless and out of control partly because he is fat, and he soothes himself by compulsive eating, which makes him fatter. Underweight children are turned against food for some reason, perhaps because of unpleasant experiences in connection with eating and/or a fear of growing up. They may fear maturity because they feel worthless, unable to succeed. In some cases, the emotional problem becomes so severe that teenagers literally starve.

In the case of both overweight and underweight children, it is vital to get at the root of any emotional problem as early as possible, and then to institute a program to alter the self-destructive behavior. Children cannot do this for themselves.

If you can diagnose your child's emotional problem yourself by looking into what in his environment might be causing tension and by taking steps to make corrections, that is ideal. Here are a few suggestions to explore:

- Is the child being helped to want to grow up, to feel himself becoming an independent and worthwhile person?
- Is he afraid of school for some logical or illogical reason?
- How does he get along with other children? If he has no friends, can you help him develop at least one peer friendship?
- Does he feel that he is low man on the totem pole in his family?

Often, however, when we are emotionally involved in problems, as we always are in close loving relationships, we can't solve them ourselves. This is perfectly natural—so, if you can't succeed in helping your child, do not hesitate to go to a professional outsider (doctor, school, or family service counselor) who can make impersonal observations and recommendations.

SEE ALSO: Self-Image; Habit Formation; Cooking; Gardening.

PLAY

What adults call "child's play" is really serious business in the educational process. Through play, children learn how to handle their bodies. They develop conceptual foundations upon which to build their formal education. Because they are not yet able to use words fluently, they express their joys, fears, goals, and worries in play action. Social skills evolve as children gradually move away from their egocentricity and play with peers.

The play opportunities children have in their early years depend almost entirely on parents. It isn't so important how much money is spent on commercial toys. What is important is that parents know what a child's play needs are for proper mental, emotional, and physical growth. The needs are varied within each developmental stage; also at different stages, children themselves emphasize certain kinds of play as their mental operations mature, enabling them to make new discoveries.

Outdoor Play

Before discussing play as it evolves through the various developmental stages, it is important to mention the importance of outdoor play for children of all ages. One often hears of the value of "fresh air and sunshine." Outdoor play offers, in addition, freedom of movement in an enlarged space without the constrictions of walls and furniture. Young children confirm their need for outdoor play by returning radiant with pleasure.

Infant Play

Infant play is not well defined, yet it accomplishes all the various tasks at hand. Infants do not decide to pursue an activity; rather, they respond to whatever attracts them. In the process, they develop their bodies, their eyes, and their coordination, and they also soak up vast amounts of information. From birth, they enjoy the warmth and love of parents and respond with delight, so one might say that social play commences very early. In play, a baby expresses his emotions with his entire body. He responds to playful attention with his arms and legs as well as with smiles. In a very few months he learns to respond to parent play with special intimacy.

A whole new world of play opens up when the baby can sit up. And when he learns to crawl and walk, there is much more to be explored. More than commercial toys, he needs unobtrusive supervision from his parents, so he can be safely free to crawl, climb, and move around.

In Toddlerhood

At this time, play is still very directly connected with exploration, body building, and coordination. Quiet play involves pulling things apart and trying to put them back together. A toddler is more successful at taking things apart, which is part of his learning, than he is at putting them together. He can manage to nest pots and boxes—which he enjoys—and he can pour sand from one container into another. Toddlers like to run and climb about from one place to another. All this apparently random activity is the step between baby play, which is purely responsive, and play with a self-directed purpose. He needs to learn the up and down of things; the shape, size, and weight of objects; and what they do when he does this or that. He is so busy thinking about exploring his world that he is almost oblivious to his peers. Toddlers will play beside one another, but they seldom play with each other. Social play is with adults and older children. There is little pretending and role playing because such play requires mental operations that are still beyond the toddler.

The Preschooler

The preschooler begins to make some more complicated mental connections. While a toddler will mimic, a preschooler will engage in elaborate *pretending* and *role playing*. He learns how to play with his peers by setting up pretend grown-up situations and acting out what he has seen adults do in similar situations. You can encourage beneficial role playing by making props and costumes available—and by staying out of the act. Role playing is as vital a part of a child's education as any course in school. It is educational to parents too, because they can see what they look like to their children. They can see some behavior patterns of their own that are almost automatic, yet are viewed by a child in a fresh light and deemed impressive enough to imitate. There can be shocking and humorous revelations.

Creative Play

A young child's creative play starts with the manipulation of tools and materials. Toddlers don't have the coordination to cut with scissors, though they may enjoy opening and closing them. Once the ability to cut develops, the fact of cutting is the whole game—just cutting for the sake of cutting. It takes the next step in mental and physical development for a child to cut for a creative purpose. The same is true in the use of crayons, paste, and other such creative tools. Toddlers explore *them*, not so much what they can create with them. Be pleased with whatever comes out of this exploration, understanding that a person has to learn about his tools before he can create with them. Unconscious attitudes do show up in a toddler's lines and splotches. They are clues to how he feels; and his having the opportunity to create them in a big way helps him feel good about himself. Creative play should be as free of adult prescriptions as possible. Coloring books and predesigned craft projects develop thinking and finger skills but do little to encourage real creativity. It is better to offer tools and raw materials, a place to play, perhaps some models and ideas, and a little help when requested; but generally, allow creative play to be directed by the child as much as possible.

Games and Puzzles

Puzzles develop thinking, concentration, small muscle coordination, and concepts of shape and direction—all of which are good preparation for reading and writing. Card and board games provide more practice in the above skills; and they are also a mechanism for learning to socialize with peers and understanding the need for rules in organized play.

Fantasizing and Daydreaming

Imagining and dreaming are mental play in which the child tries to build mental connections between and among phenomena. During the preschool and school years, daydreaming is a great pastime. The child projects himself into possible situations and then plays with alternatives. Daydreaming and fantasizing are the beginnings of motivation to learn, so teachers take advantage of the resulting questions. We are all familiar with children's questions that start with, "What if . . .?" This kind of mental play never completely vanishes as a form of mental projection, but it will diminish as the child reaches eight or nine if his education stimulates him to learn about the real world and if his family and peer relationships are fulfilling.

All of the above forms of play have their purposes. Opportunities for each type should be the concern of parents. However, one must remember that play is play only when it is self-directed. Organized activities and lessons are fine for their purpose as the child matures, but all through childhood it is important that time be spent in self-directed play.

SEE ALSO: The Fertile Environment; Pretending and Role Playing; Friendship; Knowledge and Skills; Toys, Games, Equipment.

PRETENDING
AND ROLE PLAYING

When a young child pretends to be someone other than himself, he is learning about himself, about others, and about how he fits into the world. He likes to put on grown-up clothes and talk grown-up talk. It is not known for sure what all goes on when children pretend, but we are convinced that pretending is a very important learning procedure.

Pretending and role playing do not begin until the child has achieved some sense of his own identity as different from that of other people. Very young children are too busy with themselves to think much about others. If they play with Mother's shoes, it is more to learn about the "shoeness" of shoes than to use them as props for acting like Mother. Baby dolls are for companionship and hugging more than as pretend babies.

In the preschool years, when a child begins to become aware of the "otherness" of other people, he likes to pretend that he *is* those other people. It is a way of learning not only what makes others different, but what makes him a unique individual himself. He "tries on" other personalities to see whether they might enrich his own, adding little bits to his conception of the person he would like to be.

In the elementary school years, role playing, although still partly pretending, becomes, in some of its aspects, more real. Group games, in which one person is "it" and the rest of the group is subordinate, give each child a turn to play the role of the individual who either dominates or is subordinate to the group. In playing "school" or "house," children usually take turns playing the dominant and subordinate roles. Sometimes, however, the larger, older, or stronger-willed child will usurp the dominant role consistently until the child relegated to the subordinate role rebels. "It's *my* turn to be teacher." When pretending in groups, children are not only "trying on" adult roles, they are working at establishing their own real life roles in relation to each other.

Parents have little opportunity to be involved in their children's pretending; in fact, their presence can put a damper on the activity. They can—and should—however, contribute understanding, equipment, space, and the opportunity for children to play together in a free and easy atmosphere.

SEE ALSO: Self-Image; Theater; Children's Books (cowboys; fantasy; hospitals, doctors and dentists; policemen).

READING WITH CHILDREN

Being read to is one of the delights of childhood. It's not only educational but also warm, cozy, loving, and relaxing. Your child will forget some of the stories—the ones that don't impress him— but others he will remember all his life—just as he will always remember pleasant times with you at story time.

Here are a few tips that may ensure successful reading and storytelling:

- Choose a reading place together—one which is comfortable, pleasant, and, above all, SPECIAL.
- Even though your time is limited, act as though you have all the time in the world. You want the child to feel that he is important to you.
- Put your arm around the child occasionally or have him sit on your lap. Parental love is important to his love of books and reading.
- Touch the child. Give him a little hug or a pat if the story is sad, or a chuckle and a fingertip to the nose if the story is funny. Count on his fingers if there are numbers in the story. Young children respond to and learn from physical activity combined with mental activity.
- Read the same story over and over if the child wants it, and gently add new stories as you go along. A favorite story is one you will want to consider buying for his own library.
- If a story turns out to be boring, don't persist; choose another, read a poem, or just chat, depending on time limitations.
- Be theatrical! Use your arms and exaggerated facial expressions, rise up in indignation, droop with mortification, cringe with fear. It's fun once you get into the mood—and your "audience." will love it.

- When the child becomes interested in learning to read, he will begin to pick out words and ask you about them. Point out words of interest to him, but don't destroy the flow of the story. Tutoring should be separate from recreational reading time.

SEE ALSO: Children's Books; Reading; Poetry.

SAFETY, FIRST AID, AND EMERGENCIES

The teaching of safety and first aid measures has to be properly timed, unobtrusive, matter-of-fact, and gradual. One can't expect a toddler to understand the reasons for certain rules that you impose for his safety. A lot of talk about the dangers he faces will, at best, go in one ear and out the other; at worst, such talk will inhibit him. He can learn what a firm "NO" means, but his mind isn't ready for, nor has his experience shown him, the possible consequences of running in front of a passing car.

A preschooler can be gradually and consistently directed to observe safe procedures involved in his own activities. Be direct and matter-of-fact. Avoid going into possible dreadful consequences and do more showing than talking as each opportunity presents itself.

School age children will begin to respond to reasons for safe procedures, though you will still want to avoid being too dramatic about the disastrous things that can happen to people. Invite your child's cooperation in keeping younger siblings (and Mommie and Daddy) safe by pointing out anything he sees in the house that he thinks is unsafe. You will be encouraging him to think about safety as a responsibility to others as well as to himself. Knowing that your school age child will be out of your sight at least part of the time, it is better to teach safe practices than to prohibit independent active play with his peers. Parents should feel responsible, if necessary in conjunction with the community, for establishing safe places for older children to congregate and enjoy unsupervised active outdoor play with their friends.

There is a national effort to have all adults know first aid and Cardiopulmonary Resuscitation (CPR) procedures. Courses are offered nationwide by the National American Red Cross. Look in your phonebook or inquire at your community hospital about your local Red Cross chapter. When a person is choking or has heart arrest, minutes make a difference. With children, choking is the more common problem, so you will be most interested in knowing what to do and what not to do in such an eventuality.

Keep emergency phone numbers, including the poison center phone number, next to your phone where they can be easily spotted. On that list, put your complete street address (not just the name of an apartment complex or development name) and your apartment number. In an increasing number of communities, the 911 emergency phone number replaces the police, fire, and hospital numbers. You will also want to include your own doctor's name and phone number on your emergency list. For details on teaching your school age child to use the phone in emergencies, see page 160.

Keep your home safe from fire: Install smoke alarms and have fire escape routes planned. Teach your children escape routes and procedures. Your local firemen will be glad to advise you and will probably have literature for you.

Keep all poisons and medicines clearly labeled and out of reach of children. Teach your older children not to play with the following items:

- Alcohol, rubbing
- Ammonia
- Anti-freeze
- Bath oils and crystals
- Bleaches
- Boric acid and other acids
- Cosmetics, creams, and lotions
- Deodorants
- Detergents, liquid and powdered

- Drain cleaners, lye
- Dry cleaning compounds, liquid and powdered
- Dyes and tints
- Fertilizers, weed killers, lime
- Furniture polish
- Gasoline, kerosene, anti-freeze, oil
- Glue
- Insecticides and rat poison
- Lighter fluid
- Medicines
- Metal polish
- Moth balls and sprays
- Oven cleaners
- Paint, unused or old and peeling
- Paint removers and thinners
- Perfume
- Plants of some varieties
- Plaster chips and powder
- Room deodorizers
- Rust remover
- Scouring powders
- Shampoos and hair conditioners
- Spray cans of all materials
- Tobacco

Keep syrup of ipecac, which is used to induce vomiting, in a special place in your medicine chest. If your child swallows a toxic substance, CALL YOUR POISON CENTER AND FOLLOW THEIR INSTRUCTIONS IN THE USE OF SYRUP OF IPECAC. Never induce vomiting without professional advice because some substances, such as petroleum products and lye, will cause further harm if vomited.

Be sure your babysitter knows what to do in case of an emergency and how to get in touch with you.

Safety for Infants and Toddlers

Keep small objects that can be swallowed, inhaled, or put into the nose or ears out of reach.

Put gates at the top and bottom of the stairs.

Inspect toys for chipping paint or parts that might splinter, come loose, cause cuts, or be swallowed.

Watch for situations in which the child might climb up and fall over or off something. A large toy in a crib or a pen can be used by a child to try to climb over the rail.

Put covers over electrical outlets.

Keep pot handles turned to the back of the stove and be aware that a dangling tablecloth can be pulled by a toddler, dowsing him with whatever is on the table.

Avoid prolonged exposure of tender baby skin to sun.

Keep plastic bags out of reach.

Safety for Preschoolers

Keep matches and lighters out of reach.

Start teaching your child to keep his toys off steps where they can cause someone to fall.

Start teaching street-crossing procedures; but do not let him cross by himself.

Have him learn how to swim.

Teaching Safety, Emergency, and First Aid to School Age Children

There have been many situations in which children have proven their competency in helping in emergencies. So one can assume that they can be taught to handle problems should they be called upon to do so. Of course, parents cannot teach children as

159

they would adults, and they cannot expect them to remember a lot of detail, but there are a few crucial bits of information with which they can cope.

Emergencies

Anyone can stay calmer in an emergency if he has been forewarned and trained. First of all, a child (or anyone), must recognize that, in an emergency, one's first reaction is to run away, to think of one's own position and one's own safety. If a person recognizes this universal impulse, then he can better take control of himself to meet the situation, which requires *thinking of the person who is in serious need* at the moment. His next thought will be *how to get help*, especially if he is a child, who has neither the knowledge nor the capability to do much himself. In our technological age, help will probably be at the other end of the telephone wire, so the child needs to know how to communicate by phone. Teach your child to use the phone as his first probable source of help. You will have a list of emergency phone numbers beside the phone. Show him how to call the fire station if there is a fire; the hospital if someone is seriously injured, ill or unconscious; and, for any other emergency, how to call the police. In communities which use the 911 emergency number, that is the only number he will need to know. When you call 911, an operator answers, asking, "Fire, police or ambulance?." Tell your child to answer with one word, depending on which service is required. At that point, usually your line will be held open, so if, for any reason, the caller must hang up or leave the phone, the call can be traced and help dispatched. Knowing this, you will not be disturbed if you cannot get a dial tone right after having placed a 911 call. Also, your child will be discouraged from experimenting with the 911 number if he knows that the call will be traced and that the police will arrive.

Once the operator knows which of the three departments the caller needs, he rings a "call taker" in that department who will identify himself, probably using an identifying number (which it is not important to remember). It *is* important to be as calm as possible and to state the problem clearly: "The couch in the living room is on fire"; or "Mom fell down the steps and can't get up." The call taker will ask questions. Tell your child to listen carefully and answer as clearly as possible. When giving your address, he should be sure to give the street name and house number and, if necessary, your apartment number. All the information should be beside the phone.

You don't want to alarm your child. Matter-of-fact practice with a toy phone from time to time will become as easily accepted as fire drills at school. A little refresher now and then will make sure that both you and he know what to do and what to expect.

First Aid

Much first aid is beyond the capability of a young child, but there are a couple of important things he can learn:

- Get professional help by phone.
- Leave a severely injured person just as you find him. If he has broken bones, moving him may make matters worse.
- Cover the person with a blanket or coat because when a person is badly hurt, he gets cold.
- Do not try to give water to an unconscious person.
- Stay nearby to be a guide when the ambulance arrives.
- Step aside out of the way and let the professionals take over knowing that you did your part of the rescue correctly.

Safety Habits to Teach

Traffic Safety. Cross at crosswalks and never run out from behind parked cars. Realize that in fog, snow, and rain, drivers cannot see very well, so take extra care. Do not play in the street or near highways. Do not expect a car to stop to avoid hitting you, because the driver may not see you until it is too late.

Self-protection. Teach your child to be polite, but to stay well out of reach of strangers who approach. Do not tease people who act strangely and do not call out or do anything to attract attention to yourself. Never accept gifts or candy from strangers and keep well away from their cars. Avoid secluded places and remote woods unless your parents are with you. If a stranger accosts you, yell as loud as you can and run to where there are other people. Tell your child that there are very few people who would harm him, but let him know that there are some and that that is why he should be cautious unless he knows the person.

Sports.   Teach your child about the rules and proper equipment for his sports. (See Sports.)

Climbing.   Avoid climbing banks along highways or beside deep water and do not climb on abandoned structures, bridges, or trestles. When climbing a hillside or over rocks, show him how to test his footing each step of the way to make sure a loose rock won't give way under him. Before climbing a tree, make sure the ground underneath is soft and free of rocks, branches, and debris. As he climbs, he should test each branch for strength before putting his weight on it. Tell him to be thinking of his way down as he goes up.

General.   Teach your child never to play in cars, in motor driven equipment, or in old refrigerators, to not be persuaded to eat leaves, flowers, fruit, mushrooms, or berries without checking first with you. Tell him not to investigate funny looking objects or guns. If he should find anything suspicious, he should tell you; if you also think it is suspicious, you will call the police.

TALKING WITH CHILDREN

Perhaps we should say we are discussing "communicating" rather than "talking," because communication between parents and children begins before the baby is able to talk at all. When he does begin to talk, the child (as well as older children, teen-agers, and adults) has much more on his mind than he is able to express in words. So what you will want to develop *in your child and with your child is real communication.*

Infants

Infants inform us of their needs and satisfactions without the use of language. Parents become quite sensitive to their baby's nonverbal communications and if they respond, the baby learns that communicating is a two-way street. If parents do not respond, the baby will be slower to learn what communication is all about. Infants learn to recognize words and their meanings before they learn to speak (they will wave "bye-bye" when they hear the word before they can say it). If you have not been one to converse with your baby from birth, start doing so when you see that he understands words; do not wait for him to talk. Use simple words that sound different from one another; use action and touching to show what you mean.

Toddlers

Your toddler is learning to walk and talk all at once. This is a pretty big order—at no time in life does a person put forth a greater learning effort than at this time. And your child's progress in speaking his thoughts vastly increases his ability to learn. Take advantage of this magnificent opportunity to enrich every activity by talking about it. Supply words he doesn't know, using proper terminology. Keep your conversation in the "here and now" because very young children do not understand yesterday and tomorrow—or even "later on today." Nonverbal communication does not disappear with the advent of talking; in fact, most parents know what their toddler means regardless of what he says.

Preschooler

When you think that he started from scratch, it is amazing how quickly a child picks up the use of language. At the young age of three or so, a child even begins to think with words, although most of his thinking is done through his *physical action* with *things*. In order to encourage your child to express his thoughts in words and to work through problems verbally, listen to him very carefully and restate what you think he means in your own (simple) words. If you understood correctly, your child will feel rewarded. If you did not, he will be encouraged to think of a way to make you understand.

When you talk with children, often bend down, stoop, or sit so he can talk "man to man" with you. If a child is to learn to make good use of language, he will benefit much more if you bend down and listen carefully than if you consistently lecture from on high, apparently showing only a passing interest in what he is really trying to communicate.

A good teacher sets up learning situations and then helps his student think and talk his way to understanding. The activities and experiences you make possible for your child to enjoy will give him things to think about and talk about. They will arouse his curiosity and present him with problems. He will come to you. You will help him best by listening carefully to his thoughts and questions and then restating them in your own words and by stimulating him to do his own thinking, using little bits of information from you. This is the recipe for good conversation with persons of any age. No one enjoys a "know-it-all"—and a "know-it-all" misses quite a lot of input from his partner in conversation. It is quite delightful—and, indeed, educational—once you learn how to really converse with children.

When sibling and peer problems arise, remember to whom the problem belongs before you start to talk. *You do not have to solve the problem; it is your objective to talk with your child to help him solve his own problems.* If you dictate the solution to the problem, you not only incur resentment, you deny your child a chance to learn through discussion. By restating his needs in your own words and by verbally helping him to explore alternatives, you will be delighted at how often your child will straighten out his own matters.

School Age Child

You want to keep the lines of communication open with your school age child. He is going to learn fast from his peers how to tune you out if you try to manipulate him. The best way to avoid the "teen-age tune-out" is to treat your child with respect, showing him that you know he is capable of making decisions and taking responsible action. When he comes to you, treat him as you would a close friend who comes to you to hash over a problem. Listen carefully; look at the problem through your child's eyes; restate it to make sure you've got it straight; listen as he works his way to a solution. When you restate his problem, be sure that you state it honestly—as you think he meant to express it. Do not play "put-down" tricks with language by saying something like, "Do you mean to tell me that you think . . .?" Actually, the solution he comes up with may be better than the one you had in mind. On the other hand, it may not be to your liking; but unless his solution is impossible (which you will find it seldom is), it will be the best because it makes sense to him. You want your child to be motivated to carry out the solution, which he will be if it is his own. If you talk a solution *at* him, he may not tell you outright, but he rebels. As children get closer to their teens, if parents keep talking *at* them, communication breaks down completely; and the child learns to seek his own solutions without the benefit of parental assistance.

It is an excellent family custom to have "talk times"—not necessarily to talk about problems, but just to "chew the fat." Such times might occur after dinner on certain evenings, while you work on the car, or when you are all piled on one bed Saturday morning—whatever suits your life style. Talk about whatever is interesting at the moment, and if the talk moves into a problem solving area, so be it. Just remember to hold up your end of the listening.

TIME

In the womb, the baby experiences neither time nor hunger; he cannot distinguish between night and day, nor between sleeping and waking. When he is born, he becomes a *being in time* from that moment, but he has neither the experience nor the mental ability to understand time until several years have gone by.

His earliest sense of time develops out of the repetition of day and night, and he gains a general time structure in everyday activities like feeding, bathing, and going to bed. Although rigid organization of family activities is neither necessary nor much fun, it does help a child develop his time sense if routine activities generally happen at the same time every day. "It's bath*time*." "It's story*time*."

Toddlers can be very adamant about the regularity of their rituals—as though they are trying to get a fix on time as part of their growing up. They know what NOW means, but they have little understanding of past and future. In fact, they will not have much sense of the distant past until around third or fourth grade, and they do not develop a realistic approach to the future until they reach adolescence. For the toddler, waiting for his lunch is about as far as he can go into the future. You can begin to tell him such things as, "We'll go to see the ducks this afternoon," and he will gradually begin to connect "afternoon" with after his lunch and before his dinner. Such short-term well-defined projections will help your child hang his idea of time on fixed familiar hours in his day.

As your child approaches school age, it is a good idea to put a big, easy-to-read clock where you can also put a paper clock with movable hands. Don't make a project of teaching hours and minutes unless your child shows a real interest—and even then, don't bore him with it. Use the paper clock to show when something interesting is going to happen. "Aunt Martha is coming over at three o'clock." Set the paper clock at three o'clock. "The paper clock says what the time will be when Aunt Martha is to come and the real clock says what time it is now." When your child asks, "Is it time for Aunt Martha to come?" you can both look at the clocks and see whether the real clock looks the same as the paper one. Point out that she will come when the little hand is on the three and the big hand points straight up, just as you have set it on the paper clock. Use only hours and do not expect much sustained interest. As you continue to use this procedure easily and casually, your child will begin to connect clock time with times when real things happen, which will be an advantage when he learns to "tell time."

The paper clock will come in handy for guessing games and reminders when your child really begins to learn to tell time in school. Help him learn how to plan his time for dressing and eating in the morning, so he will gradually take over the responsibility for being on time for school. After he has learned to tell time reasonably well, you may want to buy him an inexpensive, large-face watch.

He will be thrilled and proud, but don't be disappointed if he forgets to look at it when it's *time* to come home.

SEE ALSO: Dawdling; Math; History; Children's Books (time).

TOILET TRAINING

The later you toilet train, within reason, the better it is for your child. During his first year, your child's muscle control has not developed well enough for him to be able to hold back his urine and stools. If you try to train him before he is developmentally ready, both of you will be under an unnecessary strain. Also, it is better to wait until your child is past the first excitement of standing and walking (when "sitting down" is the last thing he wants to do).

Here are a few guidelines:

- You don't want your child to get distorted ideas about elimination, so you will want to be easy and matter-of-fact about toileting.
- You don't want your child to get into a failure habit, so you will want to wait for toilet training until the child is old enough to be able to succeed.
- Because organs for elimination are located close to the sex organs, you don't want overemphasis, shame, and failure to affect his attitudes toward sex.
- Since you can't have control over your child's elimination, you don't want to get into the situation of having your child use his control of elimination as a way of rebelling. How you and your child get along generally will have an important part in preventing lingering elimination problems.
- Upsetting events, illness, and tension can cause problems after a child seems to be trained. It is important to help the child with the cause of the problem and not add to his discomfiture by scolding and shaming him.

Parents usually begin training with bowel movements at eighteen to twenty-four months of age, depending on the child. Figure out your child's schedule and put him on the potty chair (near toilet paper) when he usually has a bowel movement—for not longer than ten minutes. Stay with him till he gets the idea of what he is supposed to do. After each movement, wipe him and put the paper in the potty, talking about it in a matter-of-fact way and praising him for his success. A potty chair is easier for the baby to use than the flush toilet and is also less frightening in the beginning.

Bladder control comes gradually, and training usually follows control of bowel movements. When your child stays dry for fairly long periods of time (when he is between eighteen months and three years of age), put him in training pants. If you time it right, you will not have to go back to diapers. Little girls may find it easier to use the potty chair. Since you need a shield on the potty chair for boys, it is more difficult for them to sit down behind the shield, so it may be easier for Dad to teach his little boy how to aim for the toilet from the start (a sturdy stool is needed).

There will be accidents until the child is into his school career—in fact, starting school can cause a temporary setback, which is very embarrassing to the child. Simply say, "You couldn't help it . . . don't worry about it . . . just don't be afraid to tell the teacher when you have to go to the bathroom."

TRAVEL

Very young children are captivated by their immediate surroundings; they have a short attention span; they tire quickly; and they have little interest in "places." The close-at-hand offers new experiences more relevant to their stage of development. When they travel with the rest of the family, they enjoy certain aspects of the trip, but they learn relatively little from what they see. You can consider using a trip as a break point for helping a child discard a habit or take on a new responsibility for which he is developmentally ready. It is when your child is studying geography, history, and nature in school that enrichment through travel is extremely beneficial, although arduous trips are still very tiring for the young school age child. Long driving trips with few stops can be awfully hard on the whole family. Fewer miles and a leisurely pace are more fun and educational.

Plan your trip well, taking into consideration your child's developmental level and his interests at the particular time (which may well be related to what he is studying in school or to some project at home).

You will want to think about:

- Season, climate, and proper clothing. When in doubt, take "layers" of clothing, so you can adjust to each day.
- Places to eat and stay overnight, or camping facilities.
- What places of interest are along the route.
- What toys, books, and equipment will make the trip more enjoyable and enriching. For example: bathing suit, binoculars, magnifying glass, bags for collecting, blunt scissors, crayons, paper, paste, camera, canteen, knapsack, pencils, boots, comfortable walking shoes, old gloves, long sleeved shirts and slacks for woods-walking, books, compass.

The best place to start planning is at the library, where you will find some fascinating books. The list of resources at the end of this section on travel will give you an idea of the wealth of available material.

You may also want to talk to a travel agent, who, if you plan to purchase tickets or to stay in hotels and motels, will be glad, free of charge, to help you plan your itinerary and make reservations for you. You can call your nearest state office building about state parks and tourist bureaus in your state. You can also write to the Chamber of Commerce in the cities you plan to visit. Ask about points of interest specifically for children.

When you plan a trip by car, choose some secondary roads to explore in areas of interest. Schedule your time to allow for stops along the way. Take advantage of wildlife preserves, zoos, guided tours, historic sites, look-outs, cavern tours, short trails, and visitor centers. You may want to take along a scrapbook into which you and your child can paste brochures, post cards, and photos. Your child can make good use of his very own camera. Take along your nature books to identify trees, birds, wildflowers, and rocks; you may want to make notations or crayon drawings in the scrapbook.

At some visitor centers and historic sites, you will find books of special interest for both adults and children in each area.

To be acceptable travelers and sightseers, there are a few things children need to learn:

- To be considerate of other people.
- To keep all trash in a bag until you reach a trash can for disposal.
- To obey signs, such as *"Please do not feed the animals"* and *"Please do not pick flowers."*
- To not touch exhibits without a guide's or attendant's permission.

As you ride along, there will be many sights to look for and talk about with your child, especially if you take some byways as well as highways:

- Bridges—suspension bridges, old wooden bridges, covered bridges, trestles.
- Roadside flowers and plants—milkweed, thistle, day lily, cactus, mountain aster, goldenrod, Queen Anne's lace, blackeyed Susan, cattail.
- Fall colors

  scarlet—black gum

  deep red—dogwood, sumac

  orange and red—sugar maple

  copper—red oak, hawthorn

  golden—aspen

  brillant yellow—birch, tulip, hickory
- Land use—crops, houses, transportation, recreation, industry, orchards, animal husbandry, logging.
- Vehicles—trucks (different ones for different purposes); tractors; antique and other interesting cars; trains; wagons and buggies; fire trucks; boats of all kinds, including tow boats with barges, sailboats, canoes, tankers, liners, freighters and all sorts of motorboats for all kinds of purposes. Young children are always very much interested in "purposes" if it doesn't take too long to describe them.
- Equipment—piledrivers, cranes, harvesters, planters, road pavers and rollers, road scrapers, plows, pumps, windmills, water wheels, cotton pickers, lightning rods.
- Structures and houses—silos, barns, firetowers on high mountains, factories, roundhouses in rail yards, log cabins, skyscrapers, solar

houses, burned down structures, and structures in the process of being built.

- Domestic animals—horses (race horses, saddle horses, work horses, ponies), cows (black and white—Holstein; black—Black Angus; orange and white—Guernsey; brown and white—Hereford; tan—Jersey; tan with long horns—Longhorn. Holsteins, Guernseys and Jerseys are dairy cattle; the rest are beef cattle), sheep, chickens, geese, ducks, turkeys, hogs.

- Wild animals—Raccoon, skunk, rabbit, ground hog, deer, opossum, squirrel, chipmunk, snake, prairie dog, badger, armadillo, bear, turtle, fox, otter, beaver.

- Birds—on or near the ground: pheasant, quail, roadrunner; in trees or on wires: bluejay, blackbird, red wing blackbird, dove, owl; high in the sky: hawk, crow, vulture, eagle; near ponds and lakes: goose, duck, swan; near the ocean: heron, gull, pelican, crane, egret, loon.

- Water—ponds, lakes, streams, waterfalls, canals (and locks), ocean, bay, dams, deltas, reservoirs.

- Land configurations—hills, mountains, valleys, plains, passes, lookouts, mountain ranges, canyons, coastlines.

- Rocks—horizontal ledges, ledges upturned by movement of the earth's crust eons ago, scouring by glaciers, waterworn rock (sometimes high on a mountain top), quarries (active and abandoned).

What you see will prompt questions, some of which you will not be able to answer. Make a brief note in the scrapbook to find out later. Try to follow up on at least some of the questions to teach your child how to "research." When you stop each night, you might ask your child a few of the things he saw that he found especially interesting to enter in the scrapbook. He will be giving you interest clues for the selection of reading material.

Family Camping

Camping as an economical and down-to-earth way of exploring the country has become *the* way of traveling for many families. It is especially suited to traveling with children because it involves a freer environment for them and a greater variety of experiences than hotels and motels. It provides an opportunity for nature study, which is also well suited to children. A well-planned camping trip teaches children the joy of working with the family in rather primitive circumstances; it also teaches them that there are many things even very young children can do to be an important part of the group. Resourcefulness and imagination are required to solve the inevitable problems that arise unexpectedly; and courage is needed in the face of dark nights, thunder storms, and bee stings. One doesn't really experience nature in a house, yet family camping keeps the security of parents nearby during both good and scary camping adventures.

Learn all you can before you start out by reading, by talking with veteran campers, and by visiting stores that specialize in selling or renting quality outdoor equipment. There are items for which investing in quality equipment pays. Then again, there are many ways to save money and teach children self-reliance by improvising. For a couple of examples: invest in a good tent and Coleman lantern; then save by thrift shop buying of cooking utensils and improvised cushions, laundry bags, and airtight food containers. Half the fun in camping is in "making do," which is almost like playing house for children. When planning, gather everyone together to assign responsibilities and gather provisions. Include everyone in decision-making and in plans of action. Along with all the other things you will all be remembering to take, don't forget binoculars, a magnifying glass, bags and plastic containers for specimens, toys and books for quiet times, and your nature identification books.

SEE ALSO: Broader and Deeper Interests.

RESOURCES

Democracy

Books

DREIKURS, RUDOLPH. *Family Council*. Chicago: Regnery Co., 1972.

GINOTT, HIRAM. *Between Parents and Children*. New York: Avon, 1969.

Booklet

Beautiful Secrets for Your Child's Hair. Johnson & Johnson Baby Products Co., Consumer Services Dept., 220 Centennial Avenue, Piscataway, N.J. 08854. No charge.

Course

Good Grooming. The American National Red Cross. A fourteen hour course designed for elementary, junior high, and senior high school students. Inquire through your nearest Red Cross chapter.

Health Habits

Books and Booklets

Baby Care Basics. Johnson & Johnson Baby Products Co., The Consumer Services Dept. 220 Centennial Avenue, Piscataway, N.J. 08854. No charge. Also available in Spanish.

FEINBLOOM, RICHARD I., M.D. and THE BOSTON CHILDREN'S MEDICAL CENTER. *Child Health Encyclopedia, The Complete Guide for Parents.* New York: Delacorte Press, 1975. Covers every aspect of preventive medicine, physical fitness, illness, safety, symptoms, and care.

FROMME, ALLAN, PHD. *The ABC of Child Care.* New York: Pocket Books, 1976, pages 139–141.

SPOCK, DR. BENJAMIN. *Baby and Child Care.* New York: Pocket Books, 1976, pages 506–11.

Government Publications

Order from the Assistant Public Printer (Superintendent of Documents), U.S. Government Printing Office, Washington, D.C., 20402.

Infant Care. 1973. HE 21.110:8/2. 017–91–00178–2. Spanish edition. HE 1.458:B11/2/Span. 017–091–00211–8.

Parents, Are Your Walls Poisoning Your Children? 1973. HE 20.2852: P75/2. 017–032–00019–4. Spanish edition. HE 20.2852: P75/2/Span. 017–032–0020–8.

Courses

Health in the Home. The American National Red Cross. A twelve hour course covering maintenance of good health, prevention of illness, and simple nursing care.

Preparation for Parenthood. The American National Red Cross. A fourteen hour course covering care through pregnancy and the baby's first year. Inquire through your nearest Red Cross Chapter.

Holidays

Books

ICKIS, MARGUERITE. *The Book of Festival Holidays.* New York: Dodd, Mead and Co., 1964.

LARRICK, NANCY, ed. *Poetry for Holidays.* New Canaan, Conn.: Garraid Publishing Co., 1966. For grades 2 through 5.

Housekeeping Habits, Duties, and Chores

Books

DREIKURS, RUDOLPH. *Family Council.* Chicago: Regnery Co., 1972.

HAINSTOCK, ELIZABETH. *Teaching Montessori in the Home.* New York: Random House, 1968, pages 21–46.

Books

Feinbloom, Richard I., M.D. and The Boston Children's Medical Center. *Child Health Encyclopedia, The Complete Guide for Parents.* New York: Delacorte Press, 1975, Chapter 3, pages 17–47.

Hatfield, Antoinette and Peggy Stanton. *Help! My Child Won't Eat Right.* Washington, D.C.: Acropolis Books, Ltd. Over 200 nutritionally sound recipes and menus to interest children.

Lansky, Vicki. *Feed Me! I'm Yours.* Meadowbrook Press, 16648 Meadowbrook Lane, Wayzata, Minn. 55391, 1974. Also, by the same author and publisher, *The Taming of the C.A.N.D.Y. Monster.* Continuously Advertised Nutritionally Deficient Yummies.

Government Publications

Order from the Assistant Public Printer (Superintendent of Documents), U.S. Government Printing Office, Washington, D.C., 20402.

Feeding Young Children. 1972. Al.68:693. 001–000–01219–3.

Food for the Family with Young Children. Rev. 1973. Al.77:5/11. 001–000–02944–4.

Play

Books

Allison, Linda. *The Sierra Club Summer Book.* New York: Sierra Club/Scribner, 1977.

Arnold, Arnold. *Your Child's Play: How to Help Your Child Reap the Full Benefits of Creative Play.* New York: Simon & Schuster, 1968.

BRENTON, MYRON. *Playmates: The Importance of Childhood Friendships.* New York: Public Affairs Pamphlet, 381 Park Avenue, South, N.Y. 10016. No. 525.

BROAD, LAURA PEABODY and NANCY TOWNER. *The Playgroup Handbook.* New York: St. Martin's Press, 1974.

CANEY, STEVEN. *Steve Caney's Play Book.* New York: Workman, 1975.

GORDON, IRA. *Baby Learning through Baby Play: A Parent's Guide for the First Two Years.* New York: St. Martin's Press, 1970.

GORDON, IRA, et. al. *Child Learning Through Child Play.* New York: St. Martin's Press, 1972.

HARTLEY, RUTH E. and ROBERT M. GOLDENSON. *The Complete Book of Children's Play.* New York: Thomas Y. Crowell, 1963. A storehouse of information on play for growth—each developmental stage is discussed from the child's first year through teen-age. Lists of toys, books, records, and hobbies. All are listed by age groups.

MARZOLLO, JEAN and JANICE LLOYD. *Learning Through Play.* New York: Harper & Row, 1972.

RADLER, D.H. with DR. NEWELL C. KEPHART. *Success Through Play.* New York: Harper and Row, 1960.

Safety, First Aid,
and Emergencies

Books

FEINBLOOM, RICHARD I., M.D. and THE BOSTON CHILDREN'S MEDICAL CENTER. *Child Health Encyclopedia.* New York: Delacorte Press, 1975.

KALT, BRYSON R. and RALPH BASS. *The Mother's Guide to Safety.* New York: Grosset and Dunlap, 1971.

Government Publications

Order from the Assistant Public Printer (Superintendent of Documents), U.S. Government Printing Office, Washington, D.C., 20402.

Young Children and Accidents in the Home. Rep. 1975. HE 1.452:Ac2.
017–091–00191–0. Spanish edition. HE 1.452:Ac2/Span.
017–091–00199–5.

Courses

Standard First Aid and Personal Safety. The American National Red
Cross. A Spanish language text is available. A student must be
age thirteen or have completed seventh grade. Requires fourteen hours.

Basic Life Support Course in Cardiopulmonary Resuscitation (CPR). A
student must be thirteen or have completed seventh grade.
Estimated required time is nine-and-one-half hours.

Basic Water Safety. The American National Red Cross. Requires
four units, a minimum of one hour each.

Basic Rescue and Water Safety. The American National Red Cross. A
student must be eleven years old and pass a preliminary
swimming test. Requires ten units, a minimum of one hour
each.

Talking with Children

Books

BIENVENU, MILLARD J., SR. *Talking It Over at Home—Problems in Family Communication.* New York: Public Affairs Pamphlet, No.
410, 381 Park Avenue, South, N.Y. 10016.

GINOTT, HIRIAM. *Between Parent and Child.* New York: Avon, 1969.

GORDON, DR. THOMAS. *Parent Effectiveness Training.* New York: New
American Library, 1975.

WHITE, JAMES D. *Talking With a Child.* New York: Macmillan Co.,
Inc., 1976.

Toilet Training

Books

SPOCK, DR. BENJAMIN. *Baby and Child Care.* New York: Pocket Books,
1976, pages 286–96.

Guides

Country Vacations. Farm, Ranch and Adventure Guides, Inc., 36 East 57th Street, N.Y., 10022.

FEDOR, EUGENE and ROBERT C. FISHER. *Fedor's U.S.A.* New York: David McKay Co., Inc., 1976. A comprehensive guide to travel in the U.S.A. Indexed by area of interest and by states.

FODOR, EUGENE and ROBERT C. FISHER. *Fodor's U.S.A.* New York: David McKay Co., Inc., 1976. A comprehensive guide to travel in the U.S.A. Indexed by areas of interest and by states.

Mobil Travel Guide. New York: Rand McNally. A series of regional guides to restaurants and accommodations in the U.S. Includes road maps, population statistics, zip codes, and some brief summaries about the towns and areas.

Roughing It Easy. Provo, Utah: Brigham Young University Press, 1974. There is also a sequel to this book.

USA Plant Visits, 1977–1978. Order from Assistant Public Printer, (U.S. Superintendent of Documents), U.S. Government Printing Office, Washington, D.C., 20402.

Your Neighbor North. The Canadian Pocket Encyclopedia. Quick Canadian Facts Limited, Box 699, Terminal A, Toronto 1, Ontario.

IV

character
and personality
development

One cannot educate a child in knowledge and skills without attention to his emotional development. A child's attitudes toward himself and toward his relationships with other people affect not only how well he learns, but also how well he uses what he has learned. Chapters nine through eleven are especially important ones for parents because, while schools can teach knowledge and skills, healthy emotional attitudes develop mainly at home.

Chapter nine contains a number of "special topics," some of which will be applicable at one time or another in every family, while others pertain to specific situations in only certain families. It will be to your benefit to read through all the "special topics" because, even if some of them do not apply to your family, they will give you a better understanding of situations in which some of your relatives, friends or neighbors may find themselves. They will also help to prepare you for eventualities which sometimes occur when least expected.

Chapter ten helps you deal with normal everyday emotions which can cause aggravation and which, if not dealt with properly, can grow to have an adverse effect on both your child and your family. On the other hand, since emotional health depends not only on learning to deal with troublesome emotions, chapter eleven describes the encouragement of positive attributes.

9

special topics

ADOPTION

Once you have gone through the decision-making, the planning, and what seems like interminable waiting, finally the day arrives when your family welcomes the new arrival with open arms. That moment is where this book commences, and it is as valid for adopted children as for natural children. There are simply a couple of additional concerns to be dealt with here.

When you adopt an infant, most of the adjustment problems will be yours and will be the same as those in any family. It is generally agreed that a child should be told that he is adopted. There are a number of good books on adoption and there are also some excellent children's books. Refer to these if you wish, and then choose an approach with which you feel most comfortable. How secure you feel in your role as your child's completely responsible parent will affect how secure he feels when you tell him about his adoption, so learn all you can.

Parents often fear that if a child knows he is adopted, he may ask some difficult questions. Facing the questions, however, is better than having your child's confidence in your integrity destroyed sooner or later. You can honestly tell him you do not know who his natural parents are, but that you are his real parents forever and ever and that you love him and will always care for him, just like all the other kids' parents. Choose your own words and repeat them often so he will have an answer for adults and children who hurt him with tactless remarks. If he asks why his parents gave him up, you can again say you don't know, but that, usually, for one serious reason or another, parents give up a child because they could not take care of him.

When you adopt an older child, his introduction to the family will most likely be more difficult for him than for you. He will be unaccustomed to your lifestyle and may suffer physically as well as emotionally for a certain period of time. How the child reacts will depend on his own nature and on what has happened to him previously. If the family expects this temporary period of adjustment, then everyone will be better prepared to be patient, flexible, kind, relaxed, and good-humored.

It is best to avoid showering your new child with attention and food and to give him a chance to settle in at his own pace. Let him follow you around while you are doing your chores and hobbies so he can learn how you do things. Be ready to hug him and to include him, but don't force him to respond to you.

The first "stand-off" happens when your child has gotten somewhat adjusted. It means that you are entering into the real parent–child relationship. How you handle this situation in the beginning is important to your continuing relationship. You want to establish right away that you are not only kind and loving, but that you are responsible and dependable and that your child can feel secure in your decisiveness even if you have to thwart his temporary desires from time to time. If your child's self-determination does not begin to exhibit itself, you will want to concern yourself with what has been called a *floating* reaction to past disappointment. Your attention to his self-image; and the security he finds with you will ultimately overcome his fears of being punished with disappointment for things beyond his understanding.

SEE ALSO: Discipline; Affection; Children's Books (adoption).

DEATH

Death has a considerable impact on children when they reach the age of three or so. Earlier, because they have only a growing sense of "going away" and "coming back," they do not realize the difference between a temporary and a permanent departure, which is why they feel abandoned when left, even for a short time, with strangers. Around three they realize that when you go away, you are coming back; but they do not understand that there is no coming back in death. For most children, early experience with death involves pets, animals, and birds. The preschool child fully expects a return in the spring along with the flowers.

Parents sometimes try to save their children the grief of having a pet die by making artificial arrangements to shield them. It is better to allow the child to grieve, to remember, to know that death has happened, and to talk about it. If possible, bury the pet with your child's participation, explaining how everything that lives and grows is part of the earth and that when the body dies, it is buried in the earth of which it is a part; yet the pleasures and happiness given by that special being will live on with us forever. Wait a few weeks to get a new pet. Replacing a pet right away denies the child the opportunity to completely feel the unique qualities of his pet in memory and to express his feelings. He should be allowed to learn, even though in sadness, that living beings are unique and wonderful and can never be replaced.

To prepare the preschool or school age child to understand death, so that they will be able to grow up without fear, it is important to be very sensitive yet honest with him every time he confronts the phenomenon. It is also important to teach about life—about birth and growing up, about getting old, about nature, seasons, and cycles—and always at his level of understanding. Teach him how to "pick himself up" and go on after a disappointment and how to be a self-reliant person. These abilities and understandings help a person to cope with death all through life.

When a child becomes aware of the death of someone's parent, how vulnerable he is comes home to him. When this happens, it is a good time to explain how parents make arrangements for the care of their children in such a situation; but take care to impress on him that most people do not die until they get old and their children are grown up. When he asks with whom you have made arrangements, tell him about it.

When a friend of the family is struggling with a terminal illness or is grieving over the death of a loved one, include your child in the preparation of flowers, food, or whatever expression of compassion you find appropriate. While you are going about it together, take the opportunity to talk about the person who is dying or has died—about how he was born and grew up to be the person you know. If the person is young, explain how it is unusual for young people to die and how it is not much fun to spend your life worrying about dying even if a few young people do die. Take a moment to give hugs, kisses, and smiles—even if the smiles are through tears. Talk about how the tears are there because it is sad to have to say goodbye forever when someone dies. Explain how the body dies; ask him to remember when his pet died and remind him about what happens to the body. It is very important to talk about your beliefs concerning the spirit of the person who has died. Talk about how the person leaves with us love, deeds, and memories and about how a person's children are very real parts of him which we still have with us.

Children take what we say quite literally. If you say someone "went away," they connect that with times that you go away: They may fear that, when you go away, you may die and never return. If you say that the person "went to sleep," your child may confuse death and sleep, which could cause sleep problems. If you have not talked about God in many other contexts, talking about Him in connection with a death may give your child the impression that God is sinister and snatches people away. If you talk about life after death, make sure your child knows that the body does not live on, so that he will not fear a physical presence hovering over him.

In recent writing about children and death, some authors say that, when a death occurs in the family, it is best to keep your child with you throughout the time of mourning. The funeral or memorial service has a purpose. It is a formalized way to bring people together to say "goodbye" and to support one another. The child needs the ceremony as much as adults. If the child is excluded, he not only suffers being denied the formal "goodbye" and a focus for his grieving, but he feels abandoned by the whole adult family at a crucial time. He might even interpret this abandonment as resulting from something he may have said or done that he imagines may have contributed to the death.

There are three major stages of grief for everyone, children included: (1) shock and disbelief; (2) anger, guilt, bitterness, and a feeling of having been abandoned; (3) resignation and the decision to get life back on the track.* If the second stage is not recognized and dealt with sympathetically, the third stage does not come about properly—the anger and guilt remain buried and influence all future thinking. No one grieves without feeling selfish and guilty. Because of their limited understanding of themselves, children are more susceptible to exaggerations of these feelings; they must be allowed to express them and be understood and forgiven. They must know that they are not evil for having those feelings. Because children confuse thoughts and wishes with actions, they quite often keep buried within them the fear that they may have caused the death; they might even fear that the person may come back to punish them. Or they might feel that the deceased person abandoned them as punishment for past mistakes. School age children tend to fantasize about death, fearing ghosts. *All of these feelings are not isolated emotional responses, so they should be understood and tenderly cared about by all parents.*

When a child loses one of his parents, all of the above problems are there and there are also additional ones. The grieving parent must take on additional responsibilities at the time when he is feeling depressed, and yet the child needs him desperately. There will be tension and distraction. You may do and say things that you both regret. Be open with your child; ask his forgiveness as you forgive him. Your young school child may find that his school friends run away from him, simply because they do not know what to say, leaving him lonely and confused. This is temporary but cruel; it can't be helped except by your support and devotion. There may be a period in which you will be struggling with a

---

*Elisabeth Kubler-Ross includes these three in her description of five stages of grief in *On Death and Dying*, New York: Macmillan Publishing Company, Inc., 1969; London: Tavistock Publications Ltd., 1973.

tendency to rely on your child to assuage your own loneliness; and you may worry excessively about his safety, when actually you both should be getting together with your own friends again. You may also be disappointed in your child's behavior, which, because of his grief, seems to regress. His school work may deteriorate and he may seem disrespectful, sullen, aggressive, and hard hearted; he may do what seems to you to be bizarre things. All of this is normal behavior under the circumstances.

The old saying that time heals is only partially true. Time heals when someone you love understands your grief, your fears, and your confusions and stays close by to help.

SEE ALSO: Talking with Children; Children's Books (death); Anger; Fear; Withdrawal; Courage; Independence.

DIVORCE

Divorce, although it is hard on both marriage partners, is *very* hard on children. Many psychological problems are traced back to broken homes, though it is not necessary for divorce to cause such problems if parents know how to help their children. It can be worse for children to live in an antagonistic, unhappy household than to suffer the separation of their parents.

Having a child for the purpose of keeping a marriage from falling apart is unfair to the child and it does not alleviate problems arising from incompatible life views. As the child grows and learns *his* life views from his parents, their incompatibility becomes more rather than less of a problem. Such a situation can be more harmful to children than divorce.

Divorce always separates children from one parent. Very often, it also causes partial separation from the parent who retains custody because of the necessity for earning money and for having a reasonable amount of time with adults. Of all the effects of divorce on children, separation is the most severe. Most of your efforts on behalf of your child will grow out of your concern about his problems resulting from the understanding he has of losing one of his parents. It takes maturity on the part of both parents to remember, in times of emotional upset, that the child needs the security of knowing, loving, and respecting *both* of his parents—no matter how they feel about each other.

If your marital problems are becoming insurmountable, there are several steps to take in behalf of your child. First, see a counselor so you will know whether or not your problems really are insurmountable and so you will learn what will be required of you as divorced parents. You may find that your troubles are fewer together, at least temporarily, than apart. Then again, you may find that divorce is the best course of action. Read one or more of the books listed at the end of this section. They will give you, in the form of case histories, models of divorce situations and child views of them.

One of the things you can do for your child ahead of the divorce, should you decide on that course of action, is to accustom him gradually to separation as he will experience it, so that, when it comes, the change will not be so great for him. Develop his peer friendships and outside activities. Do everything possible to set up a stable situation that you will be able to maintain for a period of time after the divorce. No matter what you do, the divorce will be hard on him, but keeping him in familiar surroundings with familiar friends and activities will lessen the impact. It is hard to keep emotions under control when marital problems accelerate, but remember that your child will suffer from being taught that one or the other of his parents is an irresponsible person. You are not related by blood to your spouse, but your child is, and he needs to know that his heritage is intact and that he need not be ashamed of part of himself.

Divorce forces the understanding of some concepts before the child is ready for them. For one thing, children believe their parents to be perfect. When separation and divorce occur, the child, not being able to see any human foibles in his parents, may take the responsibility on himself for the departure of Mommy or Daddy. Also, the child does not understand the permanence of an irreversible situation. He will fantasize and hang on to the hope that the whole problem will go away or that some strange arrangement can be thought up to make things the same as they were. You will find it necessary to explain patiently and sensitively, over and over, that he is not in any way to blame for what has happened, that you will continue to live in separate houses, and that both his parents love him dearly. Much is beyond his level of understanding, but your patience will calm his fears and he will gradually learn to understand.

Vital to your child's development is the confidence that he can rely on both his parents even though they live in different places. Care must be taken to fulfill obligations to your child, which means more than just financial obligations, as crucial as they are. Barring the absolutely unavoidable, never disappoint him when you promise to be with him and never deny him the promised time to be with his other parent.

Divorce requires that your love for your child enhance your ability to control the all too destructive emotions that want to burst forth in divorce. Everyone concerned needs to go on as a complete person, uncrippled by rancor and guilt. Nothing can be more important.

DRUG ADDICTION
AND ALCOHOLISM

Prevention begins in early childhood. The reasons for teen-age and adult drug addiction and alcoholism should be known by parents of young children because some suspected causes are rooted in childhood. Self-image develops very early in children, when parents are the child's only consistent reflection of himself. Life goals, also, are closely related to parental expectations. Family values become the child's values. If, through years of early childhood living, a child has learned that he is not a very acceptable person, if he feels that he can't measure up to expectations, if he has not absorbed a sense of values, then when peer pressure leads him to try drugs or alcohol, all he knows from his initial experience is that they produce a feeling of well-being, of power that he relishes. He has no defense against the temporary euphoria.

How can parents immunize their children against the tragedy of addiction? We still have much to learn about some of the possible physical causes of addiction, but this much cannot fail to be a deterrent to recognized emotional factors:

- Show your child in ways he can understand at each developmental level that he is a valuable individual, deserving of your love.
- Encourage self-direction. Avoid overdirecting and excessive criticism.
- Listen to your child, when he comes to you with problems, with a sensitivity to *his* timing; don't put him off for your convenience.
- Teach him how to cope with disappointment.
- Teach him how to set reasonable goals and how to reach them through skills and concentration.
- Encourage close peer friendships.
- Accept his weaknesses and help him compensate.
- Encourage self-discipline.
- Help him develop *his* interests.
- Do not laugh at drunkenness in movies or on television.
- Use medicine sparingly, only for illness, and only under a doctor's supervision.

SEE ALSO: Self-Image; Discipline; Talking with Children; Friendship; Independence; Community; Human Ecology.

HUMAN ECOLOGY

Random House Dictionary defines *ecology* as "the branch of biology dealing with the relations between organisms and their environment." Every living creature, including humans, is an organism, hence the new educational reference to "human ecology." When we are teaching our children, we want to keep in mind the environment that they, as human organisms, are going to be relating to all their lives (they may live vital lives for over a hundred years). It is important that parents not be down in the mouth about the future: It is terribly unfair to their children. It is hard to foresee all ecological problems, but there are a few we are dealing with now—and there are some things we can teach children to help with solutions. Some of what we consider "problems" may not seem so difficult for our children, because they will have grown up accepting different (and quite possibly better) ways of living.

There may well be a need for activities to fill up the time now spent in energy-consuming activities. There may be less gas to get around and less money to put into impulse buying and costly recreation. Teach your child to engage in activities that are, as much as possible, creative. Buy good quality toys. Teach your child to enjoy the intrinsic quality of what he uses, not just the activity of buying. The activities in this book consume very little in relation to the enjoyment to be gained from them.

In a highly mobile society, which we have now and expect to see continue, it is hard to form lasting friendships. Teach the child early to want to maintain old friendships regardless of distance. This means teaching him to do the things that let a friend know that he cares and that he does not want to lose contact. If your child develops a good self-image, if he enjoys doing interesting things, and if he has learned to value people, he will be able to move into any new group and find friends with compatible values and interests.

There may be a shortage of food. Rather than teaching your child to eat a lot, teach him good nutrition for better health on less consumption. Growing vegetables is just one thing that gives children a better understanding of the value of food.

With the population explosion, we will be overcrowded and the quality of life will decline. Most Americans are aware of population problems and are limiting their families—this trend is beginning to show in a drop-off in school population. In most areas of America, the main problem is not so much physical crowding as it is carelessness and lack of respect for people. The closer we live together, the more considerate we have to be.

Teach your child to respect the entire environment, to look beyond his own immediate interest. Teach him not to litter and not to throw things into streams and rivers; teach him how to be thoughtful of his neighbors, how to work patiently with others on behalf of his community, and how to enjoy activities that do not infringe on the rights of others.

We're going to be run by machines and computers. In old-time America, people spent most of their time working and taking care of the necessities of life. People, not machines, did almost everything and people who served were also friends—bankers, shopkeepers, delivery boys. Those days are passing away rapidly and, in retrospect, it seems sad. Today's children, however, are at home with machines. They need to be taught (1) to make efficient use of machines; (2) to use their time to develop themselves and to do interesting things; and (3) to use their time and interests to enrich their communities and enjoy their friends.

SELF-IMAGE

Perhaps the most precious gift you can give your child is a positive self-image. The happy and intelligent behavior that results from a person's knowing who he is—that he is a person of value—is *almost miraculous*. Likewise, the damage a negative self-image can do to intelligence and personality is *almost unbelievable*.

Because parents represent virtually the entire world of people to the infant and the young child, it stands to reason that the child's picture of who he is depends a lot on the way he is treated by his parents. How parents react to the child day in and day out either builds the child's feeling of capability and worthiness or tears away at the self-image he is struggling to develop. The damaging things parents do are not intentional—they are normal adult ways of reacting. So what is needed is a few pointers on knowledgeable and reasonable parent reactions to very normal childhood situations.

Infancy

Because the newborn baby is utterly dependent on his parents for his comfort and acceptance, it is vital that he be handled with loving care if he is to develop a feeling of security with people. Security is necessary for the development of a positive self-image. Insecurity in infancy leads to tense and withdrawn or aggressive behavior, which, in turn, alienates other people, causing a further deterioration in self-image. It is a vicious cycle. On the other hand, a child who feels secure and loved by his parents meets other people on an equal footing. He assumes that he is as worthy a person as they are and that it isn't necessary for him to have to prove himself in order to gain their respect.

Toddlers

Instinctively, the toddler seems to work hard on being an individual with power to direct his own life. While this great adventure is going on, don't "rain on his parade" by standing off at a distance constantly shouting, "NO." You don't want him to get the idea that he should not participate in life, that he should not try to direct himself, and that he is constantly doing the wrong thing— always making other people mad at him. Instead, arrange for his safety; and, when necessary, rescue him from danger by physically removing him (with hugs and kisses). Give him many ways to develop himself. Self-respect comes with self-development without a lot of criticism.

Toddlers are not much aware of the true existence of other people. They don't quite realize that, when damaged, other people hurt—just as they do—so they don't hesitate to inflict wounds. A firm denial of the right to hurt others will keep the development of the toddler's self-image reasonably on target.

Preschool and Young School Age Children

Teach your child *how* to contribute to the family. Positive self-image requires being one of the gang, and being a knowledgeable contributor is important to being accepted.

Listen to your child so that you can help him dispel fantasies he might have about guilt and fear of doing the wrong thing. He needs to learn that he is in charge of his own behavior and that there is no demon or irredeemable guilt in him. He needs to know that everyone makes mistakes.

Give your child opportunities to develop his motor skills so that he will be able to physically keep up with his peers. Self-image in children depends a lot on physical abilities.

Be understanding and encouraging. Follow necessary criticism with something positive.

Help your child with his deficiencies in a matter-of-fact way. Teach him that everyone has certain deficiencies which require extra effort. Some people have more problems than others; it is often those people who develop the strongest characters.

Look for good things in your child and commend him for them. His self-image depends a lot on how proud you are of him.

Minimize mistakes and accidents, pointing out that such things happen to everyone. The important thing is to learn from mistakes and then to put them behind us.

Help your child maximize the things he enjoys and can do well. It is very good for his self-image to be able to do something that others appreciate.

Be honest about your own mistakes. Don't pretend to be perfect. If your child thinks he has to be perfect to be worthy, he will never think himself worthy.

Trust your child. Being trusted develops the child's self-image as a trustworthy person.

Give your child the right to get angry. One cannot be expected to accept everything, no matter how obnoxious, unless he accepts himself as a nonentity, undeserving of consideration.

Give your child as much "experience" as you can. What is considered intelligence is often knowledge and skill resulting from "experience." And feeling reasonably intelligent is necessary for a positive self-image.

Never turn your back on your child. Never say you can't forgive him. Never consider a mistake irrevocable. Never put your child in the position of not knowing how to redeem himself. Never let guilt feelings fester.

Love and security, hope and redemption, acceptance and capability—all these come from parents to young children, and it is upon all these that a positive self-image is built.

SEE ALSO: Child's Room; Perception; Pretending and Role Playing; Sibling Rivalry; Independence; Decision-making; Children's

Books (self-image; Black children); Toys, Games, Equipment (self-image).

SEX EDUCATION

There are two elements in sex education. One is the physical—how the body functions. The other involves sexual morality and attitudes. The development of sexual morality and attitudes begins at birth and interest in the physical parts of the body develops soon after.

Infants

Since the infant is completely dependent on you, his attitudes toward affection and bodily functions will depend on you. Sexual morality, therefore, grows along with love and respect for others; and your child's love and respect for others grows out of your love and respect for him.

Toddlers

Even before toddlerhood, your baby will begin to examine and feel different parts of his body, just as he examines and feels his rattle and his cradle gym. Toes are wiggled and feet are put into the mouth. Ears and nose are discovered and there is an effort to put things into them. The navel, the nipples, the penis, and the vulva—it would be odd if they were not also examined, especially when one considers that touching the latter organs produces a special kind of pleasure. In his enthusiasm and innocence, the toddler's touching himself in public may be embarrassing to older children and adults, but it is a necessary part of his total development and should not cause you to overreact. Rest assured that, as he matures, your child will grow out of this behavior if it has been dealt with casually. Gentle distraction is the best way to divert your child when he, in his innocence, does things in public that are not acceptable in polite society.

The sexual development of the young child is as real and important as the rest of his development. One does not try to train it out of him. Rather, it is of vital concern that parents teach sexual morality. Without a word or action related to sex, you will be teaching sexual morality if you teach your child to respect other people. Your attention to his self-image will help him grow up without the emotional need to hurt or to use others. *Not wanting to hurt or to use people is an important part of sexual morality.* And, of course, your affection and love for your child will show him *how* to be affectionate and loving, which is also an important aspect of sexual morality.

Preschoolers

Obviously children find pleasure in touching their sexual organs, but previously it had been thought that they took no interest in the opposite sex. It is now observed that at the age of three, four and five, children may well be sexually attracted to their parents of the opposite sex. Here is a type of behavior that is really not acceptable, though the child does not understand that—so it is again necessary for parents to ignore the behavior and distract the child. It will be a temporary phenomenon unless a parent takes an unhealthy attitude, either by too much encouragement or by too much abhorrence. It is a time when Mommies can help develop their son's masculinity by admiring his masculine characteristics and Daddies can encourage their daughter's feminity— all the while gently discouraging sexually aggressive behavior.

This is the age when language becomes particularly fascinating to children. For the first time, tricky puns, jokes, and word inventions will include "bathroom humor." Again, you are dealing with a developmental phenomenon that will diminish unless you make too much of an issue out of it. Once you have explained that you find such language objectionable, ignore it.

This is also the age of many questions. A parent must stop and ask himself what it is that the child is asking. Although a parent wants to be truthful (in order not to create the lamentable credibility gap), he also wants to be sure that he is answering what the child is really meaning to ask. A misunderstanding such as the following can make a simple situation difficult: A child asks his parent where he came from. The parent launches into an erudite discussion on sex and marriage. The child responds a half hour later that he finds that all mighty funny because his friend, Joey, says he came from Pittsburgh.

One of the fears of the preschooler may be that of losing a penis. When boys realize that girls do not have a penis, they wonder what happened to it and fear that it has been cut off. They fear that the same thing may happen to them. Girls may also have the same sort of fear—that they should have a penis and that it has been lost or cut off. Because this fear is so common and can have such detrimental effects, it is one to deal with whether or not your child verbalizes such thoughts. Look for an opportunity to explain about how boys have a penis and girls have a vagina; explain that girls also have a uterus, which is the special place inside where babies grow when girls are grown up and ready to be mothers.

When the question arises about how a baby starts growing in the mother's uterus, it is good to have gone through the exercise of growing a flower from a seed. It is perfectly truthful and logical to the child to explain that babies grow from a tiny seed, something like the seed he planted and watched grow into a flower. Breeding pet animals is an excellent way to teach about gestation and birth.

When the child asks how the seed gets planted in the mother's uterus, it isn't unusual for parents to panic in the face of discussing intercourse with a young child. Actually, a child cannot begin to understand the nuances of intercourse. His question is purely mechanical. You might tell him that Daddies have seeds inside them, that a daddy puts the seed in the mother's vagina with his penis, and that this is done when a Mommy and Daddy love each other and want to have a baby. There are different ways of telling the story. You might know of one you like better.

When he asks how the baby gets out of the mother, he can be told simply, and as a matter of fact, that the vagina can stretch to let the baby out. Parents often fear that all this information may lead to sex play. But sex play may—and probably will—occur anyway, and the best way to handle it is to have enough other activities of interest to keep it to a minimum.

This, too, is the age of playing "investigating" games. Although the toddler was interested in his own sex organs and did not really play *with* other children, preschoolers are learning that there are people in the world who are different from themselves and different from one another. Sexual differences are very intriguing and, of course, sex play feels good. Here again, don't make a big issue of it. The best deterrent is to have plenty of other interesting things to do.

Young School Child

Once the ice is broken with some discussion of the most difficult questions, you and your child should be able to talk over all future questions without embarrassment. Because you will have answered your child's questions truthfully, you will have laid the groundwork of trust. Your child will feel that, whenever he has a question on sex or on anything else, he can come to you for a straight answer. There is nothing more important in sex education than this.

As your child becomes more aware of things he sees on television, at the movies, at the corner drug store, and in the newspaper, you may be asked some disturbing questions. "Dad, what's rape?" "What is a child molester?"

No matter how you try to protect your child from disturbing sexual material, there is no way of predicting what he is going to see on the newscast, in the paper on the street, or on the movie marquee. Such situations put parents on the horns of a dilemma. They cannot tell a falsehood, but they also cannot explain a disturbing concept to a child whose mental development makes it impossible for him to understand. He may make illogical assumptions that can haunt him all his life.

It is best, when talking with young children about rape, child molestation, and so on, to explain that there are a few people in the world who do things to hurt people. Take the opportunity to explain that it is because of these few people that we have locks on our doors and that we do not let people we don't know come into the house. And we do not go with strangers in their cars, nor do we talk with them on the street—and we never accept candy or presents from them. Tell your child that if a stranger should come near him, offer him candy, or try to take hold of him, that he should run away as fast as possible to where there are people; he should do this because persons who want to hurt someone are not apt to do it in front of other people.

Such serious talk is honest and relevant to the child's question, but it avoids the sexual connection, which the young child cannot understand. Be sure to repeat that there are few people who want to hurt other people; you don't want your child to become overly fearful and suspicious of everyone. Also, put your arm around your child—because such thoughts are bound to be frightening.

Generally, the young school child is not terribly active sexually, possibly because he is well occupied with his adjustment to school. He seems to go through a period of solitude and thinking about his new life. Later, in the fourth grade, he begins to notice girls in a different way; this activity intensifies as your child approaches sixth grade and then seems to diminish again till puberty. Although you will have introduced him to the subject at home, your child will learn the physical side of sex in school. The parts of sex education that only you can teach are the love, the respect, and the caring that makes human sexuality beautiful.

SEE ALSO: Affection; Discipline; Safety; Swearing and Obscenity; Toilet Training; Children's Books (sex education).

RESOURCES

Adoption

Books

DE HARTOG, JAN. *The Children*. New York: Atheneum, 1969. In 1967, Mr. de Hartog, writer and ex-sea captain, then fifty-three, adopted two little Korean girls, aged five and three.

This book contains practical advice for anyone adopting a child of another culture, but it is also a delightful and sensitive description of a man's adventures as the father of two little girls.

LeShan, Eda J. *You and Your Adopted Child.* New York: Public Affairs Pamphlets, No. 274, 381 Park Avenue, South, N.Y.: 10016.

Government Publications

Order from the Assistant Public Printer (Superintendent of Documents), U.S. Government Printing Office, Washington, D.C., 20402.

Tips on the Care and Adjustment of Vietnamese and Other Asian Children in the U.S. 1975. HE 1.452:V 67. 017–091–00210–0.

Death

Books

Egleson, Jim. *Parents Without Partners.* New York: Dutton, 1961.

Grollman, Earl A., ed. *Explaining Death to Children.* Boston: Beacon Press, 1967.

Kubler-Ross, Elizabeth. *Death: The Final Stage of Growth.* Englewood Cliffs, N.J.: Prentice-Hall, Inc., 1975.

LeShan, Eda. *Learning to Say Goodbye: When a Parent Dies.* New York: Macmillan, 1976.

Stein, Sara Bonnett. *About Dying, An Open Family Book For Parents* and *Children Together.* New York: Walker and Company, 1974. Talking about death with a small child whose grandfather has died.

Wolf, Anna W. *Helping Your Child Understand Death.* New York: Child Study Association of America, 1973.

Organizations

Parents Without Partners. 7910 Woodmont Avenue, Washington, D.C. 20014 (301/654–8850). For information on publications, contact your nearest chapter.

Divorce

Books

DESPERT, JULIETTE LOUISE. *Children of Divorce.* Garden City, New York: Dolphin Books, 1962.

EGELSON, JIM. *Parents Without Partners.* New York: Dutton, 1961.

GROLLMAN, EARL A. *Explaining Divorce to Children.* Boston: Beacon, 1969.

MINDEY, CAROL. *The Divorced Mother, A Guide to Readjustment.* New York: McGraw-Hill, 1969, pages 88–150.

STEINZOR, BERNARD. *When Parents Divorce, A New Approach to New Relationships.* New York: Pantheon, 1969.

Organizations

Parents Without Partners. 7910 Woodmont Avenue, Washington, D.C., 20014 (302/654–8850). For information on publications, contact your nearest chapter.

Drug Addiction and Alcoholism

Government Publications

Order from the Assistant Public Printer (Superintendent of Documents), U.S. Government Printing Office, Washington, D.C., 20402.

Drug-Taking Youth, An Overview of Social, Psychological and Educational Aspects. 1969, pub. 1971. J24.2:Y8. 027–004–00014–8.

Human Ecology

Books and Pamphlets

BERLAND, THEODORE. *Noise—The Third Pollution.* No. 449. New York: Public Affairs Pamphlets, 381 Park Avenue, South, N.Y., 10016.

CARSON, RACHEL L. *The Sea Around Us.* New York: New American Library, 1954.

CARSON, RACHEL. *Silent Spring.* New York: Fawcett Library World, 1973.

Information on Recycling. Aluminum Company of America, 507–G Alcoa Building, Pittsburgh, Pa. 15219.

MANNIX, DANIEL PRATT. *All Creatures Great and Small.* New York: McGraw Hill, 1963.

POTTER, VAN RENSSELAER. *Bioethics, Bridge to the Future.* Englewood Cliffs, New Jersey: Prentice-Hall, 1971.

SNOW, C.P. *The Two Cultures and the Scientific Revolution.* New York: Cambridge University Press, 1961.

TOFFLER, ALVIN. *Future Shock.* New York: Random House, 1970.

Government Publications

Order from the Assistant Public Printer (Superintendent of Documents), U.S. Government Printing Office, Washington, D.C., 20402.

Conservation Activities for Girl Scouts. Al.68:1009. 001–000–02593-7.

Books

BRIGGS, DOROTHY CORKVILLE. *Your Child's Self-Esteem.* New York: Dolphin Books, 1975.

HARRIS, THOMAS A. *I'm OK—You're OK.* New York: Harper and Row, 1969.

Sex Education

Books

FLANAGAN, GERALDINE LUX. *The First Nine Months of Life.* New York: Simon and Schuster, 1962. The story of the prenatal development of a child, told in words and illustrated with photos, written for the general public.

STAFF OF THE CHILD STUDY ASSOCIATION. *What to Tell Your Children About Sex.* New York: Child Study Press, 1973.

STAFF OF THE CHILD STUDY ASSOCIATION. *What Shall I Tell My Child?* Introduction by Theodor Reik. New York: Crown Publishers, Inc., 1966.

10

feelings and behavior to understand

ANGER

Young children cry, bite, kick, hold their breath, and throw themselves around when they are angry because they are limited in other ways of expressing themselves. Also, there is so much that they do not understand; and lack of understanding causes frustration.

It is important that the child express his anger, even though he may appear to you to be completely unreasonable. Anger turned inward lies buried, only to erupt later. Then, to everyone's surprise, it surfaces in angry teen-age or adult behavior. A long spell of pouting may mean buried anger. Bring it out into the open and help your child deal with it.

You cannot have adult discussions with a very young child; his anger often seems unreasonable by adult standards. He is simply not old enough to understand. Forbid him violence to animals, people, and property, *but* be sure to give him harmless outlets for his anger. Supply him with a large stuffed animal, with paper bags to pop, with a big rubber clown with a heavy base, or with something to bang in his rage.

Throughout his development, the child will go through stages in which he is more susceptible than usual to outbursts of anger, because each new period of growth and awareness upsets his equilibrium, making him tend to be insecure and irritable. When this happens, recognize it as a step forward and know that there will be a calmer period before too long. It, too, will be followed by another leap forward and loss of equilibrium causing insecurity and outbursts of anger.

As the child matures and learns, his apparently unreasonable anger should gradually diminish; his desire to better his situation in more creative ways should develop. The more you talk with him and the more he learns, the less he will lash out in anger. As the child begins to be able to express himself by talking, writing, and painting and in harmless physical activity, he should be encouraged to use these modes of expression. They are legitimate outlets for anger.

You will set your child a good example if you apologize to him for your own outbursts and if you explain to him what really caused your anger. Surely, there isn't a parent living who has not lashed out in anger at a child who happens to do an awkward thing just when everything else is going wrong. An apology means a great deal to your child: It means that you respect him as a person.

Your child needs a close and trusted friend who will sympathize and who will, in many cases, dissolve his anger by helping him to understand. You are that friend.

SEE ALSO: Blaming; Conflicts; Disappointment; Jealousy; Death; Sibling Rivalry; Talking With Children; Children's Books (anger; growing up).

BLAMING

The more insecure a person is, the more he is apt to blame unfortunate happenings on someone else. When young children find themselves in situations that turn out badly, they learn quickly to try to wiggle out of responsibility by blaming others. Also, it is easy to learn to put another person down by pointing out everything he does wrong in order to improve one's own position. Blaming and telling tales can become a lifelong habit for a person who is not comfortable with his own abilities, for one who has not learned to be responsible.

The best way to deal with blaming and tattling is to show little interest in it. At the same time, however, show a lot of interest in your child's self-image, in what he does right and well. Be discriminating when you feel you must point out *his* mistakes so he will not be looking for others' mistakes in imitation of you.

Often, when a child blames a brother or sister for first one thing and then another, he is telling you of anger resulting from jealousy or frustration. Help him find and express his true feelings and make sure he feels as important as everyone else in the family.

SEE ALSO: Self-Image; Sibling Rivalry; Anger; Jealousy.

COMPETITION

Talents and inclinations are so individual that encouraging competition among children in general education is unfair to some and falsely stimulating to others. Whether or not a child competes well is very often no measure of his intellectual capacity.

Because life demands a certain amount of ability to cope with competition, it is necessary to help a child learn to compete successfully. On the other hand, competing just to set oneself above others—having a compulsion to win at all costs—deprives a child of rich experience. A child who wants to win all the time is looking for peer approval, but, sadly, he finds that friends drop away from compulsive winners.

To teach a child to compete successfully, help him define his goals as having a dimension other than just winning. Then help him develop the skills he needs to achieve his goals. Encourage him to compete against his own past performance. Once in a while, as a game, encourage him to do part of his homework against a timer as practice in gaining speed. Colorful charts and graphs keep a tantalizing record against which to work.

Do not talk about what other children do or compare his performance with theirs. Give him plenty of time to explore and learn about things in depth, to think and talk, to create and have friendships in a noncompetitive atmosphere. Then add games and sports for the spice of competition with an emphasis on fun and good sportsmanship.

SEE ALSO: Conflicts; Jealousy; Withdrawal; Self-Image; Sports; School.

CONFLICTS

Conflicts between young children are common, noisy, and annoying, but they are also understandable. Children have to mature to learn that others exist as individuals in their own right. Bring two immature individuals together and you are bound to have battles. The conflicts, however, are learning experiences which teach children how to maintain their self-respect while still respecting others. This is why playing with other children is a necessary part of education. It is like learning to ride a bicycle. The only way to get the hang of it is to do it, taking the bumps and bruises along the way.

If your child is not holding his own, you will want to look into the reasons why. He may be too young, too small, or too immature to deal successfully with the other child. There may be a personality clash, causing them to never want to do the same thing. You will want to remove your child from a situation that is constantly frustrating because such a situation will be damaging to his self-image. It will deny him the positive learning experience he should be having with other children. Try to find more congenial friends for him.

Otherwise, if the rumpus is not on top of you, try to ignore it (admittedly, this is not easy when you have a headache and it has been raining for three days). If you are called into the fracas, don't participate in the argument and don't get drawn into taking sides. Just separate the children and suggest that they not play together for a while. Then, after the emotions have cooled, encourage them to talk with each other and with you about what caused the problem. Through gentle suggestion and guidance, help them find their own practical solutions.

SEE ALSO: Sibling Rivalry; Competition; Anger; Jealousy; Cooperation.

CRYING

From the moment of conception, babies are individuals with their own physical and emotional configurations, so it is difficult for anyone to generalize about why any one baby is crying at any one time. All babies cry when they are hungry, cold, or in pain; some babies cry when they are wet and some don't. Then there are babies who have daily periods of crying during the first three months, and no one has yet figured out the reason, other than that we do know that such babies are often healthy, active, and alert. They may be of a more tense nature and they may have difficulty in adjusting to life out of the womb.

Do not hesitate to comfort a crying infant. The danger of spoiling him is less than the danger of his feeling insecure. Be sure to give him loving attention when he is not crying so that, as the months go by, he does not connect attention specifically with crying. The fact that first babies seem more prone to crying spells in the first three months tells us that the more parents understand babies, the less nervous they are and the less nervous the baby is inclined to be.

In a few months, as the baby is becoming more responsive to his surroundings, there will be less noisy crying and some fretting over mild discomfort or boredom. For some babies, sleep is impossible without a brief crying spell to relieve tension. Parents can begin to differentiate among the various cries, learn what each expresses, and react accordingly. Older babies cry over pain, hunger, and tension, but they begin to cry in anger sometimes. When babies learn that they are making the crying noise themselves, as a precursor of talking, they sometimes cry just to hear themselves.

Between infancy and toddlerhood, babies begin to assert themselves in a desire to be independent. This is an excellent indication, but at the same time, the baby becomes aware of his dependence on his parents for security, so he is apt to fear separation. These ambivalent feelings make him cry at one time if he is constrained and at another because of fear and loneliness. Sometimes, during toddlerhood, children become fearful of sleep because it means separation. They may sob disconsolately in their loneliness and fear. Gentle consideration with understanding firmness is needed to help the child through this passing phase without spoiling him *or* damaging his sense of security.

As the ability to talk gives a child a better way to express his desires and feelings, crying to communicate diminishes if he has been given plenty of loving attention during infancy. If not, he will have developed the habit of crying for attention. When he enters school and begins to associate with peers, he will be at a disadvantage if he has the habit of crying over every little thing. Nobody likes a crybaby.

The best way to help a child who cries over every little bump or disappointment is to give him loving attention when he does not cry and, when he cries over a small hurt, to comfort him and patch him up without being overly sympathetic. Do not, however, shame him for crying, because there will be times in life when he will need to let himself go, without guilt, and cry.

SEE ALSO: Affection; Habit Formation; Speech; Disappointment.

DAWDLING

A dawdling child can be exasperating when parents are tired or in a hurry. But there are reasons for dawdling, reasons which parents should understand.

Much of what seems like dawdling is related to a child's very rudimentary time sense. He does not understand hours and minutes. He goes by his interests and appetites rather than by a clock. When he is hungry, he eats faster; when he is full, he slows down. The struggle with his coat buttons tires his fingers and gets boring, so he slows down. When there is no end in sight—no understandable goal—time stretches out. Adults know that the quicker and better one does a job, the sooner they can get to other things. Little children haven't learned that yet and have to be taught. A young child does not realize that he is getting slower and slower, so he shouldn't be accused of dawdling. In effect, when you introduce the word to his vocabulary in an accusatory way, you give him a mechanism to use against you.

Instead of scolding, it is better to realize that dawdling means that the child is getting bogged down, that he has lost sight of his goal. Help him over the hump and make the goal more obtainable. It also helps to give him something attractive in the way of an activity to look forward to once the goal has been achieved.

Rebellious Dawdling

If a child figures out that his dawdling is annoying to his parents, he may use it to express his unhappiness. Parental admonitions only make matters worse. It is necessary to get at the cause of the child's problem, to find out why he is expressing negative feelings this way. Perhaps he is jealous or frustrated. Maybe he is bored or feels left out. Look over the other material in this chapter to see if you can find a possible source of your child's unhappiness. Once you find the cause and relieve the basic problem, then you can help your child set his own goals and get on with achieving them.

SEE ALSO: Time; Anger.

DISAPPOINTMENT

Disappointment is cataclysmic to young children. Their faces turn sad and fierce all at once, in an awesome grimace. Older children and adults who have not learned to handle disappointment are usually considered rather immature.

With young children, it is best to go out of your way to avoid disappointment, never promising that which you may not be able to produce. You cannot explain reasons for broken promises to the very young. They simply will not understand. Don't intimate possibilities that you may not be able to carry through. When disappointment cannot be avoided, don't expect your child to swallow it without saying anything. Help him express his disappointment by talking with him and letting him know you understand. Encourage him to engage in active play so he can vent his anger and frustration and his feeling of having been put down.

When a child is mature enough (toward school age), to recognize that he isn't the only person in the world to be dealt disappointment, you can help him learn to be somewhat objective and to think creatively about ways to compensate. First, gently but firmly, help the child to recognize that the disappointing situation cannot be altered. False hope prolongs the turmoil and delays creative thinking. Once past this very important first step, go into an "imagineering" session with your child. Encourage him to come up with feasible alternatives instead of getting hung up on his disappointment. Often the child will admit later that the alternative was better than what he had wanted in the first place. Your response to such an admission would not be, "I told you so," but: "That was a very grown-up way to handle what I know was very disappointing. I'm glad it turned out well for you."

SEE ALSO: Crying; Anger; Creativity; Talking With Children.

FEAR

We have seen on television how cautiously astronauts react to gravity after having been weightless for a few days. The first fear a newborn baby knows in this world originates in his total inexperience with gravity. But, in his inexperience, he doesn't recognize that he has a fear, so he struggles and learns rapidly how to cope.

If adults were to put themselves in the position of a child at each stage of mental and physical development, they might become obsessed by fear. When one considers how small and vulnerable children are, how inexperienced in worldly ways and how undeveloped their thought processes are, it seems remarkable how fearlessly they meet challenges. Their fearlessness is partly due to their lack of experience and is responsible, on the whole, for their ability to meet challenges and to learn rapidly.

On the other hand, fear is a protective mechanism and as such, is part of the learning process. As a child matures, he learns from experience what he needs to watch out for and which of his earlier fears are groundless. He also learns *that* he fears. As he develops the understanding that he feels fear, he needs to be developing the understanding that he is capable of managing his own affairs, so that he will be motivated to deal with his fears.

Parents naturally protect their children from situations that are dangerous at each stage of their child's development, and they try to assuage fears that are groundless. It is important to remember that fears which are apparently groundless to adults are very real to the child. If parents recognize a child's thought processes and capabilities at each stage and deal with him accordingly, the child will gradually work his way through his childhood fears. It takes patience, gentle encouragement, and education. It takes a complete absence of ridicule.

The following is a list of *possible* fears. Not all children react the same way to the same situations. We certainly do not want to introduce problems; rather, we simply wish to present parents with a reference should they encounter some mysterious behavioral manifestations.

Infants

Falling.   Before birth the infant is suspended in the amniotic fluid, so has no experience with gravity. After birth his body must become acclimated to the pull of gravity every time he moves a muscle. Sometimes he feels as though he is falling as he moves his arms and legs around, trying to organize his muscles to keep everything from flopping. Even his jaw gets away from him from time to time. He is tense when he is handed from one person to another, showing his insecurity.

Loud Noises. After a person has lived for awhile, he becomes accustomed to the noises in his environment and unconsciously sorts out threatening noises from all the others. Infants react to all loud noises as if they were threatening because they have no experience to tell them otherwise.

Pretoddlers and Toddlers

Bath. If a child has slipped under the water and choked, overcoming his fear may require sponge baths for a while, followed by a gradual reintroduction to the tub, starting with very little water. Sometimes a child is afraid of going down the drain when the stopper is pulled. Since he doesn't understand relative sizes, he does not realize that he can't fit in the drainpipe. You may have to wait to pull the plug when he is well away from the tub and engaged in another activity.

Toilet Flushing. At this age, a child feels that his bowel movement is a part of him, so he may panic when he sees it flushed away. Also, he may fear being sucked away by the rushing water. The use of a potty chair may help, especially if you are not too quick to dump the movement into the toilet and flush it. You don't want this fear to cause constipation.

Gagging. Instinct makes a baby panic when he can't get his breath for any reason. He does not understand what to do or that the condition can be corrected. He just reacts. Some children gag more easily than others, perhaps because of a little slower muscle development. Be patient. Feed slowly and introduce chopped food carefully at the proper time, encouraging him to use his fingers to feed little bits to himself at his own speed.

Separation.   As a child becomes aware of both his indepen-dence and his dependence on his parents, he may fear losing sight of them for even a moment. Before this stage arrives, comfort your child when he is upset by holding him close and repeating the words, "You're all right." Teach your babysitter (with whom you leave the child regularly) to use the same procedure and words. When the fearful stage arrives, keep the same babysitter (if possi-ble) and continue to leave the baby regularly. If he is very sensitive to your absence, however, don't leave him for very long until this stage passes.

Strange Objects, Sudden Movements, Noisy Equipment.   A child may be somewhat concerned about a ringing telephone and terrified of the vacuum cleaner. He has become aware that the object is making the noise—perhaps as it moves about—but he does not understand that it is not alive. In time, with gentle encourage-ment, he will begin to see that the frightening object is under the control of his parents. For a while he may accept the object when he is with his parents and be afraid of it when he is with strangers.

Animals.   A toddler is not very big and he is not too steady on his feet. Relatively speaking, even a small dog is large and, in addition, it is unpredictable in its movements. The dog is near the level of the child's face and often "kisses" the child, an unpleasant experience for one who cannot turn quickly enough to avert the wet doggie kiss without falling down and becoming even more vulnerable. Don't allow these things to happen.

Going to Bed.   This manifestation around toddlerhood is a result of a fear of separation. Be gentle and understanding. Keep everything in and around the crib familiar, use a night light, or crack the door. Show the child where you will be spending the evening (nearby) and point out your bed, telling him that you will be retiring soon, too. You may need to stay by his crib a few nights until he falls asleep; when he seems more at ease, sit in the same place in a nearby room so that he will become confident of your accessibility.

Constipation.   If a child has had a painful bowel movement, he may fear going to the toilet, and this may cause chronic constipation. Consult your doctor about ways to avoid painful movements and do a little distracting while the child is on the toilet until he forgets his fear.

Preschooler

Mutilation and Death.   At this age, a child becomes aware of other people's bodies, of how they are different from his own. Yet he does not understand why some people are missing a leg or an arm. He may fear that something is wrong, which it may or may not be, and that what is wrong may happen to him. Because he is still quite egocentric, if he becomes aware of serious injury, illness, or death, he takes the experience right to himself. He can sustain a painful bump rather bravely, but scream with terror at the sight of a little blood. You need to calmly and methodically dress his wounds, all the while telling him he is all right. Do not make too much of an issue of illness and minor injuries but don't hesitate to comfort when the distress signals go up. Mental development, gentle explanations, and experience will bring this fear under control.

Animals.   Bad experiences keep this fear alive. Gradually introduce your child to small, quiet animals, holding them yourself until your child can have time to decide to touch them. Don't force him to touch them.

Wetting.   All small children have wetting accidents. If a child is shamed for wetting, he may develop a fear that burdens his play and keeps him from sleeping soundly at night. Nervousness from the fear may actually hinder the development of control.

Dark.   At this age of fantasizing, a child can imagine all sorts of threatening things lurking in the dark. He hasn't sorted out what is real and what is imaginary. Avoid scary stories and television programs and don't force total darkness at bedtime.

Dreams. To a young child, dreams are real, so a bad dream is as frightening to him as any real experience would be. Understanding this, parents will want to be as considerate and comforting as they would be if the experience were real, holding the child close so he can feel the reality of his comforter's warm body.

Losing Love. The manifestation of this fear is particularly acute when a new baby arrives. A young child does not understand the limitless quality of love, so he fears that, if he has to share your love with another child, your love for him will diminish. Except for certain times during the day, the new baby has less need for your attention than your fearful child.

School Age Child

School. A child often doesn't know why he fears school, so parents have to do some figuring. It may be the children. Or perhaps he can't understand the teacher. There may be a spooky shadow in the hall, the custodian may look like someone he saw in a bad dream, or an unidentifiable noise may seem to portend disaster. He may fear leaving his parents, especially if there is a new baby at home, whose presence he fears will take their love from him. If parental expectations are unreasonably high, he may fear being embarrassed or not being able to please. A conference with the teacher and loving talks at home are necessary to set matters straight. Don't force the fear inside, assuming that because the child stops talking, he is rid of his fear. Try hard to get at the root of the problem, so you can help with a real solution.

Other Children. Unfortunately, there are some children who tease younger children. Perhaps your child is up against such a child either at school or in the neighborhood. Your calm intervention may be necessary in order to convince such a child that he must leave your child alone.

Imaginary Creatures, Ghosts, Weird Things. Even though a school child is learning to separate fact from fantasy, the process is gradual. Children this age have a certain fascination with ghosts and other supernatural beings. They have fears which can trigger near panic under circumstances which seem spooky or weird to their inexperienced minds. Yet their pride often keeps them from talking. It is good to take time to try to get the problem out in the open and help get to the truth without ridicule.

Fear of Fear. If a child has been ridiculed for being fearful, he will think it to his advantage to avoid talking. If he has been led to believe that to express his fears to his parents is a sign of weakness, he will, from here on, keep his fears locked up inside. Peer pressure to be fearless will intensify the situation, especially for boys. If he has no one to help, his fears may grow into debilitating phobias. Keep the communication lines open. Never underestimate or downplay your child's fears. Help him express them, understand them, and deal with them.

SEE ALSO: Children's Books (fears; friendship; growing up; hospitals, doctors, and dentists; handicaps); Independence; Jealousy; Death; Perception; Sibling Rivalry.

JEALOUSY

Everybody feels jealous sometimes and no amount of talking or being made to feel guilty will get rid of it. In fact, when a person feels jealous, he is already feeling unhappy with himself, so being made to feel guilty only makes him feel more inadequate.

Children's jealousy of their brothers and sisters is discussed under Sibling Rivalry (see page 218). However, a child can also be jealous of a parent—or even of a pet or a cooking project—if it takes away attention that was formerly given to him. When children become jealous, all they know is that they are miserable. They do not understand what is wrong and they don't know how to react. So they do things that, on the surface, seem to have no connection with anything. When parents observe behavior that appears to be plain orneriness, they will want to ask themselves whether their attention has been diverted for some reason. The following are a few possibilities, though these occurrences do not always make a child feel jealous.

- A new baby, either expected or arrived.
- Parents' attention to each other.
- Peers or siblings who seem smarter, stronger, "better."
- Illness in the family.
- Any person, such as a houseguest, who takes parent attention away from the child.
- The telephone, vacuum cleaner, and so forth, if the parents give these objects too much attention.
- Any adult activity that occupies more than the usual amount of time.

If, when a child does something objectionable because of jealousy, parents punish him or tell him he should be ashamed, the child may learn not to express his jealous feelings, but he won't get over being jealous. His parents will have confirmed his suspicion that he is not worthy of their love because he is so *bad*. Instead of feeling that he is bad, a child needs to learn to recognize what is bothering him so he can deal with it.

First, as when dealing with any objectionable behavior, parents need to hold back their criticisms and ask themselves if there is any cause, real or imagined, for the child to feel jealous. When you broach the subject, don't start by telling your child that he is bad; rather, say, *"I don't like what you did"* (poured milk on the baby, pinched the cat, dug up the beans, or whatever). Though you won't act pleased at the time when he pinches the cat, you will want to make sure that your toddler is generally getting his share of family attention and affection.

A preschooler may become temporarily jealous of one parent or the other. Don't aggravate the situation by showing a lot of affection for your spouse in front of your jealous child. This stage will pass.

As your child learns to express himself verbally, help him to work through his own jealous feelings. After you tell him you don't like what he did, don't *tell* him he is jealous and don't try to convince him that he has no reason to be jealous. That is a put-down to him in his frame of mind, so there may be no end to the argument you get. Instead, recognize that your child wants your love and support, that he feels he doesn't have it, and that he doesn't know how to get it. He needs to be encouraged to tell you all that, and, in telling you, he will be learning to understand his problem.

Listen carefully to your child when he pours out his troubles to you. Pick up any clue you can. Repeat the clue out loud, so *he* can begin to think and clarify what is behind his problem. Don't be tempted to make any explanations. Just keep him talking and thinking by sympathetically repeating each point he makes. Once you get the hang of this procedure (it takes practice), you will find that your child will not only tell you that he is jealous, but also he will begin to sort out reasons why he shouldn't be. This is the kind of mental "working through" you want him to learn. He may tell you what he would like from you. Then you can work together to come up with a way to change things that will be reasonable to you and satisfying to him.

SEE ALSO: Sibling Rivalry; Anger; Fear; Affection; Fairness; Talking With Children; Children's Books (baby in the family; anger); Self-Image.

SIBLING RIVALRY

There are a number of reasons why rivalries exist between siblings. The first child is bound to feel threatened by the arrival of the second. All of a sudden he has to share his parents. It is a shock for which there is no adequate preparation, yet there are things a parent can do to make it easier for the older child. How severely he feels threatened depends on the stage of his own development and on how his parents have helped him to become independent. The older he is, the further into his own interests and friendships he should be and the less dependent he should be on his parents for his entire existence. The younger sibling needs understanding, too. He has never known what it means to have all the attention from his parents, so he has no adjustment to make, but he does have to fend off his older sibling who will sometimes take unfair advantage of him.

The older sibling may be quieter and more serious, having lived in exclusively adult surroundings in his very early childhood. He may not relate to other children as well as the younger sibling, who has been accustomed to living with another child from the day he was born and who may be less serious, more outgoing, and more socially adept. The older child may suffer from comparisons of his awkwardness with the younger child's social skills. On the other hand, the older child is apt to have higher standards and to be the better student, having had most of his early learning from adults, in situations uncluttered by the irrationality of siblings. The younger child, then, may suffer from unfavorable comparisons of intellectual ability. How much each child is affected by his position in the family depends both on inherited characteristics and on the help he gets from his parents.

Sometimes differences in personality, inclination, and learning patterns put one child or another more in tune with parental expectations. This is why parents want to avoid tunnel vision in respect to their children's potential. It may turn out that the less favored child develops the strongest character in response to his adverse situation; but the hurt may alienate him from his family. Or, as often happens, the less favored child may not develop to his full potential because of a poor self-image. With a stunted childhood, he may try desperately to compete in insignificant or even destructive ways, so that, year by year, he becomes more alienated. And, into the bargain, what has left one child underdeveloped also leaves the favored child with a distorted self-image which may well cause him trouble with his peers.

Here are a few tips for developing a wholesome relationship between your children while helping each to reach his maximum potential.

- Keep your children out of unfair competition with each other by concerning yourself with the development of each child as an individual.
- Let your children know that you understand their jealousy and don't make them feel guilty about it. Be gentle with them when they want to hurt each other, but don't let them.

- Pay careful attention to each child's self-image (see Self-Image, pages 191–94).

- Give your children harmless ways to work off their anger with one another—plenty of physical activity and outdoor play.

- Be pleased with your children when they show concern for one another.

- Stay out of minor conflicts. Let them work on their own ways of getting along.

- Avoid comparisons. They are harmful to everyone concerned.

- Guide your children into constructive activities. Boredom leads to squabbles.

- Accept weaknesses and enhance strong points in every member of the family, parents and children alike.

- Behave toward your spouse as you would want your children to behave toward one another. Bickering is contagious.

- Teach respect for privacy. Your older child will want time to himself and time with friends his own age.

- Teach your younger child to respect your older child's belongings.

- Teach your children ways in which they may be helpful to each other and expect them to be so.

SEE ALSO: Affection; Anger; Fear; Fairness; Conflicts; Self-Image; Talking With Children; Children's Books (baby in the family).

SWEARING AND OBSCENITY

Preschool children like to experiment with words. They use words they hear without really knowing what they mean, although they do notice a sort of special effect on other children when they use "bathroom words." If you ignore the use of such words, your child will eventually stop using them. On the other hand, if you join in his playing around with alliterative words, funny words, and made-up words, he will have a legitimate outlet for his diversion.

When school children begin to use swearwords and obscene

language, they are telling you that they are trying to be grown-up and independent. One of the things they are saying is that they want to be part of the peer gang. A little shared naughtiness makes a childhood gang more cohesive.

The use of language your school age child knows you find objectionable is early evidence of the tug of war between home values and those of the world—a conflict which your child will be struggling with for many years. So the way you react to this early manifestation of peer influence, coupled with the urge for independence, will be similar to the way you will react to a lot of future situations involving clarification of family values.

First of all, we know that people who feel secure in their own capabilities do not need artificial macho mechanisms. Also, studies have shown that even the most rebellious teen-agers, as they mature, tend to revert to family value patterns. Unless swearing simply becomes a habit, it reflects the insecurity of youth more than anything else. How parents deal with profanity and other value-related behaviors, beginning with young school age children, will make the difference between open lines of communication and teen-age rebellion.

When your child introduces an objectionable expression, which usually happens when he is in first or second grade, don't laugh it off; and don't tell your child how bad it is and forbid him to use it. Tell him instead that *you* don't like it and that *you* don't want to have to hear it. This approach puts the discipline problem on his shoulders and starts him evaluating. Scolding and punishing do not accomplish these ends; they put you in the position of being the bad guy instead of the gentle but firm defender of family values. You want your child to know your values, which he learns as much by the way you act toward him as by what you tell him. You want him to have the freedom to think and to choose for himself. You can rest assured that, if you give him that freedom, along with a firm definition of family values, plenty of affection, and sympathetic talk time, he will grow up thinking seriously about his choices.

SEE ALSO: Speech; Friendship; Independence; Morality; Discipline; Poetry; Talking With Children; Self-Image.

WITHDRAWAL

For older children and adults, occasional withdrawal for medita-
tion and renewal is healthy. However, habitual withdrawal as a
defense mechanism against what seems to be an unmanageable
world is a serious behavioral manifestation.

When very young children feel frightened by a situation, they
withdraw, either to the comfort of parents' arms, or, if such comfort is not forthcoming, they hide. Hiding is a lonely form of withdrawing, so children use it only when there is no alternative. It is
desperate and always devoid of positive human learning experience. If a young child is denied the comfort of a loving protector
and, in addition, is made to feel guilty about his retreat, he will feel
devastated in his solitude. A continuation of such behavior sets up a
habit pattern you don't want for your child. So whenever your child
indicates that he needs your protection, assume that his need is
valid. Offer him the comfort of your protective body while you
help him assess the frightening situation. Knowing that he can
count on you and that you understand his dilemma, he can be encouraged to figure out how to deal with his fear better the next
time around. As you help him with each situation, his capability
grows and his need for withdrawal diminishes.

As children grow older, their reasons for withdrawal are more
psychological, less a direct reaction to fear. They feel rejected and
resort to withdrawal when every other effort to make themselves
acceptable has failed. The seriousness of this kind of withdrawal is
often overlooked because, when a school age child withdraws, he is
unobtrusive. A noisy child, whether at home or in the classroom, is
the first to be dealt with, when actually it is the withdrawn child, the
child who has left the group, who needs the most concerned attention.

Every young school age child daydreams and fantasizes, but if
his real life is taking shape properly, such fantasizing should diminish and become manageable with maturity. If a child uses withdrawal as a defense mechanism against a severe feeling of inferior-

ity, he loses ground in his real developmental experiences. His feeling of rejection and his fantasies of imagined rather than real capabilities separate him more and more from his family, his peers, his education, and his real development.

Almost everyone withdraws and fantasizes to some extent. Parents are never able to understand every situation in which their child feels threatened. All they can do is be as sensitive as they can to the child's view of contingencies. First and foremost, parents need to make sure that their children grow— from infanthood through childhood—increasingly confident that, no matter what, they are acceptable. This is the foundation for healthy emotional development. Then, when their children meet rejection, they need to assess the reasons for that rejection seriously. At any one time, the reason may be a simple one, such as incompatability due to the interests of a limited group of friends. For example, a child who is rather studious may be rejected by an athletic group with whom he just happened to be thrown. The child has no way of knowing that his experience is limited and that his being studious is also quite acceptable. It is up to parents to be sensitive to such situations and to do a bit of environmental rearranging, to search out more compatible friends for their child. On the other hand, maybe your child cries over every little thing, is overbearing, or exhibits some other kind of behavior that would turn anybody off. When a child becomes thoroughly confused and bogged down in his school work, if he knows only expectations and receives no help, he may withdraw. If you keep your lines of communication open, you can work with your child to get at the root of such problems before they overwhelm him. Read through this part of the book (Part IV) on *Character and Personality Development* and the section in Chapter 8 on *Talking with Children*; then encourage thoughtful exploration of every vexing situation as it arises. When a child has a loving friend and counselor with whom he can communicate, he will not need to take the extreme route of withdrawing.

SEE ALSO: School; Friendship; Self-Image; Anger.

RESOURCES

Books

BRICKLIN, BARRY, PH.D. and PATRICIA BRICKLIN. *Bright Child, Poor Grades*. New York: Delacorte Press, 1967, pages 14–29.

REDL, FRITZ and DAVID WINEMAN. *The Aggressive Child*. New York: Free Press, 1957.

SPOCK, DR. BENJAMIN. *Baby and Child Care*. New York: Pocket Books, 1976, pages 22–23, 368, 370–372, 400–403.

Competition

Books

BRUNS, WILLIAM and THOMAS TUTKO. *Winning is Everything*. New York: Macmillan, 1976. A plea to put *recreation* back in children's sports.

Conflicts

Books

DREIKURS, RUDOLPH. *How to Stop Fighting With Your Kids*. New York: Ace Books, 1975.

FABER, ADELE and ELAINE MAZLISH. *Liberated Parents, Liberated Children*. New York: Avon Books, 1974.

GORDON, THOMAS. *P.E.T., Parent Effectiveness Training*. New York: New American Library, 1970.

Books

Spock, Dr. Benjamin. *Baby and Child Care.* New York: Pocket Books, 1976, pages 215–224, 303–304, 387–393.

Books

Briggs, Dorothy Corkville. *Your Child's Self-Esteem.* New York: Dolphin Books, 1975, pages 209–222.
Spock, Dr. Benjamin. *Baby and Child Care.* New York: Pocket Books, 1976, pages 375–385.

Books

Spock, Dr. Benjamin. *Baby and Child Care.* New York: Pocket Books, 1976, pages 375–385.

Books

Briggs, Dorothy Corkville. *Your Child's Self-Esteem.* New York: Dolphin Books, 1975.

11

feelings and behavior to encourage

AFFECTION

Real love means more than just a show of affection. It sometimes means caring enough to insist that a child suffer the discomfort of immunization injections, that he hang up his coat, or that he be denied something he wants. It is the show of affection, however, that keeps the child secure in the knowledge that what you do, whether agreeable or not, is motivated by your love for him. We don't know what effect love has on the unborn child other than that the physical care he receives in the womb greatly affects his health and intelligence. And physical care shows love.

Every child has a gentle life in the womb. He "belongs" because he is physically attached to his mother. Once this physical attachment is severed traumatically at birth, only the family's substitution of physical affection can ease the separation. So from birth, whatever else affects the child's development and intelligence, love and affection are a necessary part of his environment. He needs to feel that he has not been cast forth into a vacuum—he needs to feel that he "belongs."

Studies have shown that by three months, mothers and babies synchronize their looking at each other and that they turn to look at each other often—*if* the mother feels affection for her baby (which most mothers do). If the mother does not feel love for her baby, neither she nor the baby maintains this connection, all of which proves that infants actively respond to affection at a very early age. All infants and children (everyone, for that matter) thrive on physical affection. For children, being *told* that they are loved is not enough. They like to be held, patted, looked at, hugged, and kissed. So be tender with your infant, hold him and caress him; and when your toddler comes and wraps himself around your leg or tries to crawl into your lap, take a moment to pick him up or bend down for a hug, no matter where you are or how busy you are. Parents are the only ones who can teach love and belonging to a baby.

Secure in his knowledge of who he is and that he belongs to his family, the toddler begins to feel the urge for independence and personhood. The more secure he feels, the more gracefully will he be able to develop his independent personhood. Since his parents still constitute a child's entire social environment, how they support his sense of belonging while responding to his learning to be independent is vital to his proper development. Since toddlers are very busy, they will not want to spend much time hanging onto you if they get a loving response when they need it.

Your child will not get this loving response from his peers. A show of affection is still lacking between peers when children are in the early school years, yet there is a consciousness of wanting to attract the friendship of peers. As the child matures during his school years, he tries to prove his personhood in order to attract friendship; and evidence of close ties to parents seems to hamper the effect he is trying to achieve. So, it embarrasses many (not all) children to be fussed over by parents in public. During this period, treat your child in a grown-up fashion in public; but remember that a lot of this is show for the purpose of impressing peers—and that your child still needs hugs and kisses and tenderness in the privacy of his home.

SEE ALSO: Self-Image; Family; Jealousy; Sibling Rivalry; Sex Education; Friendship; Children's Books (family; animals; baby in the family; cooperation; friendship; grandparents; holidays and special days).

COOPERATION

It is really fun to be a part of a group, tackling a job that goes fast with many hands. The uncooperative person, suspicious that he may be taken advantage of, misses the fun—as well as the work— and finds himself not very popular. It is one thing to enjoy working alone and quite another to refuse to cooperate in those life maintenance activities that must be done at home, at camp, on the boat, at school, and so on. In order to grow up feeling responsible and acceptable, every child should feel a part of not only the security and the fun, but also of the work of the family.

Young children seem naturally to want to help—so much so that they often bumble into mishaps while trying to be helpful. To scold when the child is trying to be helpful is hurtful and discouraging to him and is no way to nurture a cooperative attitude. Parents need to recognize good intentions and to take time to help the child succeed by showing him how to do what he is trying to do.

The school child may put up a fuss about family cooperation, but in spite of all his big talk, he needs the security of a strong family. It is important, however, while taking a strong lead, that parents recognize the maturity of the school child. Since he is too mature to accept being *told* what to do, he will rebel, if dealt with that way, rather than cooperate. Talk over home requirements with him, making the assumption that there is going to be a time when the whole family gets together to dispatch certain obligations. Plan the time of the event to suit him as well as everyone in the family. Expect that everyone will be present and ready to work at the mutually agreeable time. Help each child learn how to work efficiently and well. Keep everyone together and keep it fun, finishing in an hour (more or less), with a snack-treat and mutual admiration of a job well done by a pretty great family.

If a child suddenly "feels ill" and cannot do his share, do not question his integrity. Have a family conference on the spot to decide whether to postpone the work for a while or to divide up the extra load. There will be some grumbling from siblings, which is natural and actually helpful. Of course, if one is too ill to do his share, everyone will agree that the snack-treat would not be good for him. If the child's self-image is intact, and if he has been taught to do a creditable job, he should decide before very long that it's more fun to cooperate.

SEE ALSO: Self-Image; Talking With Children; Housekeeping; Children's Books (cooperation).

COURAGE

Courage comes with a zest for living. A baby wants to walk so badly that he will get up after a painful tumble to try again. Children run to meet life in spite of skinned knees and chins. Although parents are always alert to real dangers to their children, they should not be maudlin over bumps and bruises. They have to allow children the rewards of success in spite of difficulties. You may hear your children telling their friends about their terribly courageous behavior. A positive self-image is absolutely necessary for courage to develop.

Some experiences are unpleasant and hard for anyone to face. In such instances, it is important for you to be near your child, where he can see you and be reassured by your presence and your calm voice. It takes maturity to understand that avoiding certain unpleasant and painful experiences will lead to trouble later. Since you cannot explain all this to a very young child, all you can do is to be calm and loving and say something like, "It's not going to be *so* bad; it's time to be brave and get it over with." Later he may tell you that it *was* bad, whereupon you agree that it wasn't any fun and that you are very proud of how brave he was. Try to keep anticipatory tension from building; show love and concern, along with a rather matter-of-fact attitude toward the ordeal; and praise your child for whatever courage he has mustered.

SEE ALSO: Illness; Self-Image; Discipline; Children's Books (courage; cooperation; fears).

DECISION-MAKING

If parents make a habit of using them, there are many everyday opportunities for children to be encouraged to make their own decisions. Guided practice in decision-making should start early. A child can learn how only by making and living with decisions.

The toddler *wants* to decide for himself, often, he doggedly resists what his parents have decided he should do. A way to get around the impasse (at least part of the time) is to offer two choices, both of which are acceptable to you. Not only will your toddler be happier and more cooperative, but you will have given him cause to think. "Do you want to ride your kiddycar in to bed, or do you want Daddy to take you piggyback?" "Do you want to wear your red or your blue overalls?" All this can cause some problems when your child becomes accustomed to making decisions on many things, because there are times when you cannot offer choices. Those *problems are temporary*, however. The *benefits* of learning to take decision-making responsibility are *long-term*.

Older children are constantly faced with making decisions when they are playing with other children. They are often hesitant to ask advice from their parents when troublesome decisions are facing them, so parents have to be alert to signals indicating troublesome situations. Such signals as irritability, withdrawal, loss of appetite, or loss of enthusiasm can mean a decision that has your child baffled. When you receive such signals, refrain from the natural tendency to produce the solution to the problem yourself. If you do that, your child will have no opportunity to learn, and what is worse, if he doesn't like your solution, he will hesitate to bring other problems to you. It is best to work through the problem with him, helping him to come forth with his own decision. Help him look for and explore the alternatives, guiding him to consider all the possible outcomes, relating them, when necessary, to your family's moral considerations.

When children are doing things together, from early childhood to adulthood, there are always decisions to be made. The child who has not had the opportunity to learn to make responsible decisions will follow the decisions of his friends, regardless of the advisability of the course of action. The child who has learned to evaluate under your guidance will most likely introduce the logical thinking he has practiced under your tutelage at home.

SEE ALSO: Creativity; Discipline; Democracy; Talking With Children.

FAIRNESS

Because the life views of young children are circumscribed by the developmental level of their mental operations, they often see "unfairness" in what adults see as perfectly reasonable consequences. Every child also has an instinct for self-preservation, so he reacts when he thinks he has been treated unfairly. It is only by communicating with you and with others that he learns the "ins and outs" of human interrelationships, so let your child express his anger and stand up for his rights. Encourage him to do so. Take your child's complaints seriously, listen attentively, and avoid jumping to conclusions. If his complaint is valid, stand up for him. If it is a result of his misunderstanding, don't lecture. Talk with him, helping him to reason his way to understanding.

Sometimes, in the press of daily living, an older child is blamed for the indiscretions of a younger brother or sister. He's told that "he is old enough to know better." A young child is *not* old enough to know better when a younger child pushes him beyond his ability to deal with the situation. He will rightly think he is being treated unfairly. Put the blame where it belongs, explaining that "younger children" just haven't yet learned that there are certain things we cannot do. Appeal to your older child's "grown-upness." Get him on your side.

By school age, children become very conscious of "fairness." Their sense of justice seems to outstrip their ability to understand. It is probably related to their new sense of *self* and *others*. Also, entering school thrusts them into new procedures and interrelationships. Teachers are bound to do things differently from what the child is used to at home. And, of course, in the press of classroom activity, what the child has come to expect from others may sometimes be overlooked, leaving him to feel that he has been treated unjustly. This is the time when he learns that there is no place like home.

Sometimes a child's sense of justice is all out of proportion to the offense. He wants you to rush off to do battle on his behalf when what has happened doesn't warrant your antagonizing neighbors or taking the teacher's time. Certainly he needs to know that you understand and are ready to go to bat for him; but he also needs to learn that some unfairness is unintentional and must be overlooked, lest we be constantly fussing with our friends. If your child is developing a positive self-image, he will learn to overlook minor offenses as not being worth pursuing.

SEE ALSO: Blaming; Conflicts; Anger; Disappointment; Jealousy; Sibling Rivalry; Self-Image; Talking With Children.

FRIENDSHIP

For a child to learn to enjoy friends, he needs to feel that, in his relationships with others, he is worthy of affection. He also needs to know how to return affection. In the very early years, his "friendship" education takes place mainly within his family, where he learns how to love and be loved. He learns that love and affection have to be unconditional, because true friendship has no other purpose than "the pleasure of the company."

When a child starts school, peer friendships begin to become very special, very meaningful, and very influential. Parents naturally feel protective of their children and want them to develop friendships with children who reflect what they consider to be acceptable family values. This is right and proper, because peer relationships from first grade on will exert a powerful influence. However, it is important for parents to examine their own motives for helping their children to choose friends and to realize that true friendship cannot be forced. They need to be open to new interests and to the new friendship opportunities their children will introduce. Parents will want to be very considerate of relationships their children develop, because true friendship is precious and immensely important to a child's emotional growth. Have confidence that, if your relationship with your child is positive, he will find that compatibility comes with shared values. He has to be allowed to find this out for himself with only the most unobtrusive help from parents.

If your child, because of neighborhood proximity, has no friend with whom he is compatible because of age or personality differences, help him find at least one friend with whom he will find unpressured companionship. You may find such a friend from among the children in your circle of friends, or you may well notice that your child has developed a strong attachment to one of his classmates. It doesn't take a lot of friends to learn the joy of a mutually satisfying relationship. When you see that your child has found a friend, be generous in including that child in your family activities. There is nothing more important to a growing child than a home that welcomes his friends and there is nothing more comforting to parents than knowing their children's chosen companions.

In our mobile society, many families change location while their children are growing up. Encourage your child to maintain friendships through correspondence, and, if possible, through visits. If your child is to learn the rewards of true friendship, then he must learn to value his friends enough to let them know he remembers them.

SEE ALSO: Self-Image; Cooperation; Community; Family; Affection; Human Ecology; Grooming Habits; Manners.

INDEPENDENCE

Education for independence begins at birth, as does the child's natural desire to direct himself. Your child's desire for and his education for independence should grow apace throughout childhood.

Parents naturally enjoy the dependency of their children. They worry about them when they are on their own and they fear they will hurt themselves. The best way to keep your child safe is to recognize his developmental level and to provide him with as much independence as you know he can handle, all the while teaching him how to care for himself. You will want to enrich his life at each stage so that he will move on to the next with self-confidence, skill, and a repertoire of growing interests. Each stage of growing independence is the foundation for the next.

Your child should grow up expecting to be an independent thinker. Accept his having views different from yours, and ask his opinions on matters of interest to him. The feeling of being respected as an individual thinker will develop his ability to make judgments independent of peer pressure as he matures.

The more your child learns about caring for himself and the more constructive activities he has learned to enjoy, the safer and more fulfilled he will be when he is on his own. Also, you will be more comfortable as he moves out into the world of school and peers.

SEE ALSO: Decision-making; Self-Image; Fears; Community.

MANNERS

If your child likes people and is comfortable with them, he will naturally be pleasant with them. This is more important than formalities, which are not easy for a young child to remember.

As the child grows older, he will benefit from knowing the formalities of his own culture, because social rituals help to make social life easier. He will find that people like it when he:

- Says "please," "thank you," "pardon me," "may I help you," "how do you do," and "it was nice meeting you."
- Introduces people to one another.
- Is considerate of the host when visiting and seeks him out to say thank you before leaving.
- Writes thank you notes and shows appreciation for hospitality (see Fig. 11-1).
- Listens to others, does not interrupt or monopolize conversation.

13

learning problems

PERCEPTUAL PROBLEMS

The earlier a perceptual problem is diagnosed and treated, the greater the chance for success in school and the less strain on the child. Perceptual problems occur in the brain. *A child may be able to see and hear well, but the messages are not processed properly.* Often such a disorder is found in highly intelligent children, so the frustration at being considered lazy or incapable can understandably cause rebellious behavior. Because the diagnosis of perceptual dysfunction is a relatively recent educational development, some people do not accept the possibility of such a condition. No matter what, many children have been helped through special training, so if your child has a problem learning, you will want to explore every possibility. Children with perceptual difficulties require patient repetitive training to build the proper neurological connections which are to replace the garbled ones. It takes know-how, time, and patience, but the effort is well worthwhile from a psychological as well as from an educational standpoint.

is a coming together of symptoms as the child develops that parents and the doctor begin to suspect retardation; and even then, there is the possibility of error if the diagnosis is not carefully made. Very often, mild retardation, which is the most common, does not become apparent until the child runs into trouble with school work.

In the past, retardation was confused with mental illness and the severely retarded were often placed in mental institutions for custodial care instead of being given special education as they are now. Also, in the past, people with normal or above normal mental capacity, but with handicaps such as dyslexia (reading disability), aphasia (speech disability), cerebral palsy, epilepsy, and hearing or sight handicaps—or even those with malnutrition, chronic infection, or cultural deprivation—were erroneously labeled retarded.

If retardation is suspected in your preschool child, your doctor may be the first to notice. At any rate, your initial conversations about your child's condition will be with him.

As with other handicaps in children, the initial responses of parents are shock, disappointment, and a resistance to believing that their child must bear a disability. There is a feeling of guilt about the possibility that they may have caused the condition and worry about planning for more children. Parents need to grow through their disappointment and guilt with the help of professionals and move on to accepting their child as he is. Then, at the earliest moment, they need to plan for his educational program and his future. Child guidance professionals are ready and willing to help, although because of heavy case loads, there is usually a waiting period of several weeks for appointments, which is understandably discouraging for distraught parents. How you choose to take care of and train your retarded child depends on the severity as well as the behavioral manifestations of the condition—and on the rest of the family.

Residential care for the retarded is no longer equated with the old asylums. There are both state and private residential schools where retarded persons enjoy professional training and noncompetitive peer companionship, both of which are important to their well-being. The decision to enter a retarded child in a residential school should not be considered with any feeling of guilt. It should be a decision based on a consideration for the best interests of the child.

Learning to love and respect the personhood of a retarded child creates a sensitivity in parents which adds a beautiful dimension to their lives. The deepening of life values brought by a retarded child is his precious gift to his parents.

SPEECH PROBLEMS

Since no two people speak the same way, it is important to know when a child's speech is normal for his age and when it is defective. If it is normal, parental fretting can *cause* problems. If it is defective, the ideal age to start therapy is three. However, that does not mean that you won't be successful in helping older children.

If, by the age of three, the child says nothing or cannot be understood at all, consult a specialist. No matter where you live, for help in locating qualified speech therapists, you can contact: *American Speech and Hearing Association, 10801 Rockville Pike, Rockville, Maryland, (301) 897-5700.*

The following are types of speech problems:

- No speech.
- Physical problems involving teeth, mouth, tongue, throat, or hearing.
- Stuttering.
- Lisping, slurring, or using the wrong letter sounds (articulation).
- Voice too high, too low, too loud, or too soft.

There have been great strides made either in curing speech problems or, when necessary, in helping the child to compensate successfully. Effective therapy relies heavily on parents' learning exactly what to do.

RESOURCES

Books

BRICKLIN, BARRY, PH.D. and PATRICIA BRICKLIN, PH.D. *Bright Child, Poor Grades.* New York: Delacorte Press, 1967.

BRUTTEN, MOLTON, PH.D., SYLVIA O. RICHARDSON, and CHARLES MANGLE. *Something's Wrong with My Child: A Parents' Book about Children with Learning Disabilities.* New York: Harcourt Brace Jovanovich, Inc., 1973.

CLARKE, LOUISE. *Can't Read, Can't Write, Can't Talk too Good Either: How to Recognize and Overcome Dyslexia in Your Child.* New York: Penquin, 1975.

CLARKE, LOUISE. *How to Recognize and Overcome Dyslexia in Your Child.* New York: Penquin Books, 1974.

SARGENT, PORTER. *Academic Underachiever.* (2nd Edition). Boston: Porter Sargent, 1970–71. Handbook of preparatory, tutorial, remedial, and diagnostic resources in independent schools, alternate programs, and clinics.

WAGNER, RUDOLPH, F. *Dyslexia and Your Child: A Guide for Teachers and Parents.* New York: Harper and Row, 1971.

Organizations

Association for Children with Learning Disabilities. 5225 Grace Street, Pittsburgh, Pa. 15236.

Retardation

Books

BUCK, PEARL S. *The Child Who Never Grew.* New York: John Day Co., 1950.

FRENCH, EDWARD L., and J. CLIFFORD SCOTT, M.D. *Child in the Shadows.* New York: Lippincott Co., 1960.

HART, EVELYN. *How Retarded Children Can Be Helped.* No. 288. New York: Public Affairs Pamphlets, 381 Park Avenue South, N.Y. 10016.

HILL, MARGARET. *The Retarded Child Gets Ready for School.* No. 349. New York: Public Affairs Pamphlets, 381 Park Avenue South, N.Y. 10016.

JACOB, WALTER. *New Hope for the Retarded Child.* No. 210A. New York: Public Affairs Pamphlets, 381 Park Avenue South, N.Y. 10016.

ROGERS, DALE EVANS. *Angel Unaware.* New York: Pillar Books, 1975.

Government Publications

Order from the Public Assistant Printer (Superintendent of Documents), U.S. Government Printing Office, Washington, D.C., 20402.

People Live in Houses, Profiles of Community Residences for Retarded Children and Adults. 1975. PR 36.8:M 52/H 81. 017–000–00143–4.

Organizations

National Association for Retarded Citizens. P.O. Box 6109, 2709 Avenue E East, Arlington, Texas 76011.

Speech Problems

Books

BATTIN, R.R. and C.O. HAUG. *Speech and Language Delay.* Springfield, Ill.: Charles C. Thomas, 1964.

VAN RIPER, CHARLES. *Your Child's Speech Problems.* New York: Harper and Row, 1961. A book by a very well-respected authority on the subject.

14

physical problems

A child with a physical handicap is not an abnormal person unless one has a narrow conception of normality. We are all somewhat trapped by our rather provincial norms; we are inclined to accept as normal those who look and act just like people within our own limited acquaintance. How absurd it is to look askance at perfectly fine people who simply look "different." Appearances and physical capabilities have nothing to do with the normality of a person unless those around behave abnormally.

There is no getting around the fact that life is harder for a child with a physical handicap. It goes without saying that not being able to see, hear, or speak; being confined to a wheelchair; or having to use artificial limbs puts a heavy burden on a child. There are things he will never be able to do. But there are two things we all know: (1) many very fine and productive people have had to struggle with physical handicaps all their lives; and (2) how a child develops is strongly influenced by the love and support he receives from his family.

Generally, a physically handicapped child needs to learn all the decision-making abilities, the self-discipline, and the handling of everyday relationships with people which all children need to learn. They, too, need to learn how to care for themselves as well as possible and to contribute to society. And they have to learn by experience just like everyone else. It takes more on the part of the family to provide a handicapped child with the experience he needs simply because of his physical limitations.

For the family to be of the greatest help, everyone has to work out his own feelings about the handicap. Parents and other children in the family need to learn to accept the handicapped child, to work out their guilt and resentment, and to avoid fantasizing about impossible expectations. Being able to do all this is not easy. It takes rethinking and finding a new orientation. Fortunately, consultation and help are available, so don't hesitate to make contact with sources of advice. Also, you will want medical care in which you have confidence; you can find such care through community resources or through your own doctor.

The more you can isolate the handicap from your child's personhood in your thinking, the better able you will be to help him deal with his special problems and the less negative influence the handicap will have on the quality of his life.

RESOURCES

Physical Problems

Books

DEMARY, HELEN CURTIS. *Questions and Answers about Ambliopia.* Washington, D.C.: Prevention of Blindness Society, 1775 Church Street, N.W., 20036.

DICKMAN, IRVING R. *Living With Blindness.* No. 473. New York: Public Affairs Pamphlets, 381 Park Avenue South, N.Y. 10016.

PRINCE, DAN, ed. *Tool Kit '76.* Washington, D.C.: Dept. of HEW. Order from Dr. Pam Coughlin, Project Head Start, Office of Child Development, DHEW, P.O. Box 1182, Washington,

D.C. 20013. An award winning publication. A well-annotated, highly readable and informative catalog of current materials, methods, and resources for working with handicapped children.

SEAVER, JACQUELINE. *Cerebral Palsy—More Hope than Ever*. No. 401. New York: Public Affairs Pamphlets, 381 Park Avenue South, N.Y. 10016.

Organizations

Alexander Graham Bell Association for the Deaf. 3417 Volta Place, N.W., Washington, D.C., 20007.

American Council for the Blind. 1211 Connecticut Avenue, N.W., #506, Washington, D.C., 20036.

Epilepsy Foundation of America. 1828 L Street, N.W., Washington, D.C., 20036.

International Association of Parents of the Deaf. 814 Thayer Avenue, Silver Spring, Md., 20910.

National Association of Parents of the Deaf-Blind. 525 Opus Avenue, Capitol Heights, Md., 20027.

National Easter Seal Society for Crippled Children and Adults. 2023 West Ogden Avenue, Chicago, Ill., 60623.

United Cerebral Palsy Association. 66 East 34th Street, New York, N.Y., 10016.

See also the books, directories, and organizations listed under Handicaps on page 244.

VI

knowledge
and
skills

Every child has his own unique combination of interests and abilities. He may follow one inclination for a while, and then shift; but over the span of his early childhood, he will develop a sense of what he most enjoys.

Your child will take an interest in what you do, but it is not a foregone conclusion that his inclinations will lead him to follow in your footsteps. It is best to avoid pushing any interest to the detriment or exclusion of others. Let your child take the lead and gain a wide variety of experiences. Enrich each experience as it comes along; observe and enrich consistencies as they develop. It will be out of these consistent interests that, much later, he will choose one for his vocation and continue to enjoy the others as avocations.

15

skills

CARPENTRY

Carpenters and cabinet makers develop a deep love for wood, the color, grain and smell of wood and its warm texture. Everyone reacts to the "soul soothing" quality of the material. Children have the same affinity for wood, so, for whatever the mysterious reason, give your child the experience of working with wood.

Your toddler, who is often beset with frustration, will find release in banging away on his toy pegs with his toy mallet, all the while improving his aim. By the time he is four or so, you can get him some sturdy little tools, and short nails with large heads and supply him with an old table for a work bench (so he won't use your dining room table). Bring him some bits and pieces of wood from the lumberyard (free in some lumberyards). Remove splinters. Teach him not to practice his carpentry on the wall and furniture—only on his work table with his own pieces of wood; and teach him not to put nails in his mouth or leave them where younger children might find them or on the floor where someone might walk on them. Be sure to pay attention to and to appreciate his creations, even if they do not resemble anything you ever saw.

Toward school age you can add to your child's collection of tools and show him how to use them: a short handled screwdriver, a vise, "C" clamps, a nonelectric hand drill, sandpaper of different grains, and a hacksaw. Show him how to drill a hole to start a screw; how to tap a nail lightly to start it; how to saw easily and straight along a pencil line; how to insert and remove screws; how to sand with the grain of the wood. Be very patient, because carpentry takes skill—and skill takes coordination and practice. Don't confuse your child by showing him too many things at once. Don't get ahead of his ability and don't expect a neat job. No matter how bad his work looks, be pleased. Offer no more than a tiny suggestion for improvement. Suggest only what you know he can understand and is able to do without tedious work. As his coordination and skills improve, you can gradually introduce such things as plumb lines and "T" squares—but don't do it until he can appreciate what you are getting at, and, even more importantly, until his coordination is good enough to make them work.

Your young child will start out making abstract constructions, which he can paint and decorate. He will move on to making plaques, key chains, and paper weights. Still later, he will graduate to building a clubhouse in the back yard and furniture for club members.

SEE ALSO: Math; Arts and Crafts.

GAMES

Games are life encapsulated, so they are very important educational tools. The right games at the right stage of development accomplish a multiplicity of objectives:

- Muscle development and coordination.
- Spatial and directional concepts.
- Understanding the reason for rules.
- Following directions.

- Participation, communication, and socializing.
- Practice in developing skills.
- Development of self-concept.
- Acquisition of general knowledge.
- Practice in thinking.
- Concentration, planning, purposefulness, and keeping goals in mind.

In spite of these objectives, games should be played for fun, and there is much to be said for taking time to relax and play with no purpose in mind. That in itself is something that many say the American people need to learn.

It is interesting to note how many children's games have been passed down from generation to generation; and although there is some variation from one culture to another, the basic games are similar, possibly because all young children enjoy and are able to do similar things at about the same age. There have been studies which try to establish theories of basic human needs as expressed in games. One such theory is that the infant has an instinctive fear of death and plays the game of "Peek-a-boo" to learn the difference between temporary separation and the permanent separation of death. Other age-old infant games include the following:

When the baby can sit up, he enjoys being bounced on your leg while you recite:

> Ride a cock horse to Banbury Cross
> To see a fine lady on a white horse
> With rings on her fingers and bells on her toes
> She shall make music wherever she goes.

He enjoys "Patty-cake." At first he simply claps his own hands together; then, when he is able, he claps hands with a partner in rhythm to a poem:

> Patty cake, patty cake, baker man
> Bake me a cake as fast as you can.
> Roll it and pat it and mark it with a T,
> And put it in the oven for Tommy and me.

He raises his arms high over his head and says, "So big" when you play the game with him by asking, "How big are you?" If you ask him a second time, he will stretch his arms even higher expecting your approval.

"This Little Piggie" is terribly amusing when you tweak each toe, going from big to little, as you recite:

This little piggie went to market;
This little piggie stayed home;
This little piggie had roast beef;
This little piggie had none;
And this little piggie cried "Wee-Wee-Wee" all the way home.

As your child grows into toddlerhood, whether he is crawling or toddling, he loves to be chased, and to be caught and hugged. He likes to play hide and seek with adults and older children (toddlers don't play anything well with other toddlers). You must pretend you don't see him as he watches eagerly for you to find him, whereupon everyone expresses great joy at the reunion (an important part of the game). The toddler likes to play ball with a big ball he can roll. Since he cannot change direction very well, you have to roll the ball right to him. He can play "Pease-porridge," which is like "Patty-cake," but is more sophisticated:

Pease-porridge hot
Pease-porridge cold
Pease-porridge in the pot
Nine days old.

The "Church and Steeple" game is appropriate for this age. Bend your fingers on both hands, then interlock them, making the "church," with your fingertips turned inside. Put your thumbs together to form the "doors." Lift your two forefingers to form the "steeple." When you "open the doors," you reveal your wiggling fingertips inside ("all the people"):

This is the church
This is the steeple
Open the doors
And see all the people!

Preschoolers are beginning to learn how to be friends. Games are a way to play with others when you don't really know how to play with them too well. Preschoolers play rough and tumble games like:

- Follow the Leader
- Ring around the Rosie

  Ring around the Rosie
  Pocket full of posies
  One, two, three, four
  We all *fall down*.

- *London Bridge is Falling Down*. Two children hold hands and form a bridge for the other children to pass under. On "my fair lady," they drop their arms to entrap whoever is under the bridge at the moment:

  London bridge is falling down,
  Falling down, falling down;
  London bridge is falling down,
  My fair lady.

- Hide and Seek
- *The Farmer in the Dell*. The children form a ring with the farmer in the middle. He chooses a wife and takes her from the ring into the middle, and so on through the verse:

  The farmer in the dell,
  The farmer in the dell,
  Hi-ho the derry-o,
  The farmer in the dell.
  The farmer takes a wife, etc.
  The wife takes the child, etc.
  The child takes the dog, etc.
  The dog takes the cat, etc.
  The cat takes the mouse, etc.
  The mouse takes the cheese, etc.
  The cheese stands alone, etc.

These games do have "leaders" and "losers," but they are a gentle introduction to the idea. Preschoolers take losing too seriously for their games to be really competitive.

It is a different story, however, for young school age children. At about six, children begin to learn to enjoy competition. At the same time, your child will also become very conscious of fairness. He will enjoy making up rules for his games and will be strict about making everyone obey them. Though he may cheat a little himself—if the going gets rough—he won't tolerate anyone else's cheating. However, since all his friends feel the same way, they straighten each other out. If the children do not seem to get the point of playing by rules, you might suggest that they play one game in which everyone cheats as much as possible so they learn what a mess *that* is. It is good to let children make up their own rules for their games, but to suggest that, once the game starts, the rules don't change. There is no logical reason why children's games have to be played by set rules when they are playing together informally. Making up rules is good practice in group decision-making and procedure-planning.

There are informal role playing games like *Cops and Robbers, Cowboys and Indians*—traditional American games which keep youngsters racing about for hours. Such make-believe games combine chasing with fantasy and give children a chance to act out exciting adventures. These games seem to fill a need to learn how to get along with peers. From here on, all the opportunities for your small child to develop strength and coordination will begin to pay off. *Hide and Seek* takes attention, ingenuity, and physical ability if one is to avoid being "it" all the time. There are all kinds of tag, including stoop tag, ball tag (dodge ball), tree tag, and so on, each with its own rules.

Games for One, Two, or a Few
School Age Children

Choosing who will be *first,* "*it,*" *leader,* or *caller:*

- Penny flip—heads or tails
- Drawing straws

Enie, meenie, mini, moe
Catch an ostrich by the toe

If it hollers, let it go,
Enie, meenie, minie, moe.

- Draw the high card from the deck
- One potato, two potato, three potato, four
  Five potato, six potato, seven potato, more.

Jumping Rope.   There was a time when jumping rope was only a boys' game; then it became a girls' game; and now, because of current interest in body building, both boys and girls are interested. There are several rope jumping games and they usually are accompanied by rhymes. Two children hold either end of a piece of clothesline about ten feet long, turning it while other children jump in, take a turn (usually while chanting a rhyme), then jump out as the next in line jumps in for his turn. In "double dutch," the rope is about twice as long and is held so that one half is turned in one direction and the other half in the opposite direction, which, of course, makes the jumping twice as fast. Some children learn to jump rope with amazing rhythm and grace.

Hopscotch.   As the children get more adept at handling themselves, they like "hopscotch," which also takes several forms. Here is one form:

Variation No. 1.   Each person takes a turn. When it is his turn, a person tosses a pebble into a box, beginning with box #1. If he misses, he loses his turn. If he gets the pebble in the box, he hops on two feet in boxes 1 and 2, on one foot in 3, on two feet on 4 and 5, on one foot on 6, and so forth to 12, where he turns (on one foot), and comes back the same way. If he gets back without stepping on any lines, on his next turn, he tosses his pebble into box #2 and then follows the same procedure. The person who works his way through 12 first is the winner.

Variation No. 2.   Each person tosses his pebble, beginning with box #1. Then he must hop on one foot, kicking the pebble into box #2, then into #3, and so forth to #12. If the pebble lands on a line or goes into the wrong box, the person goes back, waits his turn, and starts over. If he succeeds, on his next turn he tosses his pebble into box #2 and procedes the same way. The first person to

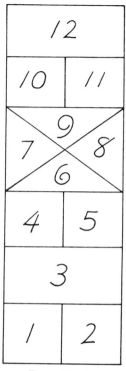

Figure 15—1.

get to box #12 wins the game.

Hopscotch and jumping rope are good city games, because they do not take much space. Usually, children draw hopscotch diagrams on the sidewalk; but you may want to paint one on your driveway or in the gameroom, carport, or garage.

Frisbee. Frisbee requires more space and skill that is best learned first hand. It is so popular with all ages of young people that in 1977, The Smithsonian Institution sponsored a frisbee festival on the Mall in Washington, D.C.

May I?. One child calls off directions and the rest of the children line up, side by side, at the starting line. The direction giver calls the name of the first child and gives him directions to take a certain number of giant steps, baby steps, or man steps. The child must say, "May I?" before proceeding. If he doesn't, he must go back to the start. Each child is directed in turn until one of them reaches the finishing line, becoming the winner—and next direction giver.

Simon Says. "Simon," one of the children, gives directions to the others, and as he does so, he performs the act he directs. Some of the time, however, he performs a different act, and the children are supposed to do what he *says*, not what he does. For example, if "Simon" says, "Touch your left knee with your right hand," but he touches his nose with his right hand, the children are to do what he says, not what he does. When a child forgets and does what "Simon" *does* instead of what he *says*, he is "out." The one who stays in the longest is the winner and becomes the next "Simon."

Parchesi and Other Board Games. Rules are supplied with the games.

Dominoes. Rules are supplied with the game.

Tic Tac Toe. Draw two vertical lines about three inches long and about an inch from each other. Cross them with two horizontal lines similarly drawn, forming a square in the middle. One of the two players starts by making an X in any of the compartments in the drawing. The second player makes an O in any one of the remaining empty compartments. The players continue taking turns until all the compartments are filled or until one player wins by creating a row of three X's or O's either vertically, horizontally or diagonally.

Ring Toss and Horseshoes. You can buy a set or create your own by pounding a dowel or piece of broomstick into the ground and making rings from something around the house (coat hangers, heavy cardboard, and so on).

Bean Bag or Ball Toss. Toss a ball or bean bag into a wastebasket or at a target with holes, much as in the ball toss carnival game.

Croquet.   The game requires a level lawn. Rules are supplied with the game.

Checkers, Chinese Checkers, Chess.   There is a beginners' chess game, called Quick Master Chess, for young children, distributed by: *Learning Games, Inc., 34 South Broadway, White Plains, New York 10601, Phone (914) 428-7336.*

Story Telling Game.   Children sit in a circle. One child starts the story, perhaps by saying, "Once upon a time there were four ———." The next child has to think up something to say—like, "alleycats." Then he continues, "These cats were good friends and they decided to ———." The next child goes on from there and so on around the circle.

Hot and Cold.   One child thinks of an object in the room, but he does not say the word. The other children guess what the object is. As each child guesses, he is told whether he is "hot" or "cold," depending on how close he comes to the location of the object.

Cat's Cradle.   There are several different games to play with strings, but they are so difficult to describe that it may be best to learn them from someone who can show you with a piece of string.

Hoops.   Maybe rolling hoops will become a popular pastime again. A few years ago, there was a Hula-hoop craze. Meantime, hoops are fun for children to roll or "Hula."

Scrabble.   There are variations for each age group.

Jacks.   Each player drops the jacks on a step or tabletop as he bounces the small ball. He scoops the jacks and releases them again as he bounces the ball, using one hand. Then he proceeds to pick up one jack at a time with each bounce of the ball. If he misses the jack or the ball, he must wait his turn to start again. If he succeeds in picking up all the jacks, one by one, he throws again, scoops again, and then picks up two jacks at a time: Each maneuver must be accomplished within one ball bounce. If he succeeds, he throws again, scoops again, and picks up three jacks at a time. The game goes on in this way until he successfully picks up the whole batch at once, thus winning the game.

Marbles.   There are several marble games, but this one is the most common. Find a place where there is flat hard dirt. Draw a three-foot circle in the dirt. Each player puts a few marbles in the center of the circle. The players take turns shooting from the edge of the circle, trying to knock the other marbles out of the circle. Some children play "for keeps" and others give back the marbles they win at the end of the game, so it may be well to warn your child to find out the rules before he gets into a game. The best way to shoot is to crook your forefinger and place your thumbnail in the crook with the marble on your thumbnail. It takes practice to learn to aim well.

Wall or Step Ball.   One child throws a tennis ball hard at a step or wall. The other child tries to catch it. If the ball is caught before it hits the ground, the thrower is "out"; if it goes over the catcher's head, it is a "homerun"; if he catches it after one bounce, the thrower has "made first base" and so on. After three "outs," the children change places.

Pick Up Sticks.   Available at toy stores.

Old Maid.   There are contemporary variations of this game.

Solitaire.   Shuffle a full deck of cards. Lay down a row of seven cards with the first card on the left face up and the rest face down. Repeat, laying the next card face up and the rest face down. Continue until each of the seven piles of cards has a card face up on top. Hold the remaining cards in your hand. Look at the seven cards showing on the table, then look at your hand for a card that is one number lower and of an alternating color. For example, if you have a red ten on the table, you will put on it a black nine, then a red eight and so on until you get down to the two. Place the cards so they overlap but do not completely cover the card underneath so you can still see the highest card. Aces are placed above the row on the table and built upon by suit. You also play the cards on the table on each other and upon the aces above. As you play cards off the

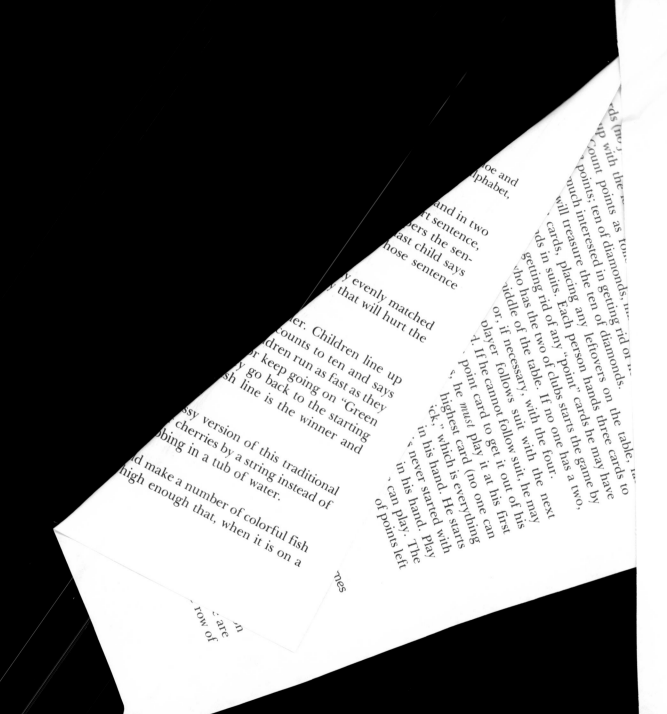

covered cards, turn those cards face up in turn and play on a
with those. Kings may be placed in empty spaces as they occur
the table. The object of the game is to end up with all the cards
by suit in consecutive order on the aces.

Go Fish.   Shuffle and deal seven cards to each person
the remaining cards in a pile on the table. Each person m
many pairs as he can from the cards in his hands. Then
player asks the person on his left for a card with which he
a pair. If the person has the card, he hands it to the play
pair is laid down. The player then has another turn. If
on the player's left does not have the card requested, h
fish," whereupon the player draws a card from the
table. If that card is the one needed to make a pair, the
and laid on the table. If not, the next person to the
turn—and so on around the table. The object is
greatest number of pairs.

Crazy Eights.   Two to four people can play,
lation deck of cards (no jokers). In this game, eigl
The object of the game is to be the first to go "o
cards in your hand.

For two players, deal seven cards to each
players, deal five to each. Put the remaining ca
table. This is the "kitty." Take the top card fr
it face up on the table.

Taking turns clockwise, each person
hand on the upturned card, either matchi
numbers. For example: If a two of clubs i
can play either any club, or the two of any su
is wild. If he plays an eight, he must name the numb
represents. If an eight has been played, the next player must
according to the number and suit the eight represents. If the player
has no card in his hand to play, he draws a card from the kitty.
When the kitty is depleted and a player has no card to play from his
hand, he forfeits his turn to the player on his left. The winner is the
first person to go "out."

chairs. When you suddenly stop the music, the children all try to
find a chair to sit on. The child who is left without a chair is out.
Remove one chair and play again. Continue the procedure until
you have one chair and two children. The one who manages to get
the chair wins the game.

Relay Races.   There are all sorts of variations:

- Carrying a hard-cooked egg on a tablespoon.
- Hopping instead of running.
- Having something to do during the race, like taking off a sh
  putting it back on again, turning a somersault, saying the a
  or counting to ten.

Whispering Game.   Form two teams. Have them st
lines. The first child in each line privately tells you a sho
which you print on a piece of paper. One child whisp
tence to the next in line until all have heard it. The
the sentence out loud as he heard it. The team w
survived best is the winning team.

Tug o' War.   Help the children to form fair
teams and be sure there is nothing in the vicini
winning team as it falls backward in victory.

Red Light, Green Light.   Choose a cal
side by side at the starting line. The caller
either "Red light" or "Green light." The chi
can; then they either stop on "Red light"
light." If they either fail to obey the order, th
line. The first person to reach the fir
becomes the caller.

Bobbing for Apples.   A less me
Halloween game is to hang apples o
having the children get soaked bo

Fishing.   You and your chi
and a decorated box with sides

table, the child cannot see in. Put a number on each fish and attach a paper clip. Put the "fish" in the box. Make a fishing line using a magnet tied to a piece of string. If a child catches more than one fish on his magnet, he may keep the one with the higher number and throw the others back in the box. The child whose fish add up to the highest number wins the game.

Treasure Hunt. Make a list of items you have hidden or items you know are in your yard. Divide the children into two teams and give each a copy of the list. The team that finds the most items wins the game.

Blow the Ball. Line up two teams on either side of a table and place a Ping-Pong ball in the middle of the table. Each team tries to blow the ball off the opposite side of the table. Lay folded strips of newspaper across the ends of the table to keep the ball from rolling off the ends.

SEE ALSO: Learning How To Learn; Everyday Teaching; Toys, Games, Equipment; Competition; Decision-making; Fairness.

MATH

Math is a simplified language using symbols and procedures to deal with quantities, shapes, space, time, and relationships. Young children learn math automatically just as they learn language. The more opportunities they have to do interesting things, and the more they learn all by themselves, the better prepared they are for formal math education. Very young children arrange toys and people to suit a purpose they have in mind: They know they have two shoes, one for each foot; they know what half a cookie is and insist, when sharing, that they get their full half; when they reach the age of three, they can symbolize three by holding up three fingers. When we stop to consider, it is surprising the number of math concepts a child learns between birth and school age.

Not too long ago, when children started school, they were

expected to learn numbers skills by writing page after page of addition, then subtraction, then multiplication, then division, then fractions, and so on. The skills were not integrated either with what the young child already knew or with each other as math operations. Also, there was little application of what had been learned through child development studies. We know know that young children are not ready for abstract symbols, and that they learn math readily when principles and procedures are presented with actual objects.

"New math" for young children is not one specific math program. There are many different ones, but generally, they involve procedures and vocabulary which form a bridge between what the young child can understand and what is to follow as the program develops into more complex abstract procedures. Numeration, algebra, geometry, decimals, and fractions are integrated from the very beginning, first using money, rods, toys, shapes, then pictures; then printed shapes; and then numerals. The aim of math educators is to find ways to help young children build a firm foundation so they can understand concepts, develop skills, solve problems, and, ultimately, be able to express themselves in the language of mathematics. Which teaching system is used depends on the school administration or on individual teachers, though with some exceptions, the vocabulary and symbols are the same (see Math Glossary in this chapter).

Help your child move naturally into the world of math by providing him with opportunities to handle shapes; to play games using numbers; to hear number rhymes and stories; to play with sand, water, and containers; to "cook;" to use building blocks; to sort and fit objects; and to match and fit objects. Talk with your child about what he is doing, but do not push. Fit the activities to his stage of development, knowing what developmental toys are useful and letting your child show you by his interest and ability what he is ready to tackle. Before first grade, he may or may not be ready to count to ten and to relate counting to enumerating sets of objects.

First Grade

Children learn to tell time in hours and half hours, to count items in sets, to write numerals, and to deal with pennies and nickels. They combine and separate sets of items and pictures, and they write number sentences using the *equal, greater than,* and *less than* signs. They add and subtract, using an algebraic equation. As the year progresses, they learn vocabulary and numerals for simple fractions and two digit numbers. They are introduced to simple geometric shapes, to linear measure (inches and centimeters), and to liquid measure (cups, pints, half liters). They learn number places (hundreds, tens, and ones); they also learn adding and subtracting in vertical form. They make use of the numberline, the abacus, and objects like Cuisenaire rods—as well as practice sheets and workbooks.

To reinforce first grade math, here are a few ideas for informal activities at home:

Activities

- Count out nickels and pennies when paying allowance or allowing the child to pay for something at the store.
- When driving, look for numerals on signs and license plates and count items like red cars, lamp posts per city block, and so forth.
- Talk about and use nickels and pennies, hours and half hours, cups and pints, metric cups and half liters, inches and centimeters. Give your child plenty of practice with metric measurement.
- Refer to the calendar whenever the opportunity presents itself.
- If you have an adding machine or calculator, let your child play with the operations he has already done by school procedures.

Equipment

- Calendar, clock, rulers, cups.
- Simple abacus, balance, ruler.
- Make a masking tape numberline, using numerals from zero to ten, to paste along the edge of your child's table or desk.
- Flannel board with felt numbers and simple geometric shapes (circle, square, rectangle, triangle).
- Cuisenaire rods or any well-designed counting objects.
- Add new shapes to building block set.
- Numbered follow-the-dot book.
- Simple puzzles—jigsaw and other appropriate manipulative puzzles.

Games

- Matching and counting games.
- Physical counting games like hopscotch, ring toss, Simon says, and "May I."
- Searching games like treasure hunt or Easter egg hunt. You hide five buttons; your child can then count off each button as he finds it. He will automatically subtract what he has found from the total number hid.
- Subtraction games like musical chairs and games in which first one person and then the next is "out."
- Counting by feeling. Put four or five apples in a paper bag. The child counts the apples with his hands without looking in the bag.
- Estimating, then counting or measuring: How many bananas do you think are in this little bag? How many inches long do you think this book is? Do you think there is a half liter of water in this pot?

Second Grade

The first few weeks of second grade are usually spent in review and reinforcement; then new material is added to the first grade foundation. The stronger the foundation, the more successfully will the child be able to move into more advanced work. It is tricky to accomplish the necessary practice for reinforcement without turning the child against math, but it can be done if parents make use of a variety of games and activities. If you have any fears of math, try not to let them influence your child's attitude toward the subject. If you don't know "new math," admit it and let your child have the pleasure (and practice) of teaching you.

Actually, the second grade curriculum follows much the same pattern as first but uses larger quantities, higher numbers, more everyday fractions, and more complex operations. The children learn quarter hours; quarters, half dollars, and perhaps dollars; liters and quarts; counting by tens; ordinal numbers; adding and subtracting two and three digit numbers; adding and subtracting when digits must be renamed ("carrying and borrowing"); introduction to multiplication.

Suggestions for reinforcement of second grade work:

Activities

- Pay allowance in pennies, nickels, and dimes, varying the distribution.
- Offer to trade pennies for nickels and dimes—or vice versa—for the penny bank.
- Talk about baseball and basketball scores or those of whatever sport interests your child.
- Talk about thirds, quarters, and halves when preparing food or cutting pie or cake.
- If the line isn't too long at the store check-out, count out what you are paying and relate the money to the numeral on the cash register. Talk about the change if it happens not to be too complicated.
- Cooking—weighing and measuring foods.

Equipment

- Compass, triangle, small T square for drawing.
- Toy cash register and play money for playing store.
- Educational calculator—but use it in conjunction with manual and mental numbers practice.

Games

- Jump rope games.
- New board games and puzzles appropriate to your child's ability.
- Counting games to pass the time in the car—dogs, flower gardens, tractor-trailors, joggers, and bikes.
- Estimating games and checking with the ruler, scale, or measure to see who made the closest estimate.
- Calculator games.

Third Grade

Children are taught to use math for problem solving ("word problems"); they learn some basics of plane and solid geometry; they learn to write thousands and millions; how to multiply and divide; how to use Roman numerals from one to ten; how to make a graph; and of course, they continue to review and integrate all that they have learned so far. Your activities at home will follow the same pattern: continual use of what has been taught over the three years, adding new games and activities to fit the child's level of development. Suggestions for reinforcement of third grade work:

- Note and figure mileage on trips.
- Give your child the money to pay a restaurant or store bill.
- Here is a game that produces giggles while it reinforces number handling skills. Count in turn: one, two three, "snerd" (or any other silly word), five, six, seven, "snerd," nine, ten, eleven, "snerd," and so on. The one who misses a "snerd" is "out."
- Make up games using what your child is learning in school.
- Note increase and decrease in elevations as you travel through mountains.
- Carpentry uses measuring.
- Some crafts, such as sewing, use measuring.

There are many more opportunities to use numbers and math procedures than can be listed here; and every day there are new educational toys and games on the market. Glance through your child's workbook or talk with his teacher to get an idea of what is to be covered and when in the school year. Then you will know what toys, games, and activities will be good reinforcements at the proper time. In math, step-by-step success is the best source of motivation to move ahead. Like a game, it is fun for a child if he is not scared of failure and if he understands how it is to be played each step of the way.

SEE ALSO: Games; Toys; Games and Equipment (math; problem-solving); Children's Books (math); Time; Writing (penmanship); Arts and Crafts; Carpentry.

TABLE 15—1
Tables of Measurement

UNITED STATES

Length	Capacity
12 inches = 1 foot	2 cups = 1 pint
3 feet = 1 yard	2 pints = 1 quart
5,280 feet = 1 mile	4 quarts = 1 gallon

TABLE 15—1 (continued)

Weight	Area
16 ounces = 1 pound 2,000 pounds = 1 ton	4,840 square yards = 1 acre

METRIC

Length	Capacity
10 millimeters = 1 centimeter 100 centimeters = 1 meter 1,000 meters = 1 kilometer	1,000 milliliters = 1 liter 1,000 liters = 1 kiloliter 2 metric cups = 1 half liter

Weight	Area
1,000 milligrams = 1 gram 1,000 grams = 1 kilogram 1,000 kilograms = 1 metric ton	10,000 square meters = 1 hectare

ROMAN NUMERALS

I	(1)	VI	(6)	XI	(11)	XVI	(16)
II	(2)	VII	(7)	XII	(12)	XVII	(17)
III	(3)	VIII	(8)	XIII	(13)	XVIII	(18)
IV	(4)	IX	(9)	XIV	(14)	XIX	(19)
V	(5)	X	(10)	XV	(15)	XX	(20)

TIME

60 seconds = 1 minute	12 months = 1 year
60 minutes = 1 hour	365 days = 1 year
24 hours = 1 day	366 days = 1 leap year
7 days = 1 week	10 years = 1 decade
52 weeks = 1 year	100 years = 1 century

CONVERSIONS (APPROXIMATIONS)

Length	
1 inch = 25.4 millimeters (mm)	1 yard = 914 millimeters
1 inch = 2.54 centimeters (cm)	1 yard = 91.4 centimeters
1 foot = 305 millimeters	1 yard = .91 meters (m)
1 foot = 30.5 centimeters	1 mile = 1.61 kilometers (km)

1 millimeter = 0.0394 inch (7 mm is a little more than ¼ in.)
1 centimeter = .394 inch (1 cm is about ⅜ in.)
1 meter = 39.4 inches (1 m is about 3 inches longer than 1 yd.)
1 kilometer = .62 mile (1 km is a little more than ½ mi.)

TABLE 15—1 (continued)
Tables of Measurement

Weight

---

1 ounce = 28.4 grams (g)	1 U.S. ton = 907 kilograms (kg)
1 pound = 454 grams (g)	1 U.S. ton = 0.91 Metric ton (t)
1 pound = 0.45 kilograms (kg)	

1 gram = 0.035 ounces
1 kilogram = 35.3 ounces
1 kilogram = 2.21 pounds (1 kg is a little more than 2 lb.)
1 Metric ton = 2205 pounds (1 t is 205 lbs. more than 1 U.S. ton)
1 Metric ton = 1.1 U.S. tons

Capacity

---

1 pint = 473 milliliters (ml)
1 quart = 946 milliliters
1 gallon = 3.79 liters (l)

1 liter = 2.1 pints (1 l is a little more than 2 pts.)
1 liter = 1.06 quarts (1 l is a little more than 1 qt.)

Area

---

1 square foot = 0.09 square meters (m²)
1 acre = 4047 square meters
1 square mile = 2.59 square kilometers
1 square meter = 10.8 square feet
1 square kilometer = 247 acres
1 square kilometer = 0.39 square miles (1 km² is a little less than ½ mile²)

GLOSSARY OF MATH TERMS AS USED IN FIRST, SECOND, AND THIRD GRADES

Addend.

4	+	2	=	6
addend	plus	addend	equals	sum

Addend, Missing. The addend in an equation that is found by subtraction.

Angle. Two rays that end at the same point:

angle A B C

Area. Measurement of part of a plane or region (the area of a rectangle or a circle).

Capacity. Often called liquid measure, though "capacity" is more accurate (2 metric cups = ½ liter, 2 English cups = 1 pint).

Closed Curve. A line that encloses a region:

A curve that is not closed:

Cube. A closed surface with six equal square sides.

Cylinder. A closed surface resembling a tube:

Diameter. Segment from one side of the closed curve forming the circle to the other and passing through the point which is the center of the circle:

Digit. A single numeral in a number (in *24, 2* is the tens digit and *4* is the ones digit).

Equals. Means "is the same as" (use in the singular):

$$2 \quad + \quad 2 \quad = \quad 4$$

(2 plus 2) *is the same as* (4)

Estimating. Calculated guessing at math computation by rounding to the nearest ten.

Example: Do you think there are a little over 20 or almost 30 in this row of beans?

Even Numbers. Numbers in which two is a factor (into which two can be divided):

$$2, 4, 6, 8, 10$$

Expanded Form. Numbers expressed by naming the place of each digit:

2 tens + 4 ones = 24

Factor. Numbers that are part of the product of multiplication:

$$2 \quad \times \quad 4 \quad = \quad 8$$

factor   times   factor   equals   product

Factor, Missing. The factor in an equation that is found by division:

2   ×   n   =   8

missing
factor   *times*   *factor*   *equals*   *product*

(*or*)

$$\begin{array}{r} n \text{ missing factor} \\ \text{factor}\quad 2 \overline{\smash{\big)}\; 8\ \text{product}} \end{array}$$

Families of Facts. The four operations of related facts using the same numbers:

4 + 2 = 6
2 + 4 = 6
6 − 2 = 4
6 − 4 = 2

Greater Than.

6 > 4

Half Units. Once a unit has been described, the half unit is that unit divided into two equal parts. For example, if the unit is four and you divide it into two equal parts, two is half of that unit. If the unit is A, the half unit is ½A.

Less Than.

4 < 6

Letter Symbols. Letter representations in an equation.

A + B = C

Line. A straight curve with no beginning or end:

Line Segment. The part of a line that lies between two points on the line:

line segment

Linear Measure. The measure of length in units. In English measure, the units are inches, feet, and so on; in metric measure, the units are centimeters, meters, and so on.

Missing addend. See addend, missing.

Missing Factor. See factor, missing.

Multiple. The product of a number and other factors:

12 and *15* are multiples of *3*

Numberline. A line with numbers labeled for use in counting and in introducing addition and subtraction:

$$\xleftarrow{\quad} \overset{\text{0 1 2 3 4 5 6 7 8 9 10}}{\bullet\,\bullet\,\bullet\,\bullet\,\bullet\,\bullet\,\bullet\,\bullet\,\bullet\,\bullet\,\bullet} \xrightarrow{\quad}$$

$$\xleftarrow{\quad} \overset{\text{0 10 20 30 40 50 60 70 80 90 100}}{\bullet\,\bullet\,\bullet\,\bullet\,\bullet\,\bullet\,\bullet\,\bullet\,\bullet\,\bullet\,\bullet} \xrightarrow{\quad}$$

Number Patterns. Groupings of related numbers created by following a defined procedure (rule):

Number Places. Number representations with their value defined by their places, as on an abacus:

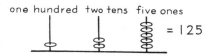

Numerals. Number names.

Odd Numbers. Numbers in which two is not a factor and into which two cannot be divided.

3, 5, 7, 9

Order of Numbers. Reading from left to right, beginning with zero and counting, as on the number line.

Ordinal Numbers. Word expressions of numbers telling position: *first, second,* and so on.

Part of a Plane. An enclosed area in a plane, such as a proscribed rectangle (see also: region).

Plane. A flat surface that extends in all directions to infinity.

Probability. The fractional expression of the likelihood of occurence.

Radius. A line segment from the center of a circle to any point in the circumference or closed curve that forms the circle:

Rectangle. A four-sided closed curve in which all angles are right angles:

Region. The area enclosed by a closed curve:

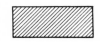

Renaming Tens. The process behind "carrying" in addition and "borrowing" in subtraction:

$$\begin{array}{ll} 40 & 30 \text{ tens} + 10 \text{ ones} \\ \underline{-2} = & \underline{\hspace{2.5cm} 2 \text{ ones}} \\ 38 & 30 \text{ tens} + \ 8 \text{ ones} = 38 \end{array}$$

Right Angle. An angle that forms identical angles in a square or a rectangle:

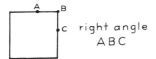

right angle
A B C

Sets. Groupings of objects, pictures, numerals, and so on:

Sets, Joining. Adding sets together to get a sum or total; addition:

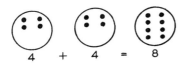

Sets, Separating. Removing sets as subtraction:

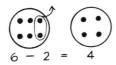

Short Form. Numbers expressed with the assumption that the placement of each digit shows its value:

$$\begin{array}{r} 40 \\ +\ 2 \\ \hline 42 \end{array} \qquad 40 + 2 = 42$$

Sphere. A closed surface resembling a ball.

Square. Same as rectangle, except that all four sides are the same length:

Sum. The result of combining addends:

$$4 \quad + \quad 2 \quad = \quad 6$$

addend   plus   addend   equals   *sum*

Two-stage Problems. Math problems requiring two sequential operations for solutions.

Unit line segment. Line segments of equal measurement: used in linear measure (inches and centimeters are units).

Unit of Area. A square unit of measurement (such as a square inch or a square centimeter).

understand something disturbing, he may find the story reassuring, or he may simply enjoy certain words and sounds. Most toddlers are not ready for the public library, though you may want to try taking him along when you are going to borrow books for yourself. Don't be disappointed if your child does not respond to large numbers of books at this age and if he doesn't care for the atmosphere of the library.

Preschoolers

Language becomes really fascinating to the four-, five-, and six-year-old. He loves puns, silly rhymes, and nonsense words. He discovers humor in words, and he dissolves into gales of giggles at his own cleverness. He uses language to converse with his peers. All this is a giant step in growing up. Look back a few months at his sense of humor and his attitude toward his peers and you will recognize what language development has taken place in a relatively short time.

Although your preschooler is intrigued with language, he still thinks in terms of things; in fact he is only beginning to see that words *refer* to things. Generally, at this age, words *are* things. You can help your child to become aware of the real purpose of words by using them in connection with things and activities. You can make a game of printing words and sticking them on things. You can stick words on pictures in magazines.

Now is the time to develop the library habit. Introduce your preschooler to the library when you have plenty of time to let him get thoroughly acquainted with the place. Show him the displays, introduce him to the librarian, show him the bathroom, chat with friendly people, let him drink from the fountain. Talk about the books. Help him look for a book like one he has at home. Help him choose one or two books to borrow on his own card (most libraries will issue a card to a child when he can print his name, with the understanding that the parent is responsible). Buy or make your preschooler a bookcase. Let your child choose a special place on his bookshelf to keep his library books. You may want to thumbtack a little plastic bag to the side of his bookcase to keep his library card safe and handy. You and he can put the due date and number of books borrowed on a piece of paper to put in the little bag with the card after each library visit.

Help him print his name in his very own books—you may even want to buy or make his own bookplates (you can find little packages of them in card stores). Your child's library need not be large, but it should be of good quality. Use the public library to find favorite books before making a purchase. These are the ones your child will come back to again and again as he learns to read.

Learn manuscript (see pages 301–2) so you can take dictation, printing just as he will be taught in school. Print stories for your child—stories about things you and he are doing, stories about pictures cut from magazines. Print short letters to relatives and friends and invitations to little celebrations. Hang his little stories on the corkboard in his room where he *may* try to read them if he has nothing more exciting on his agenda. Don't force. Encourage relatives and friends to send your child notes and picture postcards in the mail.

At this age, your child will learn letters and words by touching and moving them about. Give him large felt letters to stick on his felt board. Let him trace letters, draw them in fingerpaint, or make them in sand. Show him how to cut Plasticine ropes and curl them around into letters. He will enjoy blocks with raised letters and sandpaper letters that he can feel. Have a treasure hunt through old magazines for certain letters, either circling them with crayon or cutting them out for a "collection." Start with *b* as in *boy*, *f* as in *fat*, or with the letter that starts his name if it is an easy one. You would not want to teach *p* as in *Phil* because *ph* (a digraph) is confusing if taught before all the simple consonants are mastered. In school digraphs are usually introduced in second grade. Collecting letters teaches the child to focus on printed material and has the added dividend of numbers practice. "Can you find three B's?"

Play word games. How many words can we think of that start with the same sound as "boy?" It is best to try to avoid calling the b sound *buh*, because we read *boy*, not *buh-oy*. How many words rhyme with door? How many colors can we think of? How many soft things can we think of? Cold things? Hard things? Things for cooking? Parts of our bodies? And so on.

When your child is ready to start school, subscribe to a children's magazine in his own name (see Magazines, pages 42–43).

Show him his name and address on the cover and read the magazine with him.

A few children start to read enthusiastically by the time they are four or five. You will not only want to keep them supplied with quality reading material, but you will also want to enrich them in experiential activities so they will fully understand what they are reading.

The Young School Child

When your child starts school, you will want to inform yourself about the reading program being used and about the amount of work the teacher expects to cover in the school year. This will give you a reference point by which you will be able to evaluate your child's progress in a way more meaningful than depending on a mark on a report card. You will understand his daily work within the larger context. You will not be too upset by details and will be better able to help informally with relevant games, stories, activities, and conversation.

Many public schools use reading programs developed by publishers such as Scott-Foresman, Open Court, Ginn, Harcourt, and so forth. The publisher supplies series of books and corresponding workbooks with instructions for the teacher. Some teachers and schools develop their own reading programs or experiment with ones that have been developed recently in universities.

If your child's school is using "tracks," that is, grouping children according to their ability to progress in reading, it is best for parents to play it down, no matter which track their child is in. Remember that some children are not physically or mentally ready to get the hang of reading at age six or seven; also remember that this does not have anything to do with future success unless parents and teachers allow it to make the child feel inferior.

The following is included to give a general idea of the way in which many schools teach elementary reading; it does not represent any one program. We include it simply to give parents and tutors a general idea of reading instruction in the early elementary grades.

Early first grade is usually spent in reading readiness activity, so the teacher may choose to use materials other than books for this period of time. If your child is already reading, advise the teacher privately.

The teaching of reading in the early grades involves both phonetics and sight reading. Sight reading is necessary because there are so many elementary words in the English language that are not spelled the way they sound. Phonics are taught too, usually starting with easy *beginning consonants* (consonants at the beginning of the word). Different children have different learning styles. Some children respond better to sight reading; others grasp the logic of phonics, so the important thing is to find which best suits your child.

Sight Reading

Children are taught to recognize whole words by seeing them with pictures; by noticing their length and general shape; and by noting synonyms, antonyms, association, context, work, and syllable combinations. Ask your child's teacher for the sight word list for his grade level; then, at home, reinforce his recognition ability. There are several ways you can do this without grueling memory work:

- Pick out the words that are names of things around the house. Put each word on a piece of paper in large letters and tape it to the item it represents. Make a game of collecting the words and then replacing them on the proper item.
- Find interesting pictures in old magazines and paste slips of paper with the printed words beside the thing the word represents.
- Keep on reading to your child, *occasionally* asking him to read a word or group of words that he is learning to recognize. However, avoid turning reading for pleasure into a lesson.
- When you and your child are out together, running errands or traveling, point out recognizable words you happen to see.

Phonics

Children understand phonics as "sounding out words." By putting together the sounds represented by letters and combinations of letters, a child can learn to read new words on his own.

First Grade.   Children are taught to *hear and recognize* simple beginning and ending consonants, starting with beginning consonants: *b*at, *r*at, *h*at, *m*at, *c*at, *s*at. Later in the year, they begin to work on ending consonants—big, bi*n*, bi*d*, bi*t*—and they are introduced to the sound and position of vowels in words. They practice substituting beginning and ending consonants to make new words. They look at and listen to easy rhyming words. You can help at home by, first of all, making sure your child hears and pronounces the sounds of the letters properly. Provide him with felt letters so he can build words on his felt board. Work with him for short periods to make sure he understands how to make a word read from left to right (this concept was learned by adults so long ago that it is easy to forget that is has to be *learned* by young children). Use the ideas and games suggested above for preschool children, adding letter dominoes. You can make or buy domino games that, instead of having the traditional arrangement of dots, use pictures, letters, words, and shapes, such as triangles, squares, and circles. The game is played in the same way as the regular game of dominoes, except that the domino markings have no numerical value. Play "I See Something" using letter sounds: "I see something that starts with *t*" (*t*able, *t*oes, *T*immy, *t*elevision, *t*ee shirt, *t*elephone, *t*ire, *t*oast, *t*oaster, *t*ool, *t*omato, *t*ooth, *t*owel, *t*ub, *t*ugboat, *t*ypewriter).

Stay with the teacher, working on (or rather playing with) the letters and sounds being worked on in school. Try to make sure your child learns each step thoroughly. Each following step depends on understanding what has been learned previously. First graders are introduced to root words and certain endings, like *s, es, ed, ing, 's,* and to capitalization and punctuation. They learn how to put words in alphabetical order and how to find words in alphabetical lists. It is helpful to have ABC books and childrer's dictionaries at home.

Second Grade. Children are taught to hear and read consonant blends (*bl, cl, fl, gl, pl, br, cr, dr, gr, pr, tr, dw, sw, tw, sc, sk, sl, sm, sn, st*) at the beginning and at the end of words. They learn to hear and read digraphs (*ch, sh, th,* voiced and unvoiced *ph* and *wh*). They learn vowels in the middle of one syllable words (man, cap, pen, pin, etc.); they are introduced to long and short vowels; and they learn the following general facts:

- One vowel at the beginning of a word usually has a short sound (itch, and).
- One vowel in the middle of a word usually has a short sound (man, hat, pin).
- One vowel at the end of a word usually has a long sound (she, go).
- A final *e* usually makes the vowel in the middle of the word long (cake, bone).

Second graders learn about contractions (can't won't), about words that double the final consonant before *ing* (cutting, batting), and about the word endings, *en, er, est.*

Third Grade. Children are introduced to diphthongs (*au, aw, our, ow, oi, oy, oo*), to the sound and reading of vowels followed by *r, l,* and *w* (*ar, er, ir, or, ur, al, aw, ew*), and to the final digraph *ng.* They also learn the following facts:

- A vowel followed by *r, l,* or *w,* is neither long nor short, but takes its sound from the final letter (ball, corner, crawl).
- The rules of hard and soft *c* and *g*:
    1. *c* followed by *e, i,* or *y* is usually soft, sounding like *s* (certain).
    2. *c* followed by *a, o,* or *u* is usually hard, sounding like *k* (cat).
    3. *g* followed by *e, i,* or *y,* is usually soft, sounding like *j* (gem).
    4. *g* followed by any other letter is usually hard, sounding like *g* (gate).
- The rules of *y*
    1. In one syllable words ending in *y,* the *y* sounds like long *i* (sky).
    2. In words with more than one syllable, ending in *y,* the *y* is short, sounding like a long *e* (candy).
    3. In the middle of a word, *y* is short, sounding like a short *i* (bicycle).

Learning facts and skills is not terribly interesting, so anything you can do to make it more fun will help your child over the monotony. Your reading to him and with him will also make it easier because he will see the consistent application of the rules. In time, without lecturing, it will all come together in understanding.

Besides teaching sight words and phonics, primary grade teachers are concerned with your child's learning to understand and remember what he reads, with his enjoying reading, with his being able to read efficiently for information, with his being able to categorize and alphabetize, and with his being able to explain what he has read. Even if your child is a late bloomer, your reading, talking, playing games, and providing all kinds of "other than reading" learning experiences will help him move successfully into reading.

SEE ALSO: Children's Books; Reading With Children; Speech; Games; Toys; Games and Equipment (prereading and writing; reading and writing); Records and Tapes; Spelling.

SPEECH

Speech development begins with the baby's first lusty cries. How parents react to those cries and to each stage in the child's development will directly influence the child's desire and ability to speak. It is vital, therefore, that the child feel secure with his parents, that he have a positive self-image, and that he is talked with.

Speech develops in stages and all children go through the same stages to one degree or another and according to their own timetables. Help your child to develop each stage to the fullest and to advance to the next stage as he is ready. The following timetable is approximate:

Birth to Four Weeks

At this time, cries begin to vary with the need, even though the crying is a reflex, not a thought-out behavior. The baby soon learns to cry for attention, so teaching at this stage involves caring for needs promptly. He can learn at a very young age that smiles and pleasant noises are to his advantage too.

Four Weeks to Six Months

Now the baby begins to react to sound. He experiments by feeling his mouth and tongue moving as he makes different sounds. He listens to himself more than he ever will again in his life, because later on speaking becomes habitual (most of us are shocked when we listen to ourselves on tape). He begins to listen to other people, too. Play babbling games with him and talk to him, but also give him plenty of uninterrupted time to experiment by himself, babbling at his toys. You will hear sounds from all the world's languages.

Six Months to Nine Months

At this age, sounds begin to resemble parts of words.

After Nine Months

Baby begins to imitate, so give him sounds to imitate—words and nonsense syllables. He begins to understand words that are repeated over and over, so choose a few that are different from one another—such as his name, comforting words like you're *all right*, and the unavoidable, *no-no* to prevent accidents and injury.

For the First Two Years

Speak in few words, well articulated, and use gestures to show what the words mean. Pick the child up and hold him close when he needs comforting, while you gently tell him he is *all right*. Remove his hand from the forbidden object as you briskly say, "*no-no.*"

Do not press the child to talk, just teach him to understand how words are spoken and what they mean. When he speaks in his few words, expand his words into a short sentence or question. "Mommy, down." You say, "Do you want to get down?"

- Talk with him about things as you do them—in simple words and sentences, gradually decreasing gestures.
- Point things out and say what they are clearly: door, ball, hat, nose.
- Do not speak for the child. Encourage him to speak for himself once he has shown that he can.
- All children start out mispronouncing words. Do not correct your child. You don't want him to become self-conscious. Teach him the correct pronunciation by casually repeating what he has said correctly. If he says, "Baw," you say, "You want your ball? as you give it to him.
- Once the child has demonstrated that he *can* say a word correctly, pretend you do not understand his mispronunciation when he asks for something incorrectly. Reward him for correct pronunciation by understanding and doing what he asked.

If your child does not speak reasonably intelligibly by the time he is three, seek advice (see Problems—Speech).

SEE ALSO: Affection; Family; Crying; Swearing and Obscenity; Reading With Children; Reading; Spelling.

SPELLING

If children are encouraged to pronounce words correctly as they are learning to talk, spelling will be easier for them. Spelling, as such, doesn't mean much to preschool children, because they are not really ready to understand symbols. However, they can become familiar with letter shapes by playing with cardboard or wooden cutouts. They may or may not be interested in learning letter names. As they approach school age, they will probably be interested in printing their own names and, perhaps, *Mommie* and *Daddy*. Reading with young children familiarizes them with the *idea of words* so that, when they start school, they will have a conceptual foundation to help them understand the purpose of spelling.

Spelling the English language is very difficult. The words that have been absorbed from languages based on Latin have different rules from the words based on languages from northern Europe. Some words, such as *pear, pare* and *pair*, sound the same but have different meanings and different spellings. Other words, such as *light* and *eight*, have similar strange spellings but they sound different. In the early grades, children are taught, as much as possible, to spell words that are not phonetically confusing. Then they are gradually introduced to exceptions and rules—and to exceptions to the rules. Follow along at home with whatever is being taught in school.

Because a child learns through all his senses, use wood, cardboard, and felt letters; a toy printing set; an old typewriter; verbal spelling; and manuscript. Use little piles of flash cards so you can separate the learned words from the unlearned ones. It is gratifying to see one pile diminish as the other one grows and it also teaches the child to spend time and effort where it is needed rather than clutter up a task with what has already been accomplished. Getting the easy words out of the way first makes it easier to face the few difficult remaining words. That way, the job doesn't look so massive.

Reading and creative writing also reinforces spelling. When your child writes, gently help him make corrections. When he has been overly ambitious and has a lot of misspellings, pick out those words he is learning in school for correction and ignore the rest for the time being. You want to reinforce what he is learning without confusing him. Corrections can be made by pasting the correct spelling over the error. He would soon lose interest in the whole project if he were made to do much elaborate rewriting.

Remember that a young child's attention span is short. You will accomplish more through several short sessions than through a long tiresome lesson. Practicing skills in a variety of ways is fun and provides strong reinforcement. Also, some children learn better verbally, by hearing and speaking, and others learn visually, by reading and writing. If you are sensitive to your child's learning style, you will be able to be the most help to him in spelling.

SEE ALSO: Toys, Games, Equipment (prereading and writing; reading and writing); Children's Books (ABC Dictionaries and Encyclopedias); Speech.

WRITING (PENMANSHIP)

Handwriting is just one way of communicating. Before telephones and typewriters, handwriting was the only way to communicate with distant friends and business associates, so the teaching of fine penmanship was naturally emphasized. Today, although children must learn to write legibly, the emphasis on elegant penmanship has disappeared. More attention is given to the thought and creativity behind the writing.

However, through a child's handwriting we can find clues to his interests and talents. There is a difference in the handwriting of the artist, the craftsman, the engineer, and the person whose thoughts run ahead of his fingers. Actually, the quality of a child's penmanship is no reflection on his intelligence; it is more a reflection of his interests and priorities.

At age six, many children are not able to use a pencil without extremely tedious effort. This is muscular and has nothing to do with the child's ability to think and learn. Patience is necessary to avoid turning the child against the whole idea of learning simply because his finger muscles are not yet ready for a pencil. All children this age enjoy making big letters in sand or on a chalkboard or tracing with a big crayon. They like to make words with cut-out letters of felt, with small lettered blocks, and with plastic or sandpaper letters.

First grade children are struggling with "right and left," and with reading and printing from left to right on a page. These are basic concepts that must be learned. Adults take them for granted.

Manuscript paper helps the child line up his words. His efforts will miss the target for quite a while, so be patient. Don't be fussy; time and practice will bring improvement. What your child needs most is your encouragement. Be proud that he is learning to write, no matter what it looks like. Show it to people who are interested, send "letters" to relatives, and keep samples (dated) so you and your child can look back to observe improvement. Observe how the letters are formed in Figures 15–2 and 15–3 so you can help your child without confusing him.

SEE ALSO: Arts and Crafts; Toys, Games, Equipment (hand and finger skills, eye-hand coordination; prereading and writing; reading and writing).

SPORTS

It is difficult to treat sports in much depth in this book because there is such a variety of them. There are, however, some general statements that can be made; and we can also make brief references to specific sports and to their suitability to the developmental levels of growing children.

Sports are to be considered an important part of a child's education because, like music and art, they offer a dimension to life that can be enjoyed in no other way. They:

- Develop body strength, coordination, and grace.
- Instill a regard for good physical health.
- Provide a nondestructive outlet for physical energy and competitiveness throughout childhood, teen-age, and adulthood.
- Provide opportunities to make friends and do things with people.
- Teach sportsmanship, realistic self-image, and good humor.

In infancy and early childhood, your main concerns will be good physical development, which will come from nourishing food, adequate rest, and plenty of active play. Most "sports" will be out of range until your child is in elementary school, yet your providing him the chance to develop his thinking, his strength, and his coordination will enhance his participation in sports when he gets older.

How a child participates in sports as he matures will depend on his build, on his innate competitiveness, on the interests of the

Manuscript

period comma quotation equals add subtract exclamation
marks

Figure 15—2.

Small Letters and Numbers

Figure 15—3.

rest of the family, on what happens to be in vogue, and on what he finds he can do with reasonable success. Do not show disappointment if your child cannot compete by making fun of an inability to succeed in a narrow range of sports. You may have dreamed of his being a football star, but he may be a natural for the theater, mathematics, hiking, and tennis.

At elementary school age, your child will begin to take an interest in sports and physical activities that, unless you involve yourself and teach him proper skills, can be dangerous. *It is important—urgent—that parents make sure their children learn the correct way to perform each sport and that they know the rules and safety precautions.*

In school, early physical education is carefully supervised and comparatively noncompetitive. Professionals know that young children have small hearts and lungs compared with the rest of their bodies, causing them to tire quickly. Children go through periods of rapid growth which render them susceptible to illness. And sometimes, their muscle development is uneven, making them vulnerable to injuries and developmental difficulties if exposed too early to contact sports like football and basketball. Primary grade children learn games, stunts, and dances that teach them walking, marching, hopping, jumping, galloping, running, sliding, leaping, kicking, balancing, ball handling, and rhythms, all of which can be a bit competitive but do not require a lot of eye-hand coordination or heavy physical contact. In second grade, children may be introduced to soccer and tee ball if their coordination permits it, with body contact still de-emphasized.

The following description of sports are meant only to introduce them as possible areas of interest and to alert parents to what they may expect to see offered in the school or community, to what is involved, and to a few specific precautions. Read it through so you will have a general idea of what is available and suitable and of what your child may find on his own in the neighborhood. You will be able to spot your child's interests and follow up on them so you can encourage him as well as supervise him for safety purposes. When your child shows a real interest in a certain activity, find information on that activity at the library, at a good sporting goods store, at a community center, or from the physical education teacher at his school.

Baseball

Baseball requires eye-hand coordination, so most children do not begin to play the real game until eight or nine. Some schools introduce "tee ball" in second grade, in which a soft ball is placed on an adjustable tee for the child to bat. Baseball is a highly competitive sport and can be harmfully so if parents involved in community teams are more interested in winning games than in children. Also, while some children thrive on competition, others are hurt by undue pressure, especially if they do not have the capability of performing well for the coach and the team. There are lots of other sports activities for such children (of whom there are many).

To familiarize your child with baseball, for his expected participation or for his enjoyment of the sport as a spectator, teach him the rudiments. A baseball board game is one good way of introduction. Organizations that sponsor community leagues include Little League, the Police Athletic League, Boys' and Girls' Clubs, and city or county recreation departments.

Basketball

Basketball is an excellent way to pass the time with the kids in the neighborhood. Some elementary schools start basketball programs at the second grade level. Supply your child with a lightweight child's basketball and a backboard with basket placed at the right height for his height and ability (somewhere between six and seven feet from the ground). It should be low enough for him to have success, yet high enough to be a challenge.

Bicycling

Humans begin very early to enjoy riding about on wheeled vehicles. Young children like to ride in cars and in the safety seat on the back of their parents' bikes. By toddlerhood your child will love his little wheeled vehicle and will push himself around with his feet. There is no doubt that this "pre-bicycle" is developmentally benefi-

for the activity; and you will certainly want to make sure you know where your child is playing. Some community ice hockey teams sponsor classes for interested youngsters.

Horseback Riding

Riding is an expensive sport, whether you live in the city, where you make use of riding stables, or in the country, where you maintain your own horses. Most riding stables prefer that children be eight or older for riding lessons, and your child should have riding lessons from some knowledgeable person before he is allowed to ride alone. Do not invest in expensive riding clothes at the outset—bluejeans, a shirt, a sweater, and hard shoes with heels are all that is necessary. *No tennis shoes.* If you can manage to have your child ride without sacrificing other valuable experiences, the caring for, understanding, and controlling of a large animal can do much for a child's self-image.

Racquet Games

A child's eye-hand coordination must be sufficiently developed for him to succeed in racquet games. You can see for yourself whether your child is ready by having him bounce a ball and hit it with a racquet. Children will vary in their rate of development, and their rate of development may have nothing whatever to do with their ultimate enjoyment of sports requiring eye-hand coordination. However, you may do damage if you push a child into a sport before he is ready for it.

If tennis is a family game, take your child with you occasionally and bat the ball with him for a little bit of your court time. If you want him to have lessons, wait till he is eight or nine, when he will be better able to succeed and will stick with practice. At that time, get him his own racquet, which should be specially weighed for children. Badminton, table tennis, and racquet ball are all similar to tennis in that they involve a court with a net and racquets of one sort or another. All require the same eye-hand coordination as tennis. Knowing technique and rules makes all these games more enjoyable, since batting an object over a net is only a small part of the game and will be boring in a short time.

Skateboarding

Skateboarding has become so popular and is so dangerous that it is a major cause of serious accidents to children. On the other hand, it is excellent for coordination and movement. Before buying a skateboard for your child, be sure you know where he can use one safely. And you will find it necessary to be serious about rules for its safe use. Many communities, in response to the alarming problems that have arisen, have begun to supply safe places for children to skateboard.

Skating

Double-blade ice skates and learners' roller skates are available for young children, who skate along with absolutely no fear of falling. Skating is good exercise and is excellent for the development of coordination. If you go to a rink, choose an uncrowded time so you and your child won't get run over.

Skiing

Since cross-country skiing need not be as demanding as Alpine (downhill) skiing, it can be enjoyed by the whole family. "Under five" children's cross-country ski sets are available. Clothes should be waterproof and windproof, not too bulky or constricting. School age children should be outfitted with skis in a good sporting goods store. Be sure to designate *cross-country* skis. Get good equipment and teach your child to maintain it properly, for preservation of his equipment and for safety. When you take your child on a cross-country skiing jaunt, keep it short. Do not let your child chill or become overtired.

Sledding

In the north, sledding is another universal and fairly dangerous childhood activity. Know where your child is sledding; be sure that it is free of rocks, trees, and traffic; and check that the snow does not have ice under it or on it. If you don't have a safe place nearby, bundle up and take a couple of children to a place in the community where sled-riding is provided for children when it snows.

Soccer

After many years of world popularity, soccer is now a growing sport in the U.S. Many schools and communities are introducing soccer for elementary school age children. You may want to take your child to a soccer match, which is fast-moving and does not last too long.

Target Sports

There are safe target games available to young children. Do not give them darts or arrows that could cause critical injury. Target games teach concentration and coordination (see also: Guns).

Trampoline

Children love trampolining and it is excellent exercise; but untutored and unsupervised play on a trampoline can be very dangerous. It might be best to leave this piece of equipment to the school where the physical education teacher will always be available for instruction and supervision when it is being used.

Volleyball

Universally enjoyed by people of all ages, volleyball can be played in the backyard, in most schools and YMCAs, and wherever groups gather for picnics. Your child will most likely learn to play it at school.

Water Sports

Every child should be taught how to swim, both for his own safety and for his parent's peace of mind, because, as he grows older, he will go places where he could find himself in deep water. Swimming is an instinctive activity. An infant has not developed a fear of water, so it is possible to teach him to swim well enough to move on top of the water by the time he is fifteen months old. However, teaching swimming to a child of any age is a tricky business because mismanagement of swimming lessons can cause fear to develop. Unless you understand swimming instruction yourself and are a patient person, it may be well to find professional help. In many communities, the Red Cross and YMCA offer swimming lessons for children. Teach your child swimming safety. Never allow him to swim alone; teach him the part of the pool he is allowed to use; show him how to get out of the pool; teach him not to run on the concrete around the pool and not to throw anything but water toys into the pool. He should also be taught never to call "Help" unless he really needs it.

All other water sports require the ability to swim, one reason to teach your child that basic skill early. A child should not be allowed to go out in a canoe, even with an experienced swimmer, unless he knows how to swim and, even then, he should wear a life jacket. Rowboats are more stable than canoes, but still the unexpected can happen, so your child should be able to swim. A reasonable swimmer can snorkle and skin dive. Teach your snorkler about underwater animals, plants, and coral, not only for the general educational value, but so he will know how to avoid dangerous and painful experiences. Scuba diving (with tanks) requires formal training by a licensed person. There is much to know to avoid trouble with deep diving.

In water skiing, the greatest danger (assuming swimming ability) comes from the motor boat propellers, which means that the boat should be handled by a responsible adult. Your child should always wear a life jacket; and you should teach him not to ski unless there are two people in the boat, one to handle the boat and the other to keep an eye on him at all times.

SEE ALSO: Toys, Games, Equipment (large muscle development and coordination); Games; Competition; Health Habits; Community; Friendship; Self-Image; Safety; Children's Books (sports).

RESOURCES

Games

Books

ARNOLD, ARNOLD. *The World Book of Children's Games.* New York: World Publishing, 1972.

GRUNFELD, FREDERICK V., ed. *Games of the World, How To Make Them, How To Play Them, How They Came To Be.* New York: Ballentine Books, 1975.

SKOLNIK, PETER L. *Jump Rope.* New York: Workman Publishing Co., 1974.

WITHERS, CARL. *The Treasury of Games, Riddles, Mystery Stunts, Tricks, Tongue Twisters, Rhymes, Chanting, Singing.* New York: Grosset and Dunlap, Publishers, 1964.

Math

Books

HEIMER, RALPH T., and MIRIAM S. NEWMAN. *The New Mathematics for Parents.* New York: Holt, Rinehart and Winston, Inc., 1965. A step-by-step introduction to "new math" with exercises at the end of each step. A good condensed review, though missing some more recent developments.

RAVIELLI, ANTHONY. *An Adventure in Geometry.* New York: Viking Press, 1966.

SWENSON, ESTHER J. *Teaching Mathematics to Children.* (2nd Edition). New York: Macmillan Co., 1973. A modern math book written for teachers, but understandable to anyone with some math background.

WIRTZ, ROBERT W. *Mathematics for Everyone.* Washington, D.C.: Curriculum Design Associates, Inc., Suite 414, 1211 Connecticut Avenue. A new approach to math for young children which you may find challenging and informative.

Reading

Books

TINKER, MILES A. *Preparing Your Child for Reading.* New York: Holt, Rinehart and Winston, 1971.

Organizations

National School Volunteer Program, Inc., 300 Washington Avenue, Alexandria, Va. 22308.

Speech

Books and Pamphlets

BRYANT, JOHN E. *Helping Your Child Speak Correctly.* No. 445. New York: Public Affairs Pamphlets, 381 Park Avenue South, N.Y. 10016.

LEWIS, M. M. *How Children Learn to Speak.* New York: Basic Books, 1959.

PUSHAW, DAVID R. *Teach Your Child to Talk: A Parent Guide.* (rev. ed.) New York: CEBCO Standard Publishing Co., 1977.

Books

BAEDER, A.P. *Complete Manual of Skin Diving.* New York: Macmillan Co., 1968.

BREWSTER, BENJAMIN. *The First·Book of Baseball.* New York: Franklin Watts, Inc., 1963.

COWLE, LUCILE. *Teaching Your Tot to Swim.* New York: Vantage Press, 1970.

FITZSIMMONS, ROBERT. *How to Play Baseball.* Garden City, N.Y.: Doubleday, 1962.

HENKEL, STEPHEN C. *Bikes.* Riverside, Conn.: The Chatham Press, 1972.

LIEBERS, ARTHUR. *The Complete Book of Cross-Country Skiing.* New York: Coward, McCann and Geoghegan, Inc., 1974.

SCOTT, BARBARA ANN and MICHAEL KIRBY. *Skating for Beginners.* New York: Alfred A. Knopf, 1969.

SLOAN, EUGENE A. *Complete Book of Bicycling.* New York: Trident Press, 1970.

Sports Illustrated Horseback Riding. Philadelphia: J. B. Lippencott Co., 1971.

16

broader and deeper interests

COOKING

In modern households, now that we are breaking away from stereotyped roles for men and women, cooking is becoming a family affair. New cookbooks are not written for women but for gourmets of either sex. It could turn out that the real gourmet in your family may be your son, not your daughter.

When you teach your child to work in the kitchen, you are not only teaching him the pleasure of cooking. You are helping prepare him to read and write, to understand math, to be creative, to contribute to his family, to organize, to be conscious of nutrition, to appreciate the fruits of the harvest, to understand how things grow, and to be a loving person who enjoys bringing pleasure to others.

Infants

Your baby will start learning to handle kitchen utensils as soon as he can sit up. Give him pots, pans, and lids for developmental play. Watch him examine them, turn them over and over, fit lids, listen to them clang, and take hold of knobs and handles.

Toddlers

Your toddler can cut little pieces of Plasticine with a plastic knife. He can make sand pies, pour water and sand, scoop water and sand, beat up bubbles with an eggbeater in a little detergent mixed with water, taste bits of what you are cooking, and lick spoons. Have a sturdy stool for your child so that he can stand up at the counter with you—on the side of the sink *away* from the hot water faucet. Keep pot handles turned to the rear of the stove. Put a tray on the counter so he can play with water without flooding the counter top. Let him play with the kitchen scales and other safe and interesting kitchen equipment. Point out words like *salt, sugar,* and *flour.* Let him taste as you cook. Let him sprinkle raisins on the salad or chopped nuts into your cookie batter. In his presence, explain to the family how he helped you with the cooking.

You don't have to put up with this mess every day when you are in a hurry or when you are preparing a dinner party. Just do it often enough for your child to learn how to handle equipment and absorb techniques, often enough for him to get a feeling of togetherness in cooking. Talk with him about foods and what you are doing with them in the market and in the kitchen.

Preschooler

The preschool child is ready to do some real cooking. With your help, he can:

- Make instant ice tea for grownups.
- Peel and slice bananas.
- Shell tiny peas and eat them raw.
- Wash and tear lettuce leaves.
- Get food from the refrigerator for himself. Have a special place in the refrigerator for prepared celery sticks, cheese cubes, and so forth. Hang a colorful sign on the wall saying, PLEASE CLOSE REFRIGERATOR DOOR. He will learn all those words in a relevant way.

Steaming vegetables is the very best way to prepare them, and since many children are not overly fond of vegetables, it is a good way to get the most nourishment out of the least quantity. Later, they will remember and tend to follow this method of preparation because they have grown up with it. Often a child will balk at vegetables prepared one way and will like them prepared in another. The following list shows just a few variations, some of which your child will be able to help prepare:

- Asparagus—Serve with hollandaise sauce (can be bought in a jar) or with melted butter and lemon juice.

- Beans (green, wax, Italian, pole)—Add bacon bits or imitation bacon bits, sliced water chestnuts, cut up spring onions, sauteed mushrooms, or seasoned salt and butter.

- Lima beans—Cooked with a small amount of thyme and bay leaf, or with bacon bits and spring onions, a dash of mustard and cut up sausage, or mix them with corn (succotash).

- Beets—Serve with mint sauce or mustard sauce or pickled (cold) with hard-cooked egg slices.

- Broccoli—Serve with hollandaise sauce, or sprinkled with lemon juice and buttered crumbs and browned under the broiler (polonaise), or sprinkled with cheese and browned under the broiler.

- Brussels sprouts—Serve them polonaise (see broccoli), or covered with thick white sauce and lots of buttered crumbs and browned under the broiler.

- Carrots—Glaze in a frying pan with a little butter and honey, or with butter and crushed mint, or serve them raw in salad or for dipping.

- Cabbage—Make coleslaw or serve cooked with vinegar, brown sugar, mustard, or bacon bits.

- Celery—Best raw or creamed and browned under the broiler.

- Corn—Serve on the cob (with kernels scored for children with missing teeth) or cut off the cob, with bacon, green pepper, or cooked ham bits.

- Eggplant—Serve dipped in egg and crumbs, and fried or with bacon, tomato, onion, and brown sugar and baked in a casserole.

- Onions—Make rings dipped in flour and french fried, or serve them fried with potatoes.

- Peas—Serve small peas raw out of the pod, or cook them with butter and crushed mint or serve with mushrooms or sliced water chestnuts.

- Potatoes—To baked potatoes, add sour cream and/or bacon bits, cheese, or sliced spring onions; make potato salad or potatoes O'Brien (diced potatoes, adding bacon bits, pimiento, chopped onion, green pepper), or fried potatoes; also, potato pancakes.

- Spinach—Serve raw in salad, or cooked with slices of hard-cooked egg; serve creamed or in souffle.

- Squash (zucchini)—Serve raw in salad, or cooked with tomatoes and onion, or in a casserole with stewed tomatoes and onion.

- Squash (acorn)—Cut in half, bake with butter and seasonings, or bake with sausage in the cavity, or with apple or pineapple in the cavity.

- Sweet potatoes—Cook and mash, put in a casserole, dot with butter and brown; or serve them baked.

- Tomatoes—Serve raw in sandwiches and salads or serve slices dipped in flour and fried; or serve stewed—plain or with onion and green pepper; halved—buttered with crumbs and broiled; or raw—stuffed with cheese and rice or with rice with ham bits and onion, crabmeat, and cheese.

Baking and Creating

Teach your young school age child the elements of bread baking, of baking cakes and cookies. Before long he will be able to do it himself. If you wait until your child is a teen-ager, he will be very busy doing other things, and you may find it hard to initiate an interest; but if you start him early, the interest will remain. Let your child create salads, using fruits and vegetables with lettuces of different varieties, adding garnishes of nuts, raw mushrooms, and coconut—whatever he thinks blends. You may find him coming up with a new taste treat. As he becomes more skilled with a peeler and knife, teach him how to peel and prepare raw fruits and vegetables.

SEE ALSO: Learning How To Eat; Nutrition; Gardening; Housekeeping, Duties and Chores; Children's Books (cookbooks, gardens, and plants).

The following are just a few simple recipes school age children can learn (with some of the recipes you will have to help with peeling, broiling, and so forth):

EGGNOG FOR ONE
Mix in blender with a couple of ice cubes:
1 cup milk
1 egg
¾ tsp. vanilla
a little honey or sugar

HAWAIIAN GRILL
Toast bread slightly. On it put a slice of pineapple, a slice of ham, a slice of cheese. Bake in moderate oven until the cheese melts.

BASIC COOKIE MIX
You can make this and store in the refrigerator in a covered can. Sift:
5 pounds flour
¾ cup baking powder
3 T. salt
1 T. cream of tartar
½ cup sugar
2 cups dry milk

Cut in: 2 pounds (4 cups) vegetable shortening until the mixture resembles corn meal.

OATMEAL COOKIES
(Using basic cookie mix)
2¼ cups mix
1¼ cups brown sugar
1 tsp. cinnamon
⅓ cup water
2 eggs
½ cup melted shortening
3 cups rolled quick oats
½ cup nuts, if desired

Stir sugar and cinnamon into the mix. Combine water, beaten egg, and melted shortening. Stir into the mix until well blended. Stir into the mix until well blended. Stir in the rolled oats and nuts. Drop by teaspoonfuls on baking sheet. Bake at 350° for about 12 minutes.

STEWED APPLES
Wash, core, peel, and quarter apples. Cook in a little water over medium heat until soft. Sugar is not necessary unless the apples are very tart. Cinnamon may be added. Applesauce can be made by putting the cooked apples through a food mill.

CHEESE CRACKERS
Put either grated or a small slice of cheese on a cracker and toast for a moment under the broiler. Watch very carefully so it doesn't burn.

HAM PATTIES
Make patties of:
3 cups cooked ground ham
¾ cup sour cream
1 cup bread crumbs
1 T. finely chopped onion
1 egg, beaten

Put pineapple slices in a baking pan and top each with a ham patty. Bake at 350° for 30 minutes. Serves four to six.

ORANGE BAKED CHICKEN
Into a buttered casserole place:
2 chicken legs and thighs
¼ tsp. salt
2 T. melted butter
½ cup orange juice
poultry seasoning (optional)

Mix orange juice with melted butter and pour over chicken in casserole. You may want to add currants or raisins. Bake for 15 minutes at 350° then turn and baste and cook for 15 minutes more until chicken is tender and brown.

CINNAMON TOAST
Toast bread, butter it, and sprinkle with a little sugar and cinnamon. Or, toast on one side in the broiler, butter, and sprinkle with a little sugar and cinnamon. Return to broiler for just a moment.

FANCY SANDWICHES

Cut day-old bread into fancy shapes with cookie cutters. Spread with peanut butter, ham spread, egg salad, soft cream cheese, or mayonnaise. Decorate appropriately with slices of olive, radishes, bits of luncheon meat, a dab of jelly, ground nuts, or a hard-cooked egg slice.

COTTAGE CHEESE PANCAKES

Beat together:
1 egg
1 T. flour
1 heaping T. cottage cheese

Make 3″ pancakes on griddle. Serve with syrup or jam. Serves one.

SESAME HONEY CANDY

In a large pan over low heat, melt ¼ cup butter or margarine.
Add:
1 cup grated coconut
½ cup sesame seeds
Stir over heat for five minutes.
Add:
½ tsp. vanilla
¼ cup honey

Mix and chill. Form into balls. Store in the refrigerator.

ITALIAN TUNA SALAD

Chill, open, and drain a small can of tuna.

Make lettuce beds in individual salad bowls.

Add bits of lettuce, tuna chunks, cut up spring onions, celery, ripe olives, and tomato wedges.

Season and add Italian dressing.

Serves two.

QUICK BAKED BEANS

Into a bean pot or casserole, put:
3 cups canned baked beans
1 cup canned tomatoes

¼ cup molasses
1 tsp. dry mustard
1 tsp. Worcestershire sauce

Bake at 325° for one hour.
Serves four to six.

PEANUT BUTTER BALLS
Mix:
½ cup peanut butter
3½ T. non-fat powdered dry milk
a bit of honey if desired

Roll into balls and refrigerate. You can add raisins, peanuts or wheat germ to the mix if you like.

BISCUITS (from Bisquick)
Mix with a fork, then beat twenty strokes:
2 cups Bisquick
½ cup water

Drop by spoonfuls on a baking sheet. Bake at 425° for 8 to 10 minutes.

CRUMB CRUST PIE
Use 8″ pie pan

Combine 1¼ cups crumbs (graham cracker, ginger snaps, or chocolate wafers) with ¼ cup melted butter.

Toss together and press into pan.

Bake about 8 minutes at 350° or chill without baking.

Fill with berries or canned fruit and instant pudding.

FRUIT BAVARIAN PIE
Mix:
1 nine ounce Cool Whip (thawed)
2 eight ounce cartons fruit flavored yogurt

Pile into crumb pie crust and garnish with fresh fruit. Chill.

BAKED FISH WITH CHEESE

Allow ⅓ to ½ lb. fish fillets per adult (sole or flounder). Wipe fish and lay in buttered baking dish.

Brush with oil or melted butter. Add salt and pepper to taste and sprinkle with grated cheese.

Bake at 400° for about 20 to 25 minutes, or until the fish flakes when you test it with a fork.

YOGURT POPSICLES

Mix:
1 carton yogurt
1 six ounce can concentrated fruit juice (unsweetened)

Insert popsicle sticks and freeze.

RELISH

Grind and mix:
1 peeled and cored apple
¼ cup cranberries
¼ cup raisins

Add 1 tsp. grated orange rind and a few drops of orange juice.

APPLE SALADS

Mix with mayonnaise:
1. Chopped apple, raisins, grated carrot
2. Chopped apple, raisins, celery cut in small pieces, nuts (optional)
3. Chopped apple, dates, nuts (optional)

FRUITY OATMEAL

To cooked cereal, add raisins, currants or dried apricots cut up in small pieces.

ORANGE TOAST

Add a few drops of orange juice to softened butter. Toast bread on one side, spread untoasted side with orange-butter mixture, then toast.

BROILED OPEN SANDWICHES

Toast bread on one side. Spread with butter or mayonnaise. Layer any of the following:
1. Tomato slice, broiled bacon
2. Ham slice, cold cooked asparagus

Lay a slice of cheese on top and place under broiler until the cheese is melted and lightly browned.

TOAST CUPS

Cut crusts from thin sliced bread. Brush with melted butter. Fit into muffin tins and bake at 400° until browned. Can be filled with creamed chicken or tuna and garnished with a sprig of parsley.

MINT APPLES

1 apple, peeled and cut in rings
½ cup water
2 T. lemon juice
3 tsp. Creme de Menthe (or mint flavoring and green coloring)

Bring liquid ingredients to a boil, add apples and simmer until barely tender. Remove from heat, cool, then chill. Good with meat.

COLD PLATE

Let your child make his own combination:
cold cuts rolled or cut in strips
cottage cheese
celery sticks
carrot sticks
olives
hard-cooked egg
dried apricots or prunes

Garnish with sprigs of parsley or watercress.

GINGER FRUIT ORIENTAL

Chill:
1 can unsweetened peaches, not drained
1 T. crystallized ginger

Before serving, add sliced bananas.

GARDENING

For preschool and school age children, gardening is a way of teaching fundamental life concepts by example and in a way they can understand. Gardening teaches children that:

- Big beautiful plants grow from tiny seeds—a fascinating phenomenon.

- Nature is cyclical. The same things happen in the same season every year.
- Plants need rain, good nourishment from the soil, space in which to grow, soil that will let their roots develop, and sunlight.
- There is no such thing as a "green thumb." A good seed, given what it needs, will grow.
- If you do not give a plant what it needs, it will not grow, no matter how much you wish it could. Fantasizing won't work.
- There is an endless variety of textures, colors, shapes, scents, and flavors in growing things. Train your child in keen observation and appreciation.
- Each plant has its own characteristics in its seeds. Marigold seeds grow into marigold plants and zinnia seeds grow into zinnia plants.
- You feel very proud and pleased when you have done all the right things and the plant rewards you by growing handsomely.

Keep your child's garden simple. Use plants that are easy to grow and that do not take too long to show results. Don't get yourself in for too much work. A few successful plants teach more than a neglected half-acre garden.

If possible, find a small patch in a sunny corner near the house. If you have no place of your own, perhaps a neighbor wouldn't mind a little beautification. There are a lot of ways to garden in the city with window boxes, with wall shelves for potted plants, or with containers you can build or buy.

You will have to do the heavy digging, the soil preparation, and the fertilizing, but make sure your child knows it is his very own garden and let him do as much of the planning and work as he can.

Outdoor Gardening

Parents' Tools.   You will need a spade, a hoe, a rake, a bale of peatmoss, and a small bag of fertilizer (keep fertilizer away from young children).

Child's Tools.   Your child will need a small trowel, a small watering can, a wagon, four wooden stakes and string to put around the garden, and a small bag of sand for seeding.

Choosing a Place.   Choose a location that is sunny, in a corner where it will not be trampled, and in a place as near the house as possible.

Soil Preparation.   Do a thorough job here and you are almost bound to have success. The soil must be porous enough for roots to develop easily and it must contain the food for the plant. Hence, dig and chop the soil about ten inches deep (easiest when it is neither too wet nor too dry). For a two foot by three foot garden, mix about half a large bale of peatmoss and a couple of cups of fertilizer with the soil. Hoe and rake the soil until it is fine and smooth on the surface, pulling stones and lumps of clay to one end to be hauled away in the wagon. Keep the other half of the peatmoss for use later as mulch.

Seeding.   Draw two lines the length of the garden about a foot apart. One packet of seeds will take care of the whole garden. Put the seeds evenly in the rows at the depth recommended on the packet, press them down, let your child cover them carefully with sand, and press again. Place stakes and strings around the garden to keep people and dogs from walking on it.

Cultivation.   Give your child the job of keeping the seedlings moist with his little watering can. Watering may have to be done twice a day if the weather is dry. Show him how to hoe gently between the rows (keeping away from the seedlings) so water can soak in. Do not try to weed until the little plants are showing in the rows. When the plants are an inch or so high, you and your child will decide which plants to pull out (the weaker ones), leaving room for the healthy ones to develop. Read the seed packet for spacing. When the plants are three inches high, weed thoroughly, water well, and make a two-inch layer of mulch all over the garden. The mulch will discourage weeds and will keep the moisture in the ground around the plants, making maintenance much easier. Keep after the few weeds that develop before they get large. Your child can do much of the cultivation, but he will need your company and encouragement.

Lettuce. Lettuce is an annual which comes in many varieties. Plant as early in the spring as the soil can be worked. You will be eating lettuce by the time you plant flowers.

Marigolds. Marigolds are annuals that are insect resistant, which is a consideration for busy parents and children, and they grow fast. A variety called "First Lady" is about 18″ tall and produces beautiful big lemon-yellow flowers. For a border or container, there are medium and dwarf varieties of marigolds in orange and lemon-yellow. You can start them indoors on a sunny window sill or plant the seeds outdoors when danger of frost is past. You can plant them between the lettuce rows because, by the time they mature, you will have eaten all the lettuce (which doesn't do well anyway in hot weather). Push the mulch aside to plant the seeds and leave it aside till the plants are a few inches tall, then tuck it back around the plants.

Daffodils. Daffodils are perennials; plant the bulbs in the fall. Dig a bed as described above in a sunny place where they won't be disturbed. Dig holes about 5″ deep and about 6″ apart (a practical lesson in inches). Plant the bulbs, flat end down. Your child can begin to look for green shoots very early in the spring, even when there is still snow on the ground. Daffodils are hardy and will come up year after year. Cut the blooms after they fade so the strength of the plant will not be used to make seed pods; but the leaves should be left to soak up sunshine until they fall to the ground. A little garden fertilizer in fall and early spring each year will insure large blooms. In a couple of years, separate the bulbs, which will have multiplied, and either enlarge the bed or give the extra bulbs to friends.

Day lilies. Day lilies are perennials. Some varieties are large and very spectacular, yet day lilies are insect resistant and require little care if they are planted properly. They can tolerate light shade, but must be placed where they will have plenty of space because they become large plants. Dig a hole about 10″ deep and 12″ wide. Add a generous amount of peatmoss and a little fertilizer to the dirt you have dug out of the hole and put some of the treated dirt back in the hole. Plant the corm so the place where the leaves begin (the crown) is about an inch below ground level. Fill in around it to ground level and water well. You and your children will enjoy these great flowers every summer for years.

Indoor Gardening

Parent's Tools and Materials.   You will need plastic to cover the windowsill or table where the plants will be placed. You can put a rim around an old table, cover the whole thing with plastic, and then spread a layer of sand or gravel; or you can use a shallow pan with a layer of pebbles. You must take charge of fertilizer; there are easy-to-handle indoor types.

Child's Tools and Materials.   Have ready flower pots with drainage holes and saucers (unless you have prepared a sand or pebble bed), a spoon or tiny spade, and an indoor watering can. It is wise to invest in potting soil because it is sterile and of the right consistency for indoor plants.

Light.   If your child's windowsill is on the south side of the house, choose plants that like the sun; if not, choose ones that like reflected light. Usually, green plants like reflected light and flowering plants like sun. *Gro-lights* make it possible to grow plants anywhere in the house. They come on stands or can be hung from the ceiling, and they are available in plant shops and hardware stores. If used with a timer, they will go on and off without attention. You will pay a little extra on your electric bill to keep the lights going fourteen to sixteen hours a day; but they will produce gratifying results in otherwise discouraging situations.

Water.   The plant should be allowed to become completely dry on the surface of the soil before watering, then it should be soaked until the water appears in the saucer. However, after the plant has drained, empty the saucer—the plant should not sit in water. Teach your child to water a little at a time till he sees the water come out the bottom, so he will not cause a flood. Plant shops sell instruments which will indicate when plants need water.

Fertilizer.   Keep fertilizer away from children. If you print or let your child print "fertilize plants" on his calendar, he will learn to read the words for a purpose—to remind *you* to fertilize *his* plants. By the time your child is in school, you should be able to let him take care of the fertilizing if he understands that he should be very careful what he puts in his mouth and that he keep it away from younger children.

Easy to Grow House Plants

Geranium.   Geraniums need plenty of sun, sandy soil, not too big a pot, and not too much water. Keep faded flowers cut. Geraniums can be started from cuttings in water or sand.

Spider Plant.   The spider plant is a popular hanging plant with pale grassy leaves. It throws out miniature plants on the end of long curved stems. It needs reflected light and not too much water. (See Figure 16–1.)

Sansevieria.   There are tall and short varieties. It is very easy to grow in any light, and with little water. (See Figure 16–1.)

Cactus and Small Succulents.   Cacti need plenty of sun. Water once a week in summer, once every two or three weeks in winter. Cacti grow in sandy soil. You can make a little dish garden with cacti using tiny bridges, houses, stones, and so on. (See Figure 16–1.)

Grape Ivy.   Grape ivy tolerates low light; avoid direct sun. Keep trim by pinching off straggling growth from time to time. (See Figure 16–1.)

Begonia.   Begonias need sun. There are many varieties, some with very large colorful leaves and bunches of flowers. Begonias can be started from cuttings and they are fast growers. (See Figure 16–1.)

Root Vegetables.   You can plant carrots, beets, turnips, and so on to produce decorative plants (no vegetables). Cut off the root, leaving an inch of the green top. Trim off excess old leaves and plant with the crown at the soil surface. Good for hanging baskets.

EASY CARE HOUSE PLANTS

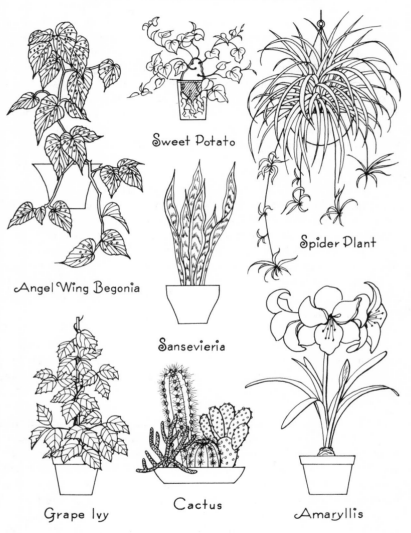

Sweet Potato

Spider Plant

Angel Wing Begonia

Sansevieria

Grape Ivy

Cactus

Amaryllis

Figure 16—1.

Sweet Potato.   In late summer or early fall, select a potato with eyes that look as though they are trying to grow roots. Let it sit for a few days for the eyes to produce the beginnings of roots. Find the end of the potato where it was picked from the mother plant. Insert four toothpicks in the side of the potato, then hang it over the edge of a jar with the end that was attached up and the other end about one-third submerged in water (this is usually the tapered end of the potato). You can continue to grow the plant in water, or, after roots and stem have formed, you can plant it in soil. Provide a trellis, which can be string or wire tacked to a window frame. The plant needs a sunny window, and you should pinch side sprouts to keep it trim. (See Figure 16–1.)

Avocado.   The Florida avocado sprouts more rapidly than the California. Find one that is very ripe (look on the reduced produce table). Rinse the seed and allow it to dry, then remove the coating from the seed. Use toothpicks, as you did with the sweet potato, and suspend the seed in water. When roots form, add soil to the water, making a thick slurry. In a few weeks, plant in potting soil, water and cover with plastic until the plant has "settled in." As the plant grows, pinch the top to encourage branching. Place it in a sunny window.

Pineapple.   Slice off the top two inches of the fruit with its spiky leaves. Plant it in sand and keep it moist, either by watering frequently or by enclosing the container and plant in a plastic bag. In a month or so, plant in potting soil.

Amaryllis.   The amaryllis is a very large bulb which should be planted in a pot that allows for at least an inch of soil around the bulb. When planting, leave one-third of the bulb showing above the soil. Water well, then *water sparingly till growth starts;* the plant will need a lot of water when it blooms. Place in a sunny window. The growth is spectacular—about an inch a day—and the blooms are huge. Snip off each bloom as it fades. When the blooms are gone, cut the stalk back to two inches above the bulb, but leave the leaves. Water and feed until October, when you cut off the leaves and lay the pot on its side in a warm place so the bulb can rest for a month. Then place in a cool place until December, when you can start it growing again by putting it in the sun and watering as before. You can keep the bulb going for years and years. (See Figure 16–1.)

Miscellaneous Ideas and Tips

- In late February or early March, bring in forsythia, flowering quince, and pussywillow to put in water for forcing.
- Make a sponge garden. Run a hanger string through the sponge with a large needle. Soak the sponge and plant it with parsley or grass. Hang by the string in a sunny window. Water by spraying.
- Try growing cherry tomatoes in a patio container.
- Cuttings: Choose geranium, grape ivy, coleus, begonia, impatiens, or ivy. Make a sharp cut about ¼ inch below a leaf node. Your cutting should be about four inches long. Remove flowers and lower leaves. Set firmly in sand or start in water. Keep sand wet. In a month or so, when roots have formed, plant in potting soil.
- In winter, when it is dry indoors, spraying plants with a fine mist keeps the leaves from drying.
- You can wash plants in cool soapy water to freshen them and to get rid of insects, either by wiping with a moistened cloth and rinsing or by dipping and swishing small plants in soapy water and rinsing. Tie a plastic bag around the pot to keep the dirt and plant from falling out.
- When you go away, put your moistened plants in plastic bags or in the bathtub under a plastic cover.
- Make a terrarium. (See Terrariums.)
- Line a glass jar with a paper towel and stuff the center with crumpled paper towel to hold everything in place. Slip different kinds of seeds between the towel lining and the glass side of the jar. Moisten the toweling and keep moist, though not soggy. In a few days you will be able to see exactly how each seed sprouts.

SEE ALSO: Cooking; Nutrition; The Child's Room; Nature Study; Toys, Games, Equipment (gardening); Field Trips; Children's Books (gardens and plants).

GEOGRAPHY

When a baby crawls out the door of his room, down the hall, past the closet door, into the living room, turns left into the dining area and then left again into the kitchen, he is learning geography. When the toddler is taken to the park, runs to the swings, then goes down the path to the water fountain, then dashes up the hill to where he remembers seeing a bird's nest in a bush, he is learning geography. The more your young child has the opportunity to explore places around home, the better will be his geographical concepts, because what he learns later about the rest of the world must be grounded in knowledge of the real, the tangible. Stories and pictures of faraway places give the child flashes of information that float free of connection with the real earth and are all right as far as they go, but "down to earth" exploration develops the context within which the differences, directions, and distances of faraway places can later be oriented.

To help your school age child learn about the earth and about directions, distances, and maps, consider some of the following ideas:

- Nature walks in different places as you travel.
- Treasure hunts: "Go to the oak tree, go south (use your compass), find the rock under which the treasure is hidden" (you have hidden the "treasure").
- Show your child how to make a diagram showing where something interesting has been found (a flower, a bird's nest), then have Dad or Mom try to find it when he or she comes home—using the diagram. "Go out the front door, take ten grown-up steps, turn right, take four steps to the pine tree."
- As a cooperative venture, make a map of the streets your child knows in the neighborhood. Include traffic signs, landmarks, and places of interest to your child.
- Make a map of his route to school.
- On an old table, make a relief map of papier mâché (see page 000 for directions). It doesn't have to be a real place, just a place with mountains, hills, flat plains, and rivers. Your child can paint farms, trees, roads, and rivers and can locate little block buildings.
- See Toys for map puzzles and games.
- Make a paper tape compass on the floor of his room, showing directions and relating them to where the sun rises and sets. If you feel so inclined, you can paint a colorful one right on an inexpensive rug as part of the room decor.

• Hang a colorful simplified map of the United States on the wall. In bold letters, print the names of the towns where relatives live and the places your child has visited. Check your local educational toy store for such a map.

When you travel with your school age child, call his attention to geographical features along the way. Stop at interesting places to observe mountaintop views, rocks, soil, streams, rivers, air temperature, sun direction, farms, and visit local geographic exhibits. Notice how the terrain changes as you come down out of the mountains, through the foothills; explain how the streams grow and slow down. Using the car odometer, check off the actual distance that makes a mile, so your child will get the feeling for what a mile really means. Read road signs telling directions and miles to nearby towns. Measure off the miles to the next town on the odometer (an exercise in addition or subtraction, depending on how you go about it). Notice how towns are often situated on rivers; how industries are clustered where the geographical features they need exist; how certain crops grow in certain places because of the soil and temperature; how the soil is black in some places, red in others, white and sandy in others. If you keep in mind that geography can be defined as the study of the physical earth and how it affects the way people live, you will find that everywhere you look you will see something to talk about. Just remember to keep the level of your child's interests in mind.

SEE ALSO: The Child's Room; Field Trips; Travel; Toys, Games, Equipment (geography).

HISTORY

Young children have little sense of time, even in the short term, so they are not able to grasp the concept of past generations having come and gone throughout the course of history. There are, however, several ways to introduce them to history, to teach them to enjoy its development into the present, and to explore its relevance to the future.

1. *Develop a sense of time passing.* Talk with your child about what he said and did when he was "little." Keep samples of his art and school work, dated, in his own "history" book. Talk about how it was when *you* were little. Encourage grandparents to tell about how it was when *they* were little. Give your child opportunities to know his grandparents and older relatives well. Help him keep records about himself by date. For example: record his height and weight on a wall chart; or make a book with a silhouette of his hand on each page, dated, from infancy to whatever age he loses interest in the project.

2. Talk about the history of his family, relating it to the history of our country.

3. Note the coming and going of seasons, how events repeat, and how, within the cycles, things grow and change.

4. Even though he cannot understand when historical events took place, develop your child's repertoire of historical stories suitable for his level of interest. If you are a history buff and a spinner of yarns, make up stories about imaginary historical children doing things the way they were done long ago. Don't be surprised if you are asked if you came over here on the *Mayflower*.

5. When your child is learning some history in school, read stories with him. Help him make early American villages, costume dolls, and so on—things that tie in with whatever he is studying.

6. Take him to historical sites and exhibits of interest to him at his level of understanding.

7. Look into the arts and crafts of the period he is studying and relate them to the state of technology at the time. For example, talk about using candles because there was no electricity; or about how spinning, food preservation, and weaving were done at home because there were no factories.

8. Be on the lookout for good historical children's movies and television shows.

9. Keep a picture diary on a big homemade wall calendar or in a notebook. Cut relevant pictures out of magazines or make little drawings. On Thanksgiving, you might draw a picture of a turkey with snow falling on it, with a caption: "It snowed today so

us dislike reptiles and insects. Try to avoid transferring your dislike to your child. Teach him to respect all animals. Teach him that all animals naturally need to defend themselves and that he should avoid cornering them or teasing them, because, when angry or afraid, they can hurt him. Teach him, too, that when people feed wild animals and birds around their homes, those animals and birds come to depend on that food supply. If one starts feeding in the fall of the year, the project cannot humanely be abandoned until the natural food supply is again abundant.

Talk about different animal habits and homes and what they eat. Notice their physical differences and how the animals use their unique body arrangements to take care of themselves. Read about how they bear and care for their young. See how some animals and birds migrate and how some change color with the seasons. If possible, put a bird feeder where your child can watch and identify birds.

NATURE WALKS

By school age, your child will become a good hiking companion, though he still has to take two or three steps to your one, so he may tire before you do (unless you are out of condition). If you don't have much background in looking for nature clues, you may want to find a nearby trail that is either well marked with information or has a trail guide. Wear sturdy shoes with heavy rough soles to avoid slipping or bruising your feet. Take a canteen of water and perhaps a backpack picnic. A magnifying glass is great for examining tiny insects, fungi, and plant life. This is a good time to teach your child how to use a compass. Pencil and paper can produce a diary of finds and reminders of things to look up at home. If your book collection does not contain guides to the identification of birds, wild flowers, trees, insects, and animals and their traces, you may want to add them to your school age child's library.

Photographing interesting observations is a good way to make a collection of records without disturbing the environment. You may want to invest in a close-up lens to take pictures of cobwebs, birds, and tiny flowers. In some areas, nature lovers have unwittingly destroyed habitats by walking off the trails and by collecting samples of plants, so it is best to stay on marked trails and avoid disturbing anything. Taking a picture is a much more humane and ecologically sensitive way to "collect" nature specimens. Use your good judgment. A twig with a cocoon taken from your own yard won't do any damage, but it is a different story on public trails where numbers of passers-by can create havoc.

When you travel, carry along your child's identification books so you won't have to wait a week or so to learn what you've seen. When you walk a trail, walk quietly (like Indians); look ahead and behind, and up and down; do not make sudden movements. Look for:

- Animal tracks. If they are fresh, they will be sharply defined and will not have leaves or debris in them.
- Nests in trees, fallen logs, hollow stumps, and under rock ledges. Be wary and don't poke.
- Beaten down or chewed brush.
- Animal scats (stools).
- Moss on the north side of trees.
- The location of the sun.
- Animals (see Figure 16–3)—squirrels can be called by making a sucking noise on the back of the hand.
- Birds (see Figure 16–6)—can be lured nearer by making kissing noises with the lips.
- Lichens, fungi, and forest floor plants.
- Wildflowers.
- Insects—nests, webs, and cocoons.
- At the seashore, observe waves, tides, undertow, and sea life cast up on the beach (avoid the man o' war, which looks like a plastic bag). Explore quiet inlets for sea creatures. Collect a few shells and pebbles to take home for collections or creations. Watch the sunrise or sunset over the ocean (depending on which ocean). Go to the beach on a moonlit night to marvel at its silvery path on the water. Look at the barnacles and pieces of coral under the magnifying glass. Hunt for driftwood. Explore the dunes for dune flowers and birds. Watch the

gulls dive for fish. If everyone can swim, try snorkling in a safe place. (See Figure 16–4.)

- When driving through mountains, allow time to stop at lookouts. Use the compass and the sun to chart directions. Talk about what you see in each direction. Observe the rocks and plants at high elevations.

- Swamps and streams have their own special plants and populations, all busily functioning in the watery environment.

- You may find rocks with fossil prints.

- In winter, look for nests in bare trees. It's easy to see animal and bird tracks in the snow. See how the creeks are frozen and note which plants are evergreen. Look at tree shapes against the sky and note winter birds.

- In early spring, look for the beginning of spring wild flowers and for the return of migratory birds. Note the patterns of the melting snow and the water beginning to flow in the creek under the thinning ice. Note the enlarging buds on trees and bushes.

- In fields, there are special grasses and sunloving flowers (daisies, morning glories, thistles), as well as insects and mice leading busy lives.

- As you drive along, look for roadside wild flowers (daisies, day lilies, thistles), and the birds (redwing blackbird, gold finch) they attract. Watch for migrating birds overhead and note birds sitting on telephone wires (doves, swallows, sparrow hawks). Identify trees. (See Figure 16–5.)

- In summer, collect leaves, identify and press them, and then find the same kinds of leaves in fall colors to add to the collection.

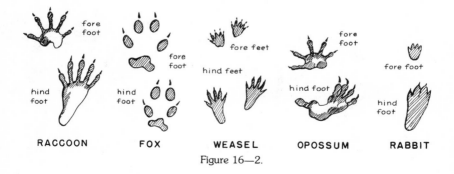

RACCOON   FOX   WEASEL   OPOSSUM   RABBIT

Figure 16—2.

WILD ANIMALS OF WOODS AND FIELDS

OPOSSUM

CHIPMUNK

BAT

BADGER

WEASEL

RACCOON

PRAIRIE DOG

SKUNK

ARMADILLO

FOX

Figure 16—3.

SEA LIFE

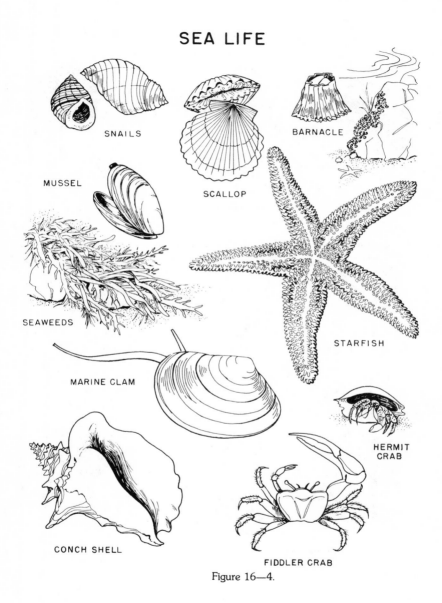

SNAILS

BARNACLE

MUSSEL

SCALLOP

SEAWEEDS

STARFISH

MARINE CLAM

HERMIT
CRAB

CONCH SHELL

FIDDLER CRAB

Figure 16—4.

TREES

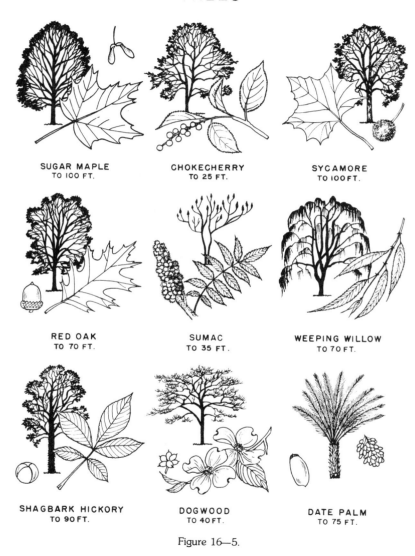

SUGAR MAPLE
TO 100 FT.

CHOKECHERRY
TO 25 FT.

SYCAMORE
TO 100 FT.

RED OAK
TO 70 FT.

SUMAC
TO 35 FT.

WEEPING WILLOW
TO 70 FT.

SHAGBARK HICKORY
TO 90 FT.

DOGWOOD
TO 40 FT.

DATE PALM
TO 75 FT.

Figure 16—5.

HOME PROJECTS

Birds.

- Bird feeder. Purchase seeds and suet from the grocery or feed store. The cardinal loves sunflower seeds.
- Throw dried corn on the ground for quail and pheasant.
- Keep your binoculars and bird book handy for identification (See Figure 16–6.)
- Try a humming-bird feeder.
- Make or buy bird houses for house wrens, blue birds, and martins.

Collections.   Items such as shells and rocks can be cataloged and arranged for storage or display.

Terrariums.   Use a large jar, an old aquarium, or a brandy snifter. Add layer of charcoal (to prevent mold), a layer of gravel, and a layer of humus or leaf mold. Plant your tiny plants, sprinkle lightly, and cover with plastic or a piece of glass cut to fit. You may be surprised to find some insect life in your terrarium. Watering is not necessary. The terrarium makes its own rain in its tiny environment.

Aquariums.   If properly outfitted and maintained, an aquarium will be a good example of an ecological system. Learn about aquariums at a good pet store.

Wildflower Gardening.   Get permission to bring wildflowers to your garden, which you can do if you can locate a wildflower haven where a new highway or building project is planned. You will be doing us all a big favor by saving the plants from destruction. Several of our species are threatened—you may want to make a special effort to rescue them from extinction. Dig plenty of native dirt along with the plant and replant it in the same kind of habitat as the one in which you found it, following the planting procedures outlined on pages 326–27.

BIRDS

HUMMINGBIRD
3" to 3¾"

MOURNING DOVE
11" to 13"

GREAT HORNED OWL
20" to 23"

RED-TAILED HAWK
19" to 25"

ROBIN
8½" to 10½"

BOBWHITE
8½" to 10½"

MEADOWLARK
9" to 11"

MALLARD DUCK
20" to 28"

Figure 16—6.

Weather Forecasting.   Do amateur weather forecasting (no guarantees):

- Light cirrus clouds (like feathers) mean fair weather, especially if the wind is from a westerly direction.
- Fluffy woolly (cumulus) clouds, not too thick, in a clear sky mean fair weather; but if they thicken and get higher (altocumulus) and if the wind shifts to an easterly direction, rain may be expected shortly.
- A veil over the sun (altostratus) means rain is coming unless the wind is westerly, in which case skies will stay gloomy without rain.
- When a dark gray blanket hovers low (stratus, nimbostratus), look for continuous rain.
- Red sun at night
  Sailors' delight.
  Red sun in the morning
  Sailors' warning.

- When the sun sets in a thick cloud bank, look for rain.
- When the barometer falls, look for a change to rain; when it rises, good weather is coming. Smoke from a chimney rises when the barometer is high, hangs low when it is going to rain. When sounds carry far, the pressure is low and the atmosphere moist, so rain may be expected.
- A rainbow in the east means clearing; to the west, it means more rain.
- Dew and frost and morning mist are fair weather signs.
- Cats sleep with their heads upside down when it is going to rain.

Ant Farm.   Ant farms can be purchased in toy stores or made. See a nature book for instructions.

Calendar Diary.   Make nature notes on a calendar to keep for reference: when you saw the first robin, the first firefly, a real luna moth, and so forth.

Cocoons.   Break off a twig on which there is a cocoon, including a couple leaves. Place in a jar. (See Pets.) When the butterfly or moth emerges, let it go near where you found it after admiring it.

Seed Collections.   Make a collage using different sizes, shapes, and colors of seeds. Grasses may be included.

Install A Weathervane.

Insects.   A few "good bugs"—praying mantis, common spiders, lady bugs, and daddy long legs—eat other bugs, such as aphids and mites, that damage our gardens.

SEE ALSO: Collections; Pets; Gardening; Field Trips; Travel; Children's Books (nature; seasons and weather); Toys, Games, Equipment (gardening; science).

PETS

Perhaps you live where children grow up surrounded by animals—maybe you live on a farm or are engaged in a business or hobby involving animals. If so, your child has a natural opportunity to learn the nuances of the animal world. He can enjoy being in a sort of adult position with another living creature. He can practice being truly giving and responsible. And, in return, he receives attention and affection. Even if some of his animals are not able to return affection, they reward their caretaker by thriving and educate him by "doing their thing."

Many of us live in urban or suburban areas where animal husbandry is not a way of life, so if children are to enjoy the aforementioned educational benefits, some special efforts are required on the part of parents. What kind of animals you can accommodate will depend, first of all, on where you live. Some people do manage to raise St. Bernards in the middle of Manhattan, but such a burden of responsibility to maintain the dog and the friendship of neighbors is not necessary.

There are generally three kinds of pets:

1. "Shelf" pets, small animals and insects kept in cages, aquariums, and terrariums. You can buy:

- Guinea pigs
- Hamsters
- Mice
- Gerbils
- Turtles
- Chameleons
- Fish
- Snails
- Crayfish
- Birds

The Humane Society of the United States recommends that you encourage your children to observe the "24 HOUR RULE" when they catch wild animals or insects. This rule means that you keep the animal for observation no longer than twenty-four hours and that you return it to the place where it was found, because, as the Humane Society puts it, these animals "have things to do"— they are an important part of the natural environment. Do not try to domesticate racoons and squirrels because they belong in their natural habitat. Also, because they are "wild," they may turn on people unexpectedly as they mature. Some animals and insects that can be kept for a twenty-four hour period are:

- Frogs and toads
- Snakes
- Insects—caterpillars, spiders, crickets, and so on
- Lizards, salamanders, and newts

2. Livestock animals often become pets to rural children, especially when the children are involved in 4-H projects. Livestock animals are a considerable responsibility; for one thing, they cannot be taken to a kennel when the family wants to go on vacation. A good neighbor is an absolute must because, even though farm animals live outside, they have specific needs that must be tended. They require daily attention and supervision regardless of the weather and regardless of other family activities. Learning to bear such responsibility is good for children, but parents must teach the

child *how* to care for each animal and must bear the ultimate responsibility for the animals' welfare. Many rural children raise money for their future education raising and selling livestock. Some of the animals children in the country can raise are:

- Horses
- Cows, beef cattle
- Hogs
- Chickens
- Rabbits
- Ducks
- Geese
- Sheep
- Turkeys
- Pigeons
- Goats

3. House pets. Only those animals which can live comfortably in the house, are not dangerous, and which do not bother neighbors should be considered.

- Dogs
- Cats
- Shelf pets

How you choose a pet will depend on where you live, on the extent of your child's interest, and on your own ability to deal with the responsibility. If, because of your own background, you have an absolute horror of certain animals and insects, you will have some compromises to make, since family life must take into consideration everyone's comfort and happiness. Be frank about your feelings, but be honest about the fact that your aversion is not reasonable, so your child will not acquire the same aversion. Whatever pets you accept into your menage will require that you accept a large part of the responsibility of their care, because, although you are teaching your child responsibility, you must recognize that a young child is not yet able to be completely responsible without help and supervision.

No matter what animal or insect you adopt, you will want to learn how to take proper care of it, not only for the sake of the living creature, but to teach your child to be humane. It would be better not to involve yourself with pets at all than to have your child become callous to suffering. For the same reason, you will never abandon a pet. Your local humane society will advise you where you can take a pet that you can no longer accommodate. You must even be cautious about returning wild animals and insects to the natural environment. If they were procured from a different part of the country, they may be a strain that should not be introduced into the country where you live. Such "accidental" introductions of species may cause considerable ecological damage.

Before and after you procure a pet, consider the following aspects of their care:

1. What is the temperature range of the animal's natural habitat? Can you provide it?

2. If it is a shelf pet, does it need sun or shade, dry or moist conditions?

3. What are the animal's habits? Many animals die in captivity because people do not know how they feed, how they sleep, how they nest, how they move about, and how much water and earth they need. Each has its own peculiarities.

4. If it is a large animal, how much exercise does it need? How much space?

5. What routine care does the animal require? How will it be cared for when you go on vacation?

6. To what illnesses and pests is the animal susceptible?

7. What are the regulations regarding this animal? Are dog licenses and rabies innoculations necessary? Is it an endangered species? It is illegal to remove an endangered species from its natural habitat. It is illegal to keep certain animals in cities and suburbs.

8. How does this animal respond to handling? What is the proper way to handle it? Does it bite?

9. What kind of pen, cage, or housing does this animal require?

10. Unless you really know dog training, plan to join your dog in training class when he is around five months old. Look under *Dog Training* in the Yellow Pages for a dog training club near

you. If your dog isn't too big, your eight- or nine-year-old child can be his trainer. It is a worthwhile experience for both child and dog.

All libraries have books on pet care; some include all kinds of pets and some specialize in the care, training, and breeding of specific animals or specific breeds. Some are written for children. If you are going in for livestock, contact the grange and the local 4-H. Pet shops and book stores have pet books. You can learn a lot by browsing through the equipment, foods, and general aids in pet shops. The humane society in your city will be more than glad to advise you, since it is dedicated to the prevention of animal suffering. You can learn a great deal from museums of natural history, from breeders, and from friends who raise an animal like the one in which you are interested.

SEE ALSO: Housekeeping, Duties and Chores; Nature Study; Children's Books (dogs and cats; horses; farm life; pets).

SCIENCE

Children are born scientists. They come with a built-in urge to explore and experiment; and after all, that is what science is all about. Infants look at, feel, and taste everything they can get their hands on. Toddlers take things apart, pull them down, push and tug, bang and hammer. The preschooler's coordination has improved, so he doesn't get into quite as many predicaments in his experimentation. However, the preschooler and the young school age child still "learn science" by discovering the physical properties of things for themselves.

Preschool

Young children love to ask questions, sometimes in a way that looks as if they are more interested in hearing you talk than to gain information. It's hard, after the fiftieth question, to take your child seriously. Yet it is how you answer his questions that will make a world of difference in your child's storehouse of knowledge and in his continuing to search for information. It takes time to stop and think of an answer that will be relevant to your child's level of understanding. You have to think about what he already knows and then build the answer on that foundation, using concrete examples, and perhaps setting up a simple demonstration for him to play with. Each successfully answered question is a milestone in your child's education.

Give your young child plenty of things to experiment with— lengths of garden hose, funnels, small plastic bags, straws, measuring containers, pieces of string and rope, sanded boards for little inclines and seesaws, sieves, sponges, corks, sand, water, soap, and toys with a scientific orientation.

School Age Child

In the elementary grades, the science program may seem haphazard because it moves about with the seasons and with whatever presents itself through the children themselves. The children observe, discover, and do; then, under the guidance of the teacher, they learn simple methods of scientific inquiry, questioning and proving their observations, and making records for future reference. You can enrich your child's school science studies by talking with him about what he is doing in school, by meshing your activities with school activities (simple experiments, nature walks, and field trips), and by encouraging careful observation and inquiry. When you explore a subject with your child, consider the following method of inquiry:

1. What is it we want to find out? (Stating the problem.)
2. Do you have any ideas about this? (Hypothesizing.)
3. How can we find out if any of our ideas are right? Can we test them? If so, let's test them; if not, where can we go for information? To a book? To a teacher? (Testing and proving an hypothesis.)
4. Do not force your child to keep written records of his findings unless he is amenable to the idea. You may want to do it for him, until he learns to write easily, as a way to encourage the scientific approach to problem solving and to encourage reading.

When your child asks a question about an animal, an object, or a happening that is related to something he already knows, try to point out the connection. It is easier to remember facts when they are tied together in categories in the brain. Another easy way to encourage categorizing is to enrich his natural urge to build collections. It is important that he collect what *he* wants to collect, because at this point, you are more interested in helping him learn to categorize and in keeping him interested than in dictating subject matter. Of course, your activities, such as nature walks, and your suggestions will open up ideas for him. Don't grab hold of his collecting with such vigor that he suspects you are trying to force something on him; rather, gently enlarge his concept of what he is doing. Help him provide space and a way to display his collection, show it to friends and relatives, find books suitable for his stage of development on the subject, and be on the look-out for additions to bring home to him.

Here are just a few demonstrations and activities that may interest your young school age child:

Astronomy

Pretend you are standing in the middle of a big glass dome. Use a compass to find north and face in that direction. Locate the north star (Polaris). The further south you live, the lower Polaris is in the sky. Use these charts to locate easy-to-spot constellations. After you find the northern constellations, turn south and locate those in the southern sky. What you find will depend on the season of the year. The charts in Figure 16–7 show the sky at about 45° north of the equator. Note the phases of the moon, the planets, comets, and northern lights as opportunities present themselves. Go to the planetarium to see and hear about the night sky and to inquire at the gift shop about a children's book on the subject. You will find books at the library too.

Physics

Physics is the science of matter and energy in terms of motion and force. Here are some sample demonstrations of several physical principles that you and your child can perform.

STARGAZING

LOOKING NORTH
ABOUT 9 P.M.

(ABOUT 45° NORTH LATITUDE)

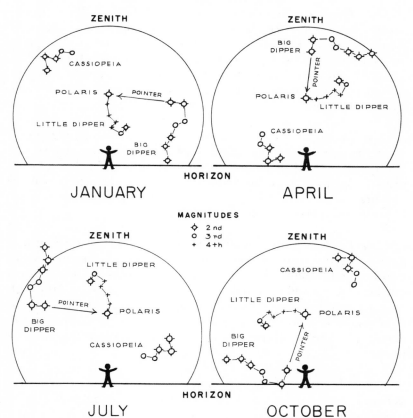

(NOT DRAWN TO SCALE)

Figure 16—7.

Water Will Not Heat Above Its Boiling Point. You can boil a small amount of water in a paper cup over a candle flame without burning the cup, as long as there is water in the cup. Paper will not burn at or below the boiling point of water and water will not get hotter than its boiling point.

Air Pressure. Place a wooden yardstick on an old table under two layers of very smooth, very flat newspaper. Allow about six inches of the yardstick to extend over the edge of the table. Have the child hit down sharply on the end of the yardstick with a bat. The stick will break before it lifts the paper. Air pressure on top of the paper and the vacuum underneath keep the paper and the stick tight to the table.

Air Pressure. Buy your child a pinwheel, and, as you blow on it, explain that your blowing makes high pressure against the slanted blades and that high pressure pushes the blades. The air pressure behind the blades is lower than on the side where you are blowing, and that lower air pressure pulls the blade. The difference in pressures makes the pinwheel go around.

Air Pressure. Put two layers of cheesecloth over the mouth of a bottle. Secure with a string. Pour water through the cheesecloth into the bottle filling it completely. Turn the bottle upside down quickly and you will find that the water will not pour back through the cheesecloth. However, do the demonstration over the sink just to be on the safe side. The cheesecloth and the water keep air from entering the bottle so the outside air pressure keeps the water in place.

Air Pressure. Hang two apples about 1½ inches apart. Blow between them and watch how your blowing through the small space causes the air pressure to drop, making the two apples bang together.

How Hailstones Build. Cut a hailstone in half and notice the layers.

Vibration and Sound. Cut a 2½ foot piece of string and have the child hold each end to touch his ears. Have him lean forward so the loop of the string is hanging free. Into the loop, hang a spoon (tie it there if necessary, though it should balance if hung by the bowl of the spoon). Tap the spoon with another spoon. The child should feel and hear the vibration through the string.

Vibration and Sound.   To make musical straws, flatten the ends of drinking straws. Cut off the corners of the flattened ends. Cut the straws to different lengths. Each straw, when blown into, will produce a different tone.

Color.   Cut a cardboard disc about 2 inches in diameter. Put two holes in the middle of the disc about ½ inch apart. Divide the disc into four sections on both sides and color two sections blue and two sections yellow, alternating. Cut two strings, each about 1 foot long, and thread them through the two holes in the disc. Twirl the disc by twisting the strings, pulling them taut, releasing, and then pulling taut again. As the disc twirls, the blue and yellow sections will blend to look green. You can do the same demonstration with discs colored red and blue (purple), and red and yellow (orange).

Reflection.   Lay a piece of carbon paper on a flat surface, carbon side up, and on top of it place a piece of paper. Print a "secret message" with a pencil with a broken point or a stick. The "message" will be in reverse on the back of the paper and will have to be held up to a mirror to be deciphered.

Chemistry

Chemistry is the science that deals with the composition and properties of substances, with the elementary forms of matter, and with how changes in the composition and properties occur. Here are a few easy demonstrations that illustrate some of the basic chemical properties and changes that are obvious enough for a child to identify. WARNING: THESE DEMONSTRATIONS RE-QUIRE YOUR SUPERVISION BECAUSE SOME OF THE MATERIALS AND PROCEDURES CAN BE DANGEROUS.

Acidic, Alkaline, and Neutral Liquids.   Test liquids with litmus paper (available at the drug store). Try water, vinegar, lemon juice, baking soda dissolved in water, and salt dissolved in water.

- Neutral: No color change in the litmus paper.
- Acid: Paper turns pink.
- Alkaline: Paper turns blue.

Magic Ink (oxidation).   Dip a small paint brush or cotton swab into lemon juice and print a "secret message" on paper. Let dry. Hold the paper over a candle flame and watch the words appear (hold the paper far enough from the flame so that you do not set it on fire). The heat makes the citric acid in the lemon juice oxidize and turn brown.

Crystals.   Evaporate a solution of salt or sugar water on a pan; then examine the crystals with a magnifying glass.

Crystals.   Collect snowflakes on a piece of dark-colored wood and examine them with a magnifying glass.

Crystals.   Make a crystal garden. Arrange a couple of pieces of broken brick or concrete or a porous rock in a shallow dish. Mix together:

- 4 tablespoons water
- 4 tablespoons salt
- 4 tablespoons ammonia
- 4 tablespoons bluing

Tell your child that the ammonia and bluing are poisonous so must not be eaten. Pour the ingredients over the rocks and set in a *safe place* to watch the crystals form over several days as the water evaporates, leaving the salt crystals on the rock.

Fire.   Let your child strike large safety kitchen matches to light candles for experiments, *but always with your supervision*. Fire fascinates children. Your allowing him to use fire under supervision will lessen your child's desire to do so on his own, especially if you have discussed fire safety, prevention, and emergency measures with him.

Fire. Focus the sun through a magnifying glass on a piece of paper in a dish until the paper scorches and bursts into flame. *Supervise carefully.*

Fire. Explain how fire needs air to burn. Explain how, if you want a fire to burn brighter, you blow air on it, and that if you want to put it out, you close off the air. Mix baking soda in a little water, then pour the fumes on a candle flame, explaining that this is how a fire extinguisher works.

Fire. Show him how throwing dirt on fire puts it out because it closes off the air; also demonstrate how throwing an old rug on a fire extinguishes it for the same reason.

Fire. Show him how to build a campfire or a fire in the fireplace; and indicate how air is necessary to get it going.

SEE ALSO: Collections; Field Trips; Travel; Children's Books (science); Toys, Games, Equipment (science; problem solving); Curiosity.

RESOURCES

Cooking

Books

PARENTS' NURSERY SCHOOL (CAMBRIDGE, MASS.), *Kids Are Natural Cooks.* Boston: Houghton Mifflin, 1974. Child-tested recipes that include child participation in preparation.

BROAD, LAURA PEABODY and NANCY TOWNER BUTTERWORTH. *The Playgroup Handbook.* New York: St. Martin's Press, 1974. Look in the index under *Cooking* for pages of preschool cooking ideas.

DENSLOW, ELAINE MARIE. *Happiness is Good Eating.* Mt. Pleasant, Mich.: Enterprise Printers, Inc., 1972. Drawings and photos, little printing. Good for preschool children, nonreaders.

KATZMAN, SUSAN MANLIN. *For Kids Who Cook.* New York: Holt, Rinehart and Winston, 1977.

Gardening

Books

Home Garden Guide. Mountain View, Cal.: Ferry Morse Seed Co. Write either to Fulton, Ky. 42041 or to Mountain View, Cal. 94042.

Simon and Schuster's Complete Guide to Plants and Flowers. New York: Simon and Schuster, 1974. A guide to both indoor and outdoor plants. Contains a color photo of each plant and has easy-to-spot symbols for water, sun, and blooming season. The photos and the symbols make it suitable for use with children.

THOMAS, ROBERT B., *The Old Farmer's Almanac.* Dublin, New Hampshire, 03444. Available at many newsstands for $1.00 for each annual edition as it is published. A little old-fashioned farmer's helper that is crammed with bits of information on weather and planting as well as other facts. Fun to read whether you live in the city or the country.

The following activity books have been written for older children:

ABEL, ELIZABETH. *Flower Gardening.* New York: Franklin Watts, Inc., 1969.

BUSH-BROWN, LOUISE. *Young America's Garden Book.* New York: Charles Scribner's Sons, 1962.

KIRKUS, VIRGINIA. *The First Book of Gardening.* New York: Franklin Watts, Inc., 1956.

SOUCIE, ANITA HOLMES. *Plant Fun, 10 Easy Plants to Grow Indoors.* New York: Four Winds Press, 1974.

Catalogs

Burpee Seed Co. Warminster, Pennsylvania 18974.

Park Seed Co., Inc. P.O. Box 31, Greenwood, South Carolina 29647.

Wayside Gardens, Hodges, South Carolina 29695 (plants).

Woodstream Nursery, P.O. Box 510, Jackson, New Jersey 08527 (wild flowers).

Geography

Books

EPSTEIN, SAM and BERYL EPSTEIN. *The First Book of Maps and Globes.* New York: Franklin Watts, Inc., 1959.

Slides

Pan American Development Foundation. 17th and Constitution Avenue, N.W., Washington, D.C., 20006. A selection of 35mm slides, accompanied by a descriptive booklet.

History

Books

WOLFE, ANN G. *Differences Can Enrich Our Lives: Helping Children Prepare for Cultural Diversity.* No. 399. New York: Public Affairs Pamphlets, 318 Park Avenue South, N.Y. 10016.

Organizations

YMCA. Inquire about Indian Guides and Afro-Guides, programs for parents and young school age children.

Books and Pamphlets

Dowden, Anne Ophelia. *Wild Green Things in the City, A Book of Weeds*. New York: Thomas Y. Crowell, 1972. Beautiful illustrations.

Hausman, Leon. *How to Attract Birds*. Birmingham, Ala.: Cornerstone, 1976.

Helpful Hints on Conserving Wildflowers. New York: The Garden Club of America. Free from Conservation Committee. The Garden Club of America, 598 Madison Avenue, New York, N.Y. 10022.

Hillcourt, William. *Nature Activities and Hobbies*. New York: G.P. Putnam's Sons, 1970. A complete nature handbook, with a project index keyed to skill, equipment, and interest levels.

Shuttlesworth, Dorothy Edwards. *Exploring Nature With Your Child*. New York: Greystone Press, 1952.

Worthley, Jean Reese. *The Complete Family Nature Guide*. Garden City, New York: Doubleday and Co., Inc., 1976.

Field Guides

Brockman, C. Frank. *Trees of North America—A Golden Field Guide*. New York: Golden Press, 1968.

Klots, Elsie B. *New Field Book of Freshwater Life*. New York: G.P. Putnam's Sons, 1966.

Miner, Roy W. *Field Book of Seashore Life*. New York: G.P. Putnam's Sons, 1950.

Peterson, Roger Tory. *A Field Guide to Birds*. (East of the Rockies). Boston: Houghton Mifflin, 1947. By the same author, *Field Guide to Western Birds* and *A Field Guide to the Birds of Texas and Adjacent States*.

RICKETT, HAROLD W. *New Field Book of American Wildflowers.* New York: G.P. Putnam's Sons, 1963.

WHERRY, EDGAR T. *Wild Flower Guide.* New York: Doubleday, 1948.

Government Publications

Order from the Assistant Public Printer (Superintendent of Documents), U.S. Government Printing Office, Washington, D.C., 20402.

Wildlife, PL21; *Insects*, PL41; *Plants*, PL44, *Forestry*, PL43; *Geology*, PL15; *Weather, Astronomy and Meteorology*, PL48.

Magazines

Audubon Magazine. National Audubon Society, 950 Third Avenue, New York: N.Y. 10022.

National Geographic. National Geographic Society, 1145 Seventeenth Street, Washington, D.C. 20036.

National Wildlife (adult) and *Ranger Rick's Nature Magazine* (juvenile). National Wildlife Federation, 1412 Sixteenth Street, NW, Washington, D.C. 20036.

Natural History (adults) and *Junior Natural History* (juvenile). American Museum of Natural History, Central Park West, at Eighty-seventh Street, New York N.Y. 10024.

Nature and Science. Natural History Press, Garden City, New York 11531.

Outdoors Illustrated. Audubon Society of Canada, 177 Jarvis Street, Toronto 2, Ontario, Canada.

Organizations

National Audubon Society. 950 Third Avenue, New York, N.Y. 10022. Membership dues support conservation efforts and give you a subscription to AUDUBON, a beautiful nature magazine that is published six times a year.

Books

BELANGER, JEROME D. *The Homesteader's Handbook to Raising Small Livestock*. Emmaus, Pa.: Rodale Press Inc., 1974.

CARAS, ROGER A. *The Roger Caras Pet Book*. New York: Holt, Rinehart and Winston, 1977.

HENLEY, DIANA. *ASPCA Guide to Pet Care*. New York: Taplinger Publishing Co., Inc., 1970.

McCOY, J.J. *The Complete Book of Dog Training and Care*. New York: Coward-McCann, Inc., 1970.

RICCIUTI, EDWARD R. *Shelf Pets*. New York: Harper and Row, 1971.

WEIDEGER, PAULA and GERALDINE THORSTEN. *Travel with Your Pet*. New York: Simon and Schuster, 1974.

WHITNEY, LEON FRADLEY. *First Aid for Pets*. Chicago: Vanguard, 1954. Also: *Complete Book of Cat Care*. New York: Doubleday, 1953; and *Complete Book of Dog Care*. New York: Doubleday, 1953.

Organizations

The Humane Society of the United States. 2100 L Street, NW, Washington, D.C., 20037. Write for a list of publications and educational materials.

Magazines

Humane Education. (Journal of the National Association for the Advancement of Humane Education). Write the Humane Society, at the above address, for information.

Science

Books

FREEMAN, MAE and IRA. *Fun with Astronomy*. New York: Random House, 1953. Easy projects for young scientists.

POLGREEN, JOHN and CATHLEEN POLGREEN. *The Stars Tonight*. New York: Harper and Row, 1967.

THOMAS, ROBERT B. *The Old Farmer's Almanac*. Dublin, N.H. Published annually. Available at many newsstands. Gives eclipses, moon phases, sunrises and sunsets, planets, and star positions, tides, growing seasons, and so on.

WATERS, BARBARA S. *Science Can Be Elementary*. New York: Citation Press, 1973.

YARDLEY, ALICE. *Discovering the Physical World*. New York: Citation Press, 1970.

Government Publications

Order from the Assistant Public Printer (Superintendent of Documents), U.S. Government Printing Office, Washington, D.C., 20402.

Geology. PL15.

Weather, Astronomy, and Meteorology. PL48.

Magazines

American Biology Teacher. National Association of Biology Teachers, 1420 N Street, NW, Washington, D.C. 20005.

The Science Teacher and *Science and Children*. National Science Teachers' Association, 1201 Sixteenth St., NW, Washington, D.C. 20036.

17

creative arts

ARTS AND CRAFTS

Your young child will benefit immensely from being given the opportunity to express himself in art forms. You will notice that your toddler's pictures are not pictures of things; rather, they are experiments with materials and expressions of his inner thinking. Encourage him without trying to get him to make pictures that look like something.

All you have to do to help your child to grow up loving art is to *make him aware of art*, to *give him tools and materials* appropriate for his developmental stage, and, as he matures, to *teach him skills*. He may not grow up to be a professional artist (then again, he may), but he will grow up more deeply and sensitively aware and will enjoy a very special dimension of life.

To develop interest, point out arts and crafts whenever and wherever you see them—in stores, in public places, and in friends' homes. Talk about colors, shapes, textures, and unique features. Point out lovely scenes, interesting combinations of shapes and shadows, colorful trees, skies, and so on. The school age child is old enough to be taken on an occasional museum trip. Each section of the country and each city has museums and shops that exhibit arts and crafts with a special cultural background. Look in a phone book or ask at a major museum for guidance. Sometimes we overlook exciting exhibits in our cities because so many new things are happening in the cultural setting. Washington, D.C., for example, has the unique Museum of African Art, which continues to expand its services to children during each year of its young existence. Next door to the museum is an African Art gift shop.

In the last few years, most museums have initiated special programs for families and they have children's rooms with art works presented in ways to reach children (and usually the children are allowed to touch the objects). If you love special art works that are in your local museum, get reproductions from the museum gift shop, show them to your child, and talk about them; then take him to the museum to see them. Hang the reproductions in his room and go back to the museum some time later to again find your treasures. Those works of art will be with him for the rest of his life. If art bores you, give your child the opportunity to be with people who enjoy it—relatives, friends, playgroups, and so on.

In creating, the young child needs to be allowed to make big movements and to be very messy. Set him up where he can enjoy himself without damaging your furniture. Cover him up with an old shirt with the sleeves cut out (you can decorate it with crayon, patch pockets, etc.). When you are called in to admire your child's creation, you will be teaching him if you (1) really look at his creation and mention something about it, (2) do not ask what it is, and (3) think of something that might inspire him to create further. You can say it reminds you of a hat you once had, how you like the way he combined red and yellow, how the picture makes you feel happy, or you may simply admire the big black spot. If your child wants to tell you the story of his picture, listen attentively. You will not only be helping him to express himself in words, but you will learn to know your child a little better.

Art for Infants

Infants, in a sense, appreciate art more than anyone, because they spend all their waking hours looking, feeling, and observing what happens around them. Nobody really knows how many impressions infants absorb, though more and more is being learned about the fertility of the infant's mind. It takes little observation on anyone's part to notice how interested infants are in their surroundings. You don't want to overwhelm your infant with a barrage of sensations boldly and constantly, but heretofore the situation has been much the opposite. Let him enjoy looking at the colorful things you have around the house. When your child is old enough to sit up, give him a variety of *safe* items to play with—not necessarily "toys"—colorful shiny items, soft cuddly things, things that change their appearance when they are moved around, pieces of fabric of different colors and textures, and translucent plastic things he can look through. *Just make sure that anything you give a baby or place near him can't smother him, cut him, or hurt him if it falls on him, and that he can't put in his ears or nose or swallow it.*

Art for Toddlers

In addition to continuing the practice of supplying your child with a variety of interesting colors, shapes, and textures to play with, you can introduce finger paints, Plasticine (nonhardening clay), and sturdy crayons. You will want to be an unobtrusive supervisor for the protection of walls and furniture.

Plasticine.   Soften it by rolling it in your hands. Show your child how to roll it into a ball between his palms, to flatten the ball into a flat round plate, to make imprints in it with spools and cookie cutters, to cut it with a plastic knife, and to roll it on the table top to make long ropes.

Finger Painting.   Buy or make safe finger paint. To make finger paint, use one box of soap flakes (not powder), one tablespoon of liquid starch, and some vegetable coloring. Mix, adding water, a little at a time, until the mixture is jelly-like in consistency; then beat well. Since this mixture will wash off, you can let your toddler paint right on a smooth tabletop (not wood), on the bottom of the bathtub, or on a reusable piece of oil cloth. If you want to keep a painting, you can press a piece of paper over it to make a print. Or you can let him make a permanent painting on a piece of smooth finish shelf paper (it doesn't have to be white).

Show your child how to get into the operation—to make big strokes, to get effects by patting or by using his arms and elbows, and to make patterns with spools and pieces of crumpled paper. Then let him go at it by himself; and be sure to admire his creations.

Crayons. Buy good quality heavy crayons (at a hobby shop, if necessary), ones that won't break and that are not more wax than color. Have a special place for crayoning and be sure he has plenty of paper and cardboard to work on so that he won't need to use the walls. Make it very clear to him where he is allowed to produce his creations. Don't expect him to draw "things" yet. Just let him make whatever he wants. You can show him how to rub the side of the crayon (with the wrapper removed) over paper with leaves, sand, coins, or textured fabric underneath to get interesting effects.

Arts and Crafts
for Preschoolers
and School Children

Junk Box. Have a "junk box" into which everyone puts little bits of this and that: ribbons, little bags of sand and gravel, pretty pebbles, beads, broken tile, clean foil, and so on. The list could go on and on—all the things that come in handy for a collage, a costume, a mobile or stabile, a clay creation, or a doll outfit. Note: *Keep small and dangerous items out of reach of younger children.*

Braiding. Tie three two-foot long pieces of fabric strips, old stockings, heavy yarn, or ribbon together at one end. With a piece of string, fasten it to a table leg. Show your child how to braid it. He can hang the braid on his wall or you can sew it into a pad for him. Or he can use it in a collage or mobile.

Clay. Plasticine is best for younger children, but when children, at around three or so, begin to want to make "things," they find it encouraging to know that their creations will be around for a while. You can buy clay in a hobby shop. Directions for its care will be on the container.

There are several ways to teach children to make pots without a potter's wheel: (1) they can roll the clay into a ball, set it on the table, and then hollow it out; (2) they can roll a rope of clay and build the pot by coiling the rope on a flat clay base (join pieces of clay by wetting the edges to be joined to make a good seal); or (3) they can make a flat slab of clay and then mold it into the shape of a pot. They may want to texture the surface of the pot by stippling it or by pressing it with burlap, chicken wire, nail heads, coins, or leaves. They may want to embellish the creation by sticking beads, shells, or some other interesting tidbits into it. Some hobby shops have marvelous collections of beads, and so forth. If a project cannot be finished in one session, keep the clay moist by covering it with a wet cloth. After the piece dries, the child may want to paint it with his tempera paint. If he wants, you can shellac it for him. The child can make pencil holders, plaques (stick a wire loop in the clay before it dries for a hanger), spoon holders, and so on—gifts for relatives. He may want to try molding animals, people, and furniture to put in the doll house or in a miniature barnyard that he is making out of boxes.

Collage.   This is a marvelous art experience and all it requires is paste (nontoxic), a piece of cardboard or plywood (you may find an old weathered treasure lying around somewhere), and a collection of "junk" of different colors and textures. Pictures cut out of magazines can also be used—in fact, just about anything that will stick and not wilt can be considered. What about some acorn caps, leaves, some sand and gravel, a piece of tinsel, or some seeds and corn? The possibilities are endless—and the child, with collage in mind, becomes very aware of colors, shapes, and textures—and of gluing and keeping qualities. Also, his finger skills improve with handling a variety of materials and putting them in place.

Crayons.   Good crayons can be used by people of any age. They can be used effectively on the pointed end, the flat end, or on the side.

1. The side can be used to create texture by underlaying the

paper with textured items as described above. Other designs and collages can be created on top of it.

2. Make colored crayon patterns all over the paper, then go over the whole paper with black crayon. Then, with a sharp point, etch out designs, showing the colors beneath.

3. Combine crayon with painting—the paint will not stick to the crayon surfaces.

4. Draw crayon designs on cloth, turn the design face down on newspaper and press with a warm iron, melting the wax into the cloth. Children can make cloth baby books for little brothers and sisters (you stitch the pages together for them).

5. Crayon designs and stencils can be done on sanded wood and then coated with shellac.

6. Leftover crayon bits can be arranged on a sheet of wax paper with other items like sand, bits of colored paper, and small leaves. Then, cover the arrangement with another piece of wax paper and press gently with a warm iron to fuse the design and the paper.

Dolls, Doll Clothes, and Doll Houses. Keep a bag of bits of fabric, laces, ribbons, trims, and yarn and be on the lookout for little boxes, wallpaper scraps, spools and beads, and scraps of soft wire—in fact, save just about anything that can either dress a doll; decorate a doll house; or fit into a small scene, such as a barnyard or fairy story scene. Help your child by cutting windows out of cartons and cutting away one side of the box, and by helping him install wallpaper if he wants it. He can paste on curtains and light fixtures; he can make people and furniture out of clay or cardboard; he can paste on costumes. Beautiful costume dolls can be made from used dish detergent bottles with foam ball heads— little or no sewing is required, just paste. Iron fabric bits before using for satisfying results. Note: "Real" doll houses, of the kind grownups like, are generally too delicate to be satisfying to very young children.

Felt Pens. Felt pens come in vibrant colors to use alone for drawings and designs or in combination with other materials. Teach your child to keep the top on the pen when not in use in order to keep it from drying out. Children's felt pens come in washable colors.

Mobiles.   Wire coat hangers can be bent into interesting shapes (you will have to help with the bending). They can be hung one from another or interlocked in assorted patterns. From these, all sorts of shapes can be suspended, balancing each other. Mobiles should be hung so they can move freely.

Needlework.   Avoid needlework that is tedious and hard on a young child's eyes. For preschool children, you can buy or make sewing cards, which have holes punched in a design for the child to thread with yarn. Tie a button to the end of the yarn to keep it in place and make a point on the other end with Scotch tape. Older children can use the same principle but can create their own free designs and can use a heavy embroidery needle. Some very unique abstract pieces can be made by covering the whole card with yarn, ribbons, and strings in different colors and patterns. Such needlework can be combined with collage and painting. Older children can also learn the running stitch, cross stitch, and blanket stitch and can begin to use the sewing machine with supervision.

Painting.   You can buy or make an easel. It can be free-standing on three legs or, to save space, you can install a three-foot by five-foot piece of cork-covered plywood on a wall. Put a three-foot by one-foot piece on the lower edge, one side to hold brushes and the other to slope the easel out from the wall at the bottom. Young children need three-quarter-inch brushes; older children will enjoy an assortment of sizes. You can buy tempera paint, in either liquid or powdered form, at any hobby shop. The liquid tends to dry out; and if you mix the powdered as it is used, you can mix in, along with the water, a touch of liquid dishwashing detergent to make laundering easier. Your child will need newspapers on the floor under the easel, a coffee can of water, a small sponge to paint with, and one to wipe up spills. His paper can be butcher paper, newspaper, or wrapping paper—almost any paper as long as it is big. Colored papers can be used for different effects. Show your child how to take a glob of paint on his brush and make big sweeping strokes. Show him how to make green out of yellow and blue, purple out of red and blue, and orange out of red and yellow by mixing the colors on the paper. Teach him how to clean his brush in the coffee can of water before dipping into a different colored paint—in order to keep his colors clean. After all that, leave him alone to his own creations.

Papier Mâché. Papier Mâché can be used to make, containers, animals, dolls, ornaments, relief maps, and so forth. Tear enough newspaper into small strips to fill a quart jar, well packed. Cover with water and soak overnight. In a cut-off gallon jug or old bucket, mix thoroughly:

- 2 cups water
- ½ cup flour
- 1 tablespoon white glue
- 1 cup of the soaked paper with the water squeezed out.

The mash should be thick but flexible enough to mold like modelling clay. Apply in thin layers to a base or frame (armature), allowing each layer to dry thoroughly before adding the next layer. The finished product can be painted with tempera paint and shellacked. To make a vase, use a cut off milk carton or plastic bottle for a base. To make figures, construct an armature out of soft wire, twisting it into the shape you want. To build a relief map, sketch a simplified map on a piece of plywood or heavy cardboard, then mold the hills, mountains, valleys, plains, continents, and so forth.

Photography. A simple camera is an enriching gift for your child when he is old enough (seven or eight) to understand how to work it, how to find the picture in the view finder, and how to make his fingers work while he holds the camera in place. Read the instructions for care and use; show your child what to do; and then have him go through the procedures as you stand by. He won't understand right away that film costs money, so you will want to caution him to use discretion in taking pictures. He will love taking pictures of animals, friends, and important events; and he should be encouraged to take his camera with him on special sightseeing trips. He can make his own album with cardboard covers, decorated with paints, crayons, or needlework.

Pressed Leaves and Flowers. On a nature walk, choose leaves and flowers that are not too thick and spongy. As soon as you get home, press them between two pieces of wax paper and place them under a stack of books. Press for about a week. Pressed leaves and flowers can be pasted in a book and labeled or they can be used in pictures under glass or as part of a collage. Collages and pictures can be made as shadow boxes inside box lids.

Printing. Printing is terribly messy, but it is real fun. Put a little tempera paint in shallow plastic pans, put a large piece of paper on a table top in a "paint proof" place and give the child spools, hair curlers, orange peel halves, bottle caps, toilet tissue rolls, leaves, a cut potato into which you have carved a design, or anything else that enters your child's mind. Langstrom Hughes' *First Book of Rhythms* introduces the idea of repeated patterns (see Children's Books—Arts and Crafts). Point out repeat patterns in fabrics, rugs, wall papers, tiles, and fish scales.

Puppets. Puppets can be made from old socks, pieces of felt, paper bags, or old mittens. Paste on yarn or shredded paper hair and button eyes; crayon or paint features. Add silly hats, noses, headdresses, jewelry, and so on. A stage can be made from a large carton (from a furniture store), by turning a table on its side, or by tacking a sheet across the lower part of a doorway.

Sculpture. A *mobile* is a moving sculpture (usually hanging) and a *stabile* is a "sculpture" that is made of bits and pieces of things stuck together to make a three-dimensional art form that is stable. It can be made with wood nailed together, pipes wired together with soft wire, or with fabric and cardboard pasted on. It can be painted or decorated with yarn or fabric strips. In fact, it can be just about anything. And of course, modeling with clay is also sculpture.

String Painting. Dip a piece of string in paint; then roll it around between the two halves of a folded piece of paper to produce a symmetrical design when the paper is unfolded.

Weaving. A simple loom is a fine gift for an older child. Modern weaving is very creative. Take your child to see some weaving at an art show or in a museum so he will get an idea of what can be done. Take time to read the directions that come with the loom so you can teach your child the proper technique—you don't want him to labor over something that won't hold together when it is finished.

If your child shows real interest and skill, be on the lookout for art shows that will inspire him and teach him. Talk to the art teacher at school about ways to advance his talent. And by all means, get him the best instruction and supply him with the best materials you can afford.

SEE ALSO: Children's Books (arts and crafts); Creativity; Anger; Perception; Holidays; Carpentry; Theater; Toys, Games, Equipment (arts and crafts).

The following are a few famous paintings with child appeal by some representative well-known artists. Some of these may have no appeal for your child. You won't know till you try a variety. Remember too, that there are many arts and crafts from Africa, Latin America, the American Indians, and the Far East available at museums and in shops. If your local museums do not have what you want, see *Resources* at the end of this section for sources of print catalogs and art education materials. Some of the commercial sources charge for their catalogs, so you may want to inquire before ordering.

- Audubon, *Mallard Ducks*
- Crite, *Parade on Hammond Street*
- Currier and Ives, *Central Park Winter*
- Degas, *Dancer on Stage*
- Dufy, *Flower Picture*
- Egyptian, *Owls and Ibis*
- Goya, *Don Manuel*
- Hals, *The Laughing Cavalier*
- Hicks, *The Peaceable Kingdom*
- Holbein, *Edward VI as Prince of Wales*
- Homer, *Gulf Stream*
- Houghtelling, *Alice in Wonderland*

- Jules, *The Circus*
- Lee-Smith, *Boy with Tire*
- Manet, *The Fifer*
- Marin, *Circus Elephant*
- Matisse, *Cut out pictures*
- Miro, *The Sun*
- Modigliani, *Girl in Pink*
- Moses, *Sugaring Off*
- Picasso, *Boy in Harlequin Jacket*
- Remington, Pictures of the old west (real cowboys and Indians)
- Renoir, *A Girl with a Watering Can*
- Renoir, *Roses*
- Reynolds, *The Age of Innocence*
- Riviera, *Flower Seller*
- Roualt, *Pierrot*
- Rousseau, *Summer*
- Van Gogh, *Sunflowers*
- Velasquez, *Infanta Marguerita Teresa*

DANCE

When your baby has just begun to walk, you may be surprised to see him hold on to something, plant his feet, and start rhythmic movement in time to music. No one has to tell him about dancing. Toddlers, in their inimitable toddler way, try to dance with boxy bouncing steps. As a child approaches school age, he can perform somewhat more gracefully.

Dancing has emotional benefits that are associated with a sense of physical well-being. Often a child who tends to be shy and introverted will blossom when the kindergarten teacher introduces him to rhythmic movement. The activity relaxes tense muscles and creates a feeling of power and control over one's physical self. Dancing is a way to express moods and feelings that can't be expressed in a child's limited vocabulary. Most informal schools emphasize expressive dancing all through the elementary grades in order to enrich a child's sense of self, to enhance his ability to express his emotions, to provide a way of socializing, and to improve coordination.

Since the rhythms and moods of music are closely associated with dance, give your child music at home and encourage creative movement. Don't worry about how the child interprets the music. Let him create his bird hops, elephant stomps, cloud floats, and hippo wallows as he imagines them. Don't embarrass him by laughing unless the dance is meant to be funny, because you don't want him to become self-conscious and tense.

Formal dancing lessons come later, when your child's coordination and attention span will allow him to learn and practice the steps successfully. Almost all children can benefit from dancing lessons. A child who is not exceptionally talented in dancing will nevertheless enjoy it if he is encouraged in expressive movement in early childhood and if he is provided later with enough formal training to give him an understanding of control and balance. In his teen years, the earlier established joy in uninhibited movement will be the foundation for confidence in learning the current social dance steps.

Most children will not follow through to become professional or semiprofessional dancers. If, however, your child shows real talent and interest, help him find the best teachers and develop his talent to the fullest without denying him the other pleasures of childhood. A good dancer finds his ability a joy to himself and a pleasure to everyone else.

SEE ALSO: Music; Records and Tapes; Creativity; Theater; Self-Image; Children's Books (music, song books; dancing).

MUSIC

As soon as your baby becomes aware of what is going on around him, he will fall in love with sound. It's amusing to watch a baby bang a rattle or spoon on a tabletop, startle and blink, and then go at it with enthusiasm. He likes it when you are enthusiastic too. This is the beginning of music appreciation, which is, after all, a love of making sounds, of listening to sounds, and of feeling rhythm.

Music To Listen To

Hang wind chimes on the porch or near a window to tinkle and glitter in the breeze. Buy a musical cradle gym or hang Christmas bells on a piece of elastic stretched across his crib where he can hit it with his feet. And of course, there are the old standbys: rattles with a variety of tones, old pots, lids, and spoons.

Play records on your record player—not just children's records, but classics, instrumentals, and folk music from many times and places. Choose gentle music for bedtime and lively pieces for playtime. Sing to your baby, pat and rock him in time to the rhythms, dance with your toddler, and play rhythm games to nursery rhymes.

Your toddler will love to have his own record player. Not all the ones on the market are sturdy enough or easy enough to handle for the toddler to manage by himself. Look for thoughtful design and quality materials. Buy records of familiar songs and sing with them. Listen and identify drums, bells, and other instruments.

Singing With Your Baby

The old familiar songs are very comfortable; and they teach rhythm, cadence, singing, and movement. Don't worry if you don't have much of a voice; your audience will love you anyway. A child learns singing as he learns to talk—by listening and by trying it out. Children who are never sung to or who never sing at home have a bit of a struggle in school to get the hang of it.

Toy Instruments

You can see the delight on your child's face when he manipulates something and it makes a noise. Without having been taught, he will laugh at a funny noise and smile appreciatively at pleasant sounds. It seems to come naturally. So, to enrich him, give him as many "instruments" as you can for him to experiment with and listen to. You can make simple instruments for your preschooler:

- Rhythm sticks: ¾″ to 1″ dowels (or a broomstick) cut about 12″ long and sanded.
- A bell bracelet for wrist or ankle, made from Christmas bells on a loop of elastic. Make sure the elastic is not too tight.
- Gong: a hanging pot lid with a spoon hung beside it.
- Flower pot bells: different sized clay pots hung from a broomstick supported by two chairs. Use heavy buttons to hold the string in the holes in the pots. Use a wooden spoon for a striker.

There are a lot more ideas in *Make Your Own Musical Instruments* by Muriel Mandell and Robert E. Wood. (See the resources at the end of this section.)

The well-known toy companies make toy instruments for pre-schoolers. Get a variety of instruments so your child and his friends can orchestrate and so they can build an appreciation of different kinds of sounds and what each adds to group playing (see *Toys— perception, music*). Describe the sounds in words. Show your child how to make different rhythms, how to dance and march, how to do whatever the rhythm suggests. Show him how to play along with his records. Encourage him and his friends to give a concert for you, perhaps after you have taken him and his friends to a band concert.

Introduce your child to concerts gradually, with his developmental level in mind. In some cities, the symphony orchestra presents concerts especially for young children. Band concerts in the park are colorful and are usually informal enough to accommodate young children. As your child matures and can sit in a concert hall for an adult performance, choose a concert that includes pieces you have played at home, ones that have become familiar. Prepare your child by playing the record and by talking about the story and the instruments; if you can, pick out the main themes on his toy instruments. Perhaps, either before or after the concert, he might like to paint a picture of his ideas about the music. Intermingling cultural media deepens feelings, increases familiarity, helps memory—and thus makes future experiences more and more relevant.

Music In School

Teachers combine singing with dancing and simple instruments in group work in the early grades. You can see how your introductory work fits with this kind of program. Teachers try to help each child "find his singing voice" if he has not already found it at home. Encourage any efforts at singing that result from the teacher's work, regardless of what it sounds like. If a child is ridiculed, he will become self-conscious and may stop singing forever. On the other hand, almost everyone can enjoy singing if he is encouraged throughout childhood.

In the early grades, children learn the rudiments of rhythm through songs with different beats and lyrical emphasis. They learn to differentiate between sounds, to match instruments to mood, to feel and move to different rhythms, and to express what they feel about music in words and paint. They listen to and accompany piano and records; they learn to plan and execute their own orchestrations.

In the intermediate grades, they are introduced to tuned instruments and to tone, pitch, melody, and harmony. When your child reaches third grade, he will have graduated from untuned toy instruments and will be enriched by a tuned xylophone or a glockenspiel. Or he may be ready for private lessons on an instrument for which he shows a preference. Don't overlook music when you talk with your child about what he is doing in school. Encourage him to play and sing for you as he continues his music education.

Private Lessons

Recently, a variety of music education programs have been developed for young children. Some of them are used in school. Ask at your library or school about the following programs: Orff, Pace, Suzuki, Yamaha, and Dalcroze. All are fairly recently developed methods of teaching music to young children.

Generally, for conventional private music lessons, it is best to wait until your child is about at the third grade level in school. There are exceptions: children who exhibit considerable musical talent very early. If you are interested in private lessons for your child, there are a series of steps to take to insure success. More failures result from parents' lack of knowledge about music lessons than from a child's lack of ability, which is why many adults lament that they didn't continue their music training.

Find a Good Teacher

Talk to school teachers, church choir directors, librarians, and musician friends about teachers. Write to: *Music Teachers National Association, 1841 Carew Tower, Cincinnati, Ohio 45202, phone: (513) 421–1420.* If you send them a self-addressed stamped envelope, they will send you a list of accredited teachers in your area, grouped by their specialties. Talk with a few teachers to evaluate how you feel they will get along with your child.

The Audition and Trial Period

The teacher you have chosen will meet with your child to evaluate his capability and to advise you on how to proceed. If the teacher feels that your child needs to mature for another year before beginning lessons, take his advice. If he feels that your child is ready to start lessons, consider the first few months a trial period during which it is advisable to rent an instrument. Inquire at your local music store about rental instruments; some have plans for applying the rental amount to the purchase of the instrument.

The Commitment

After a few months have gone by and the novelty of the instrument has worn off, set a time to make the decision about whether to continue in earnest for several years, about whether to postpone lessons, about whether to consider a different teacher, and about whether you and your child really have no interest in continuing private lessons. Once you commit yourself and your child to a program of lessons, expect to continue for at least four years. Of course, circumstances may arise to alter the commitment; but if your child has four years of training, his feeling for playing or singing will be much like that of riding a bike or swimming—he will always be able to pick up the training easily at a later date.

The Instrument

Once you and your child are committed to a program of private instruction, talk with his teacher about quality instruments. It is important to put your money in a good instrument because your child will learn by what he hears as he progresses. A poor instrument provides poor feedback. If your budget is limited, opt for mechanical and tone quality over appearance. You may consider a used instrument, which can save money; but be sure to have it checked out by a professional before buying. A piano technician will charge for an examination, but it is well worth the expense to be sure of what you are getting.

Practice

Most adults remember music training as long hours of tedious practice, yet they wish they had continued. It takes stamina, imagination, and persistence on the part of parents to keep the ball rolling until the child gets to the point where the music is its own motivation. Start gently with short practice periods, using token rewards which lead to a new record, a live concert, a tape recorder, or to some other music-related present. Do not be wishy-washy about practice. Choose a good time, perhaps in the morning before school when your child is fresh and when the "music" will not interfere with other family activities. Once your child gets in the habit of practicing at a certain time, it won't seem to him to be so much of an interference. During the rest of the day, do not talk about practicing, do not make him show off to your friends, and do not nag. But do keep interested and be supportive. Make sure your child enjoys his teacher; if he doesn't, find another. Unless you run into really extenuating circumstances, do not give up.

A love of music—all kinds of music—provides pleasure in solitude *and* a way of communicating with friends. A person always remembers fondly the music with which he became familiar in childhood. Teen years may bring unfamiliar and distressing sounds into your home, but early music education is seldom lost. It often remains during adolescence and almost always becomes more deeply appreciated with maturity.

SEE ALSO: Toys, Games, Equipment (music); Children's Books (music, songbooks, dancing).

POETRY

Hey, diddle diddle, the cat and the fiddle,
The cow jumped over the moon.
The little dog laughed to see such a sport,
And the dish ran away with the spoon.

We read and say nursery rhymes with little children; then, when they outgrow nursery rhymes, we sometimes forget the magic they loved in rhythm, rhyme, alliteration, repetition, and combinations of words that create mental images like paintings at an exhibition.

By the shores of Gitchie Gumee,
By the shining Big Sea-Water,
Stood the wigwam of Nokomis.
Dark behind it rose the forest,
Rose the black and gloomy pine-trees,
Rose the firs with cones upon them.
Bright before it beat the water,
Beat the shining Big Sea-Water.

From "Song of Hiawatha"
Henry Wadsworth Longfellow

Besides *Mother Goose* and perhaps "Song of Hiawatha," you and your child may want to make a space for Robert Lewis Stevenson's *A Child's Garden of Verses*, Edward Lear's *Complete Nonsense Book* for sillier moments, one of several anthologies of poetry for children, and certainly, a few contemporary books like Mary O'Neill's *Hailstones and Halibut Bones*.

When you read poetry with your child, make your voice rise and fall, sway and croon. Make your voice utter round sonorous words with depth and dignity, and nimbly snip off cold and brittle words. Accentuate the rhythms and special effects. It isn't really hard to do. Your audience will love your performance no matter how amateurish you think you are.

Be sensitive to your child's poetic efforts. A child who is going to enjoy language and literature is going to play with language before he can write. You can encourage your child by writing his nonsense sayings and rhymes for him. You will both enjoy reading them later. When you read a poem your child likes, he might enjoy painting it into a picture. Or he may make a poem about a picture he likes—or a scene or a happening. One of the books on the poetry shelf may well be your child's collection of his own poems and favorites by other poets. You may want to make him a present of a bound book with blank pages (available at book stores and stationery shops). His illustrations and poetry (dated) in that book will be a real family treasure.

> First it starts to sprinkle
> Then it starts to pour
> Then again it sprinkles
> Then it rains no more.
>
> *Laurie Rice Saunders (at age six)*

SEE ALSO: Writing (creative); Creativity; Children's Books (poetry); Reading With Children.

THEATER

Because little children love to fantasize and pretend, they naturally love theater. They respond to costumes, masks, and exciting adventures of the make-believe world. Fortunately, there are many ways to enhance this dimension of childhood, which is much more enriching than sitting in front of a television.

"Dress-ups" naturally lead to theatrical productions, especially if children have seen a play on a stage. Keep a boxful of costume material handy and help arrange a stage with an old sheet for a curtain. Your child and his friends will be busy for hours putting on plays. You can hang the sheet on curtain rings over a wire or rope in the back yard in the summer (after the children have decorated the "curtain" with paint and crayon). They will combine arts and crafts and music and dancing in their productions if they have been introduced to them. Perhaps a gentle suggestion on the part of a parent will open the floodgates of creativity. For the most part, however, it should be a children's production.

Puppet shows are another form of theater that children love. If you have been reading stories with your children, they will have plenty of plots and characters to work with.

Most cities and towns present children's theater at some time during the year, often around Christmas. By all means, take your child occasionally. For him to get the most out of the experience, tell him a little about what he will see (without spoiling the outcome of the plot), because a little familiarity enhances your child's understanding and enjoyment of any new experience.

SEE ALSO: Pretending and Role Playing; Music; Dance; Arts and Crafts; Self-Image.

VOCABULARY

Words are the tools of thought and language. Adults do most of their thinking with words, so the richer the vocabulary, the greater the dimensions and clarity of thought.

A child's first use of words will be exactly like his parents', since he learns by imitation. He will use their words, pronunciations and inflections. He may learn a lot of what are considered to be regional colloquialisms or words in a language other than English. *This is all right.* It is more important to teach a child to talk by talking unaffectedly with him than to be artificial and strained. Since good basic English is important to participating in the mainstream of American life, you will want your child to learn it eventually, but, in the preschool years, it is more important that you and your child communicate and enjoy each other unfettered by feelings that cause artificiality. Reading quality children's books to your child is one way to introduce him to English usage without strain. Doing things together and talking about what you are doing add new words to everyone's vocabulary in a very natural and relevant way. Keep a dictionary handy and cultivate the habit of looking up words you don't know as they come along in conversation, on television, or in reading.

When your child starts school, he will begin formal instruction in basic English. Keep in touch with what he is learning so you can help him become familiar with the words and their meanings by using them yourself informally whenever the opportunity presents itself. Encourage your child to experiment with the use of new words without fear of being embarrassed if he makes a mistake. Saying, gently and seriously, "You mean   ?" is a way of correcting without ridicule.

There are a lot of commercial games and flash cards on the market for the development of vocabulary. Or you can make flash cards to match the school vocabulary assignments. You might tape current assignment words to the bathroom mirror for instant review every morning and evening. Adults learning a new language use this trick. Under a sign, "Words I Know" on the back of his door, you might tape the words he has learned, so he can be proud to see the door become covered with words. From time to time throughout the school year, you can have a game of making sure none of them has been forgotten.

Keep reading with your child. Reading is the most efficient and pleasant way to increase vocabulary. Seeing and hearing words within the context of different stories gives them a deeper and more memorable meaning than learning vocabulary words solely from a list of definitions. You want your child to be really familiar with words, not only to know simple definitions, but also to absorb all the shadings and nuances contained in them.

SEE ALSO: Children's Books; Reading With Children; Reading; Talking With Children; Speech; Spelling; Writing (creative).

WRITING (CREATIVE)

Since writing is another form of talking, and since children talk before they write, the lead-in to creative writing is creative talking during the preschool years.

Creative writing also needs skill with tools. Pencils and typewriter, of course, but even more importantly, words and grammatical structures. Remembering that the child has plenty of time to develop these skills, parents will want to keep the creativity flourishing through verbal expression and with considerable help to the child in getting creative ideas down on paper. Don't hesitate to write things down for your child.

Pictures and drawings, decorations and colorful papers, all combined with a few words of his very own—that you print in manuscript—make the idea of putting original ideas on paper appealing to a young child. Since young children are generally purposeful in their activities, finding reasons to communicate through the mail to friends and relatives adds incentive. When your child is sick and must be kept quiet, take advantage of the time to write with him. Let him know that you consider his writing (actually your penmanship) important enough that when he says something worth writing down or asks you to write for him, stop what you are doing, if at all possible, and *write*. Keep a book of his "works," perhaps a bound book (available at book and stationery stores), and date each addition to the collection.

Reading well-written children's prose and poetry provides your child with models to emulate. The drama and rhythm you use when reading aloud enrich your child's sense of structure, while the material itself expands his knowledge.

When preparing a young child to write creatively, remember that the mechanics of penmanship are developing more slowly than his creativity. Your help, to avoid the deadening effects of drudgery, will keep his creativity alive as he gradually develops penmanship and typing skills.

SEE ALSO: Reading With Children; Creativity; Poetry.

RESOURCES

Arts and Crafts

Books

ARNOLD, ARNOLD. *The Crowell Book of Arts and Crafts for Children.* New York: Thomas Y. Crowell Co., 1977.

Children's Crafts. Menlo Park, Cal.: Lane Publishing Co., 1976.

JOHNSON, JANN. *The Jeans Book.* New York: Ballentine, 1972. Tells you lots of creative things to do with blue jeans.

LEWIS, HILDA, P. ed. *Art for the Preprimary Child.* Reston, Va.: National Art Education Association, 1916 Association Drive.

MAYNARD, FREDELLE, PH.D., *Guiding Your Child to a More Creative Life.* New York: Doubleday, 1973.

NAGLE, AVERY and JOSEPH LEEMING. *Fun with Naturecraft.* Philadelphia and New York: J.B. Lippencott Co., 1964.

PELS, GERTRUDE. *Easy Puppets.* New York: Thomas Y. Crowell C., 1951.

RAINEY, SARITA R. *Weaving Without a Loom.* New York: Sterling, 1972.

REID, BOB and PAT REID. *Sand Creatures and Castles: How to Build Them.* New York: Holt, Rinehart, and Winston, 1976.

ROTTGER, ERNST. *Creative Clay Design.* New York: Reinhold, 1963. This book has pictures of coil, pinch, and slab pots.

SLADE, RICHARD. *Modelling in Clay, Plaster and Papier Mâché.* New York: Lothrup, 1968.

STEIN, SARA BONNETT. *The Kid's Kitchen Takeover.* New York: Workman Publishing Co., Inc., 1975.

Reproduction Catalogs and Sources of Art Education Material

Art-Full Picture Frame Co., 856 Cliff Street, Pacific Palisades, California 90272.

Indian Arts and Crafts Board, Room 4004, U.S. Department of the Interior, Washington, D.C. 20240. Ask for their source directory of Indian and Eskimo art.

Metropolitan Museum of Art, Fifth Avenue and 82nd Street, New York, N.Y. 10028.

Museum of African Art, 316 A Street, N.E., Washington, D.C. 20002.

Museum of Modern Art, 11 W. 53rd Street, N.Y. 10019.

National Art Education Assn., 1201 16th Street, N.W., Washington, D.C. 20036.

Oestreichers Prints, Inc., Catalog Dept., 43 West 46th Street, New York, N.Y. 10036.

Pan American Union, Development Foundation, 17th and Constitution Avenue, N.W., Washington, D.C. 20006.

Music

Books

MANDELL, MURIEL and ROBERT WOOD. *Make Your Own Musical Instruments*. New York: Sterling Publishing Co., 1970.

MAYNARD, FREDELLE, PH.D., *Guiding Your Child to a More Creative Life*. New York: Doubleday, 1973.

PAPE, MARY. *Growing Up with Music: Musical Experiences in the Infant School*. New York: Oxford University Press, 1970.

SWANSON, BESSIE R. *Music in the Education of Children*. (3rd edition) Belmont, Cal.: Wadsworth Publishing Co., 1969.

Organizations

Dalcroze International School of Music, 161 East 73rd Street, New York, N.Y. 10021.

National Piano Foundation. 435 N. Michigan Avenue, Chicago, Ill. 60611.

Suzuki Association of the Americas. P.O. Box 164, Mendham, N.J. 07945.

Books

HOPKINS, LEE BENNETT. *Let Them Be Themselves.* New York: Scholastic Book Services, 1969.

LARRICK, NANCY, ed. *Poetry for Holidays.* New Canaan, Conn.: Gerrard Publishing Co., 1966. Grades 2 through 5. Ms. Larrick has compiled a number of children's poetry books.

JOHNSON, FERNE, ed. *Start Early for an Early Start, You and the Young Child.* Chicago: American Library Association, 1976, pages 69–99.

Books

PELS, GERTRUDE. *Easy Puppets.* New York: Thomas Y. Crowell Co., 1951.

Books

HOPKINS, LEE BENNETT. *Let Them Be Themselves.* New York: Citation Press, 1969. Ideas for teachers (but easy to adapt to home projects) in literature and creative writing.

PETTY, WALTER T. and MARY E. BOWEN. *Slithery Snakes and Other Aids to Children's Writing.* Englewood Cliffs, N.J.: Prentice-Hall, 1967. Contains a list of children's books; also contains an adult bibliography for parents of school age children.

index